Global Mindsets

T0330809

Global Mindsets seeks to tackle a topic that is relatively new in research and practice, and is considered by many to be critical for firms seeking to conduct global business. It argues that multiple mindsets exist (across and within organizations), that they operate in a global context, and that they are dynamic and undergo change and action. Part of the mindset(s) may depend upon the place, situation, and context in which individuals and organizations operate. The book examines the notion of "mindset" as situational and dynamic, especially in a global setting, why it is important for future scholars and managers, and how it could be conceptualized.

The book includes conceptual chapters that push the current boundaries of research on the topic and empirical chapters that demonstrate how different organizations in different countries apply mindset perspectives in their management practices. It seeks to help academics, consultants, and researchers understand what has been said and studied about global mindsets in action and to gain insights into possible directions and challenges that the field may face in the future.

John Kuada is a Professor of International Management in the Department of Business and Management at Aalborg University, Denmark.

Routledge Studies in International Business and the World Economy

For a full list of titles in this series, please visit www.routledge.com

Global Mindsets

Exploration and Perspectives

Edited by John Kuada

Routledge
Taylor & Francis Group

NEW YORK AND LONDON

First published 2016
by Routledge
711 Third Avenue, New York, NY 10017

and by Routledge
2 Park Square, Milton Park, Abingdon, Oxon OX14 4RN

First issued in paperback 2018

Routledge is an imprint of the Taylor & Francis Group, an informa business

© 2016 Taylor & Francis

The right of the editor to be identified as the author of the editorial material, and of the authors for their individual chapters, has been asserted in accordance with sections 77 and 78 of the Copyright, Designs and Patents Act 1988.

Library of Congress Cataloging-in-Publication Data
Names: Kuada, John, editor.
Title: Global mindsets : exploration and perspectives / edited by
  John Kuada.
Description: New York : Routledge, 2016. | Series: Routledge studies
  in international business and the world economy ; 64 | Includes
  bibliographical references and index.
Identifiers: LCCN 2015051346 | ISBN 9781138831773 (hardback :
  alk. paper) | ISBN 9781315736396 (ebook)
Subjects: LCSH: Management—Cross-cultural studies. | Organizational
  behavior—Cross-cultural studies. | Corporate culture—Cross-cultural
  studies. | International business enterprises. | Multiculturalism. |
  Globalization.
Classification: LCC HD62.4 .G5456 2016 | DDC 658/.049—dc23
LC record available at http://lccn.loc.gov/2015051346

ISBN 13: 978-1-138-61715-5 (pbk)
ISBN 13: 978-1-138-83177-3 (hbk)

Typeset in Sabon
by Apex CoVantage, LLC

Contents

Tables and Figures

Tables

Figures

Acknowledgments

In 2008, the Poul Due Jensen Foundation had donated DKK 2.5 million to Aalborg University for the promotion of research into cross-cultural management. This brought together five professors, John Kuada, Olav Jull Sørensen, George Tesar, Nigel Holden, and Nancy K. Napier, and initiated discussions about global mindset. Our discussions revealed that although the concept was then relatively new in the academic literature, it had gained substantial attention, especially in the practitioner management literature, and was considered by many top executives to be critical for firms seeking to conduct global business. We also noted that the concept was open to many interpretations and lacked unified frameworks and theoretical guideposts for academic investigations. This awareness encouraged us to explore the concept in greater detail with a view to helping researchers determine areas of high potential research needs and to give them theoretical anchors for their research endeavors.

We have received excellent cooperation and support from our colleagues at the International Business Centre's Department of Business and Management right from the time we started this exploration process. They have individually and collectively engaged in stimulating intellectual conversations with us about the project, thereby providing us with an enriching academic atmosphere. Our sincere thanks go to all of them. We would also like to thank the Poul Due Jensen Foundation for the generous financial support it has offered the project. Particular thanks go to these individuals: Niels Due Jensen and Olav Ballisager (of the Poul Due Jensen Foundation) as well as Birgitte Gregersen, (head of the Department of Business and Management, Aalborg University) for their personal interest and support.

About the Contributors

Andreea Ioana Bujac is an Assistant Professor at the International Business Centre's Department of Business and Management at Aalborg University. Andreea received her BA in international economic relationships from Babes-Bolyai University, Romania and her MSc degree in international business economics from Aalborg University. She also received her PhD in international marketing from Aalborg University in 2014. Her primary research interests are in the field of consumer marketing. Specifically, she is interested in branding, consumer behavior, country-of-origin effects, and consumer ethnocentrism.

Kelsey Crow recently graduated from Boise State University with a BA in English/Writing. Along the way, she studied at the University of St Andrews in Scotland and the University of Washington in Seattle. Now, Kelsey works at a small branding agency in Seattle as a project manager.

Vuong Quan Hoang (PhD, Université Libre de Bruxelles) is a Senior Researcher at Centre Emile Bernheim, Solvay Brussels School of Economics and Mangement, Belgium and the co-founder of the Hanoi-based applied research firm Vuong & Associates. He has published in academic journals such as the *Vietnam Journal of Mathematics*, the *Vietnam Journal of Mathematical Applications*, *Economic Studies*, *Pacific Affairs*, the *Management Research Review*, the *International Journal of Transitions and Innovation Systems*, *Statistics Applications & Probability Letters*, the *International Journal of Intercultural Relations*, and *SpringerPlus*. His opinions have also appeared in international media such as the *Dow Jones Newswire*, the *Wall Street Journal*, BBC, Reuters, *Roubini Global Economics*, AFP, Stratfor, BullionVault, *Forbes*, *La Repubblica*, *Voice of America*, and the *Los Angeles Times*. As a member of the Hanoi Stock Exchange Index Committee, he advises on technical matters relating to a number of important indexes such as HNX30, the HNX Index, and the Government Bond Index. He was the recipient of Vietnam's National Book Award 2007 and National Journalism Award in 2010.

Nigel Holden retired from full-time academic life in December 2010, having previously held professorships in cross-cultural management in the UK,

Denmark, and Germany. In May 2011, he joined the Centre for International Business at Leeds University Business School as a Visiting Research Fellow. In 2007, he helped to co-found the *European Journal of International Management*, of which he is an associate editor. He was a contributor (with Snejina Michailova) to the first special issue on language in the *Journal of International Business Studies* in 2014 and he was a senior academic editor of the *Routledge Companion to Cross-Cultural Management* published in 2015. He is an adjunct professor at Aalborg University and was appointed a Visiting Professor at the University of Regensburg in 2015.

John Kuada is a Professor of International Management in the Department of Business and Management at Aalborg University in Denmark. His research interests include enterprise development in Africa, management in Africa, export marketing, and intercultural management. Professor Kuada is the author and co-author of fifteen books and over 100 peer-reviewed articles and book chapters. In addition to teaching and research, he has consulted with businesses and international organizations in Europe and Africa, including the Danish International Development Agency and International Finance Corporation (a World Bank affiliate). He serves on the editorial review boards of a number of marketing/management journals focusing on business and management in Africa and Asia.

Hamid Moini is a Professor Emeritus of Finance at the University of Wisconsin-Whitewater. He received his PhD in financial economics and MA in finance from the University of Alabama. He joined the University of Wisconsin-Whitewater in 1985. Currently, he is a Professor Emeritus of Finance at the University of Wisconsin-Whitewater and a resource person specializing in the globalization of small and medium-sized enterprises. Over the past 30 years, his research has focused on the development of global market entry strategies for smaller firms and management education in the contemporary global context. He has published two books and numerous refereed articles in the leading journals on finance and international business.

Nancy K. Napier (PhD, Ohio State University) is a Distinguished Professor at Boise State University (U.S.) and an Adjunct Professor at Aalborg University in Aalborg, Denmark. Her research and experience is wide ranging, from managing Boise State's $8.5 million, nine-year capacity-building project at the National Economics University in Hanoi, Vietnam, to working with multi-sector groups on how to boost creativity and performance. Her recent books are *Insight* (2010), *The Creative Discipline* (2008), and *LIVEculture: How Creative Leaders Grow the Cultures they Want* (2015), co-authored by a "gang" of highly creative, high performing leaders from very different fields. She has published in academic and practitioner journals, ranging from the *Journal of International Business* and *Creativity and Innovation Management* to *Organizational Dynamics* and *Human Resource Management*. She blogs for the *Idaho Statesman* on creativity and leadership.

Olav Jull Sørensen has been a Professor of International Business at Aalborg University since 1991 and the head of the International Business Centre since its establishment in 1984. Today, the Centre hosts three graduate programs within the field of international business, a PhD program, and a core team of 14 researchers. His main research interests are the internationalization of companies, international industrial dynamics and value chain analysis, and government-business relations. The topics are being researched from a developed market perspective as well as a developing/transition country perspective. He is a member of the Academic Council for Social Sciences at Aalborg University and the Council of the Department of Business and Management. He is also a council member of the Nordic Center at Fudan University, China, and has been the director of the Sino-Danish Center's Innovation Management Program in China since 2010 comprising a graduate program, a research program, as well as collaboration with the business community in China.

George Tesar is a Professor Emeritus of Marketing and International Business at Umeå University in Umeå, Sweden and Professor Emeritus at the University of Wisconsin-Whitewater. Professor Tesar has a doctorate from the University of Wisconsin-Madison and an MBA from Michigan State University. He is a mechanical engineer with several years of industry experience. He served on several boards and is professionally active as a consultant, training academics, executives, and managers in technology transfer, internationalization, and foreign market entry strategies. He is a founding member of the Product Development and Management Association, a professional association focusing on technology transfer and new product development. He is active in international student and faculty exchanges and is a member of the Fulbright Association. Professor Tesar can be reached at tesarg@uww.edu.

1   Mindsets and Global Organizational Strategies

John Kuada

Introduction

In 1983, Theodore Levitt argued persuasively that globalization was a powerful force driving the world towards a "converging commonality" (Levitt, 1983: 92). In his view, mankind was in a process of creating a world where differences would disappear. In contrast to the Levittian perspective of a globalized world, cultural sociologists (leaning on social identity theory) argued that as long as nations maintain their cultural identities, the organizations located in them will subscribe to values and administrative practices that are unique to these cultures (Hofstede, 1980; Schein, 1992; Trompenaars and Hampden-Turner, 1997). Employees' expectations and their interpretation of their organizational environment will correspondingly be different. Thus, many of the difficulties associated with cross-border business operations may be traced to differences in culture (Schein, 1992). International companies must therefore develop information processing capabilities that will enable them to acquire the knowledge they need to overcome their psychic distance as well as liabilities of foreignness to be able to operate effectively in foreign markets (Zaheer, 1995; Johanson and Vahlne, 2009). In other words, managing international business environments successfully requires continuous learning. It also requires the development of mindsets that are globally oriented (Levy, Beechler, Taylor and Boyacigiller, 2007). It has been argued that the more global the mindset of an organization, the easier it is for it to adopt and successfully implement a global strategy (Bowen and Inkpen, 2009; Javidan and Walker, 2012).

But because individuals are not blank sheets of paper on which culture writes its scripts, they do not totally adopt culturally prescribed mindsets. The general understanding is that, due to their cognitive endowments and different role identities in the various situations, individuals may reject some culturally prescribed rules of behavior or find their way around them in order to find creative solutions to specific personal and/or organizational problems. Thus, it is the reflexivity of employees as individuals over their daily interactions with others that shapes and gives meaning to the cultures of their organizations (Kuada, 2015). This perspective, therefore, acknowledges the existence of "multiple realities" that emerge through employees' actions and therefore allow for multiple learning and innovative processes within organizations. It means one cannot discuss the internationalization processes of firms without taking cognizance of individual employees and mindsets. Individuals that demonstrate global mindset are described as those who exhibit openness as well as the cognitive capacity to mediate and integrate multiplicity.

These perspectives have encouraged the adoption of the "global mindset" by scholars and practitioners as a summary construct that captures the manner in which individuals and organizations with global outreach think and act. The understanding is that the more global the mindset of an organization and its employees, the easier it is for them to adopt and successfully implement a global strategy. This entails the development of cognitive and behavioral repertoires that ensure the awareness, understanding, and adjustment to cultural variances and managing people with a variety of values, attitudes, beliefs, and standards in different operational environments. Individuals develop these repertoires through a continuous process of learning from experience. Thus, scholars such as Kedia and Mukherji (1999) describe global mindset in terms of a manager's openness and an ability to recognize complex interconnections, manage uncertainties within the international space, and to balance tensions that arise between the needs for universal corporate policies and local peculiarities. Similarly, Paul (2000) emphasizes the need for managers to acknowledge and endorse cultural diversity and, at the same time, strive to achieve some degree of cultural diversity.

This book provides an overview of the contemporary discourses in this emerging field and gives researchers a base to ground their thinking. It also provides a jumping-off point for possible new research directions. At face value, the notion of mindset connotes something that is set or fixed. But in practice, the chapters presented in this volume suggest that mindset can be aptly perceived as a dynamic construct. The contributions lean on the growing body of literature in the field to forward the general understanding that global mindsets are both collective (i.e., organizational) and person specific. Furthermore, it is emergent (i.e., continuously changing) as individuals and organizations continuously learn and then adopt strategies that enable them to manage uncertainties within the international space and to balance tensions that arise between the needs for universal corporate policies and local peculiarities.

Structure of the Book

The book includes both conceptual chapters that push the current boundaries of global mindset research and empirical chapters that demonstrate how different organizations in different countries apply mindset perspectives in their management practices. Given the fluid nature of global mindsets in action, we have adopted a flexible and somewhat wide-ranging approach to the discussions in the various chapters. But together, they all reinforce the contemporary understanding that, in order to succeed in a global business environment, managers need to have a global vision and a complementing strategy that help them transcend existing geographic and competitive boundaries and leverage worldwide resources in order to sustain their competitive positions.

In terms of structure, we have organized the discussion into two major sections. The first section consists of five chapters and discusses issues such as where we are now with respect to our knowledge in the field and what conceptual frameworks guide our thinking. The second section contains six chapters and provides empirical evidence about how different organizations in different parts of the world practice global mindset in different aspects of their managerial functions. Summaries of the chapters are presented here for a quick overview.

Because research into global mindsets is relatively recent, it makes sense to step back, create a summary of what is known about it, and reflect on where ideas might—or could—go next. The first major review of the global mindset literature was published by Levy and her colleagues in 2007. Their study provided a synthesis and a critical evaluation of the available literature on the subject at that time and provided a useful classificatory framework for subsequent investigations. Leaning on the literature available at that time, they presented global mindset as a multidimensional construct operationalized by the facets of *cognitive complexity* and *cosmopolitanism*. Since then, no other scholar has attempted an elaborate review of the global mindset literature. Andreea Ioana Bujac and John Kuada's contribution to this volume helps fill the gap. They do so in Chapter 2 by reporting the results of a systematic review of 28 papers that have studied the global mindset orientation in the period from 1995–2014. The review traces the development of the global mindset construct in order to provide scholars and practitioners with an analytical assessment of the existing research on the topic. The findings suggest that the field has experienced significant progress over the last decade. The number of empirical research has increased and studies have been conducted in a variety of countries and contexts. They also showed that two themes have dominated the research—"global mindset and leadership" and "global mindset and internationalization"—and most of the researchers were found in North America and Western Europe. They have also identified a number of knowledge gaps that should receive the attention of future researchers.

In Chapter 3, Nancy K. Napier and Kelsey Crow propose a process framework that can guide executives in their efforts to deliberately shape the development of a global mindset within their organizations. They argue that many major international organizations consider it appropriate for their employees and organizations to manifest global orientations in their interactions with their stakeholders. However, they remind us that frequently there are gaps between what leaders want or desire for their organizations and what they actually get. The key challenges they identify in their process framework include: (1) articulating an organization's specific, workable version of a global mindset, (2) making that version concrete enough for employees to understand and use in how they act, (3) communicating the mindset using multiple methods, (4) evaluating employees' ability to comprehend and execute the version, and (5) comparing actual outcomes and behaviors to intended ones.

Nigel Holden explores the shifting perspectives on the global mindset construct in the 21st century in Chapter 4. In his view, globally oriented leaders must exhibit high levels of diplomacy in their interactions with other people. Their profiles must reflect attributes such as the ability to show empathy, to emotionally connect to people from other parts of the world, and to be able to work effectively with them. These attributes allow individuals to build trusting relationships with people who are different from them, bring divergent views together, and develop consensus among different parties.

In Chapter 5, Olav Jull Sørensen also provides a review of the concept of global mindset and then proposes a framework for capturing the essence of the concept. He applies a two-dimensional matrix to explore the construct. One dimension of the matrix features global mindset as "a state of mind" defined and nurtured by the top executives in an organization. The other dimension sees global mindset as an organizational capability. This perspective emphasizes the evolutionary characteristic of global mindset—as a "continuous state of becoming and being aligned to a dynamic context". Furthermore, he argues that in practice, global mindset entails the development of "situational capabilities", i.e., the capability to sense (quickly), reflect (constructively), and act purposefully (for mutual benefit). The practical usefulness of his conceptualization is illustrated with a Danish MNC.

George Tesar and Hamid Moini have made two contributions to the volume. In Chapter 6, they explore the incipiency of the "global mindset" as a construct in international management among smaller manufacturing enterprises. Their underlying argument is that a careful examination of the initial managerial activities undertaken in smaller manufacturing enterprises during the early stages of their exporting operations can provide indications of the incipiency or otherwise of a global mindset in such firms. Therefore, they developed a conceptual model for research that could detect the early traces of a global mindset with the hope that this may potentially contribute to an understanding of their subsequent international activities. They follow up on this discussion in Chapter 7 by comparing the potential of the three types of top decision makers managing smaller manufacturing enterprises to form global mindsets, and to assess the motivations, or reasons, why decision makers develop global mindsets related to the needs of their unique smaller manufacturing enterprises. They argue, on the basis of their analyses, that there is a relationship between different types of smaller manufacturing enterprises managers and their individual propensity to develop a global mindset.

In Chapter 8, Quan Hoang Vuong introduces the concept of "mindsponge processes" to provide a framework for studying global mindset among Vietnamese firms. The "mindsponge processes" seeks to describe a global mindset as a "dynamic" process of inducting and expelling socio-cultural values. This process poses varieties of challenges and it behooves management to understand the mechanisms that individuals and/or organizations adopt to learn from their environments and shape their global mindset. The chapter provides guidelines to management in its effort to understand and influence the process within an emerging economy context, using Vietnam as an example.

I have earlier argued that culture has been frequently presented as a defining construct of global mindset in most studies. To the extent that organizations are seen as products of their society's culture, and are rooted in its deeper patterns, they socialize their managers and employees to use these cultural values and characteristics as reference points in their engagement with other people in other parts of the world. This strengthens their conviction in the management practices that have proved successful in their cultures and encourages them to transfer these practices to their collaborative partners. But it also carries the risk of discouraging them from questioning the assumptions that govern their behaviors. This understanding has motivated my study of culture's consequences of Danish-Ghanaian interfirm collaborations in Chapter 9. The key argument is that partners in cross-border relations must demonstrate high levels of cultural intelligence in order to operate successfully. The empirical evidence discussed in the chapter shows that cultural intelligence is even more important in relationships between partners from very dissimilar cultures and when there is an imbalance in the resources of the collaborating partners, making one partner more dependent on the other. Following Earley and Ang (2003), I argue that culturally intelligent individuals avoid employing automatic cognitive processing mechanisms in new situations—i.e., they suspend judgment partially when they operate in new contexts and/or are assessing situations. The ability to suspend judgment reduces the incidence of cultural errors in highly sensitive business situations where mutual suspicion tends to be rife.

Chapter 10 discusses the challenges of building a global mindset from the ground up and uses evidence from a Danish company to illustrate it. It is a joint contribution from Olav Jull Sorensen, Nigel Holden, Nancy K. Napier, George Tesar, and myself. We argue that some MNCs tend to initiate their corporate global mindset development process from the helm of their companies. When the adoption of a global mindset is initiated by top management, this takes the form of "sensegiving" (Maitlis and Sonenshein, 2010) whereby other organizational members are encouraged to construct new meanings of their interactions with others. The weaknesses of this approach have been illustrated with evidence from a Danish company where the employees in both headquarters and subsidiaries expressed reservations about top management "imposed" mindsets. We therefore argue that it is more appropriate for MNCs to allow their corporate mindset development process to be driven less by structure and more by interactive process of managers and employees engaged in a wide variety of activities and at multiple levels of the company. We further advise that the composition of the top management team and the board of directors ought to reflect the diversity of markets in which the company wants to compete. In terms of mindset, a multicultural board could help operating managers to facilitate reflection and learning through providing a broader perspective and specific knowledge about new trends and changes in the environment. Recruiting from diverse sources worldwide supports the development of a global mindset. A multicultural top management, as described previously, might improve the company's chances of recruiting and motivating high-potential candidates from various countries.

I discuss the issue of expatriation and global mindset development in Chapter 11. Expatriation has been described as a specific and unique example of employee socialization, comprising (1) knowledge acquisition or learning, and (2) adjustment to the requirements of new work and non-work environments. To be successful, expatriates are expected to develop social skills and networks, and gain local, cultural, and work-related knowledge. The discussions further suggest that the overall capability to operate successfully in a new cultural setting depends on the following interrelated factors: (1) personality of the expatriate, (2) the expatriate's degree of global orientation, (3) home country cultural characteristics, and (4) culture of the international organization.

Chapter 12 pulls together the emerging questions with no clear answers from the different chapters and provides some directions as to where we might go from here in terms of research. In this chapter, I reinforce the earlier arguments presented in the preceding chapters that the practice of global mindset can also present paradoxes in international management. These paradoxes include the simultaneous accommodation of divergent perspectives of mindset at different levels of organizations to allow for individual interpretations of organizational values to fit local contexts, but at the same time to achieve a certain degree of strategic cohesion.

Conclusions

Put together, this book tackles a topic that is relatively new in research and practice, and is considered by many top executives to be critical for firms seeking to conduct global business. The main message emerging from the various contributions is that mindset shapes the perception of management and thus determines which strategies to pursue and how to implement them. The mindset is usually influenced by the type of organizational structure the company has chosen, its administrative heritage, top management composition, and the degree of international experience of its key employees.

Attributes such as nimbleness, mindfulness, agility, openness to foreignness, awareness of cultural diversity, and ability to handle this diversity are considered important to managing successfully in global environments. These attributes are compromised when top management insists on a universal adoption of its values and practices in local subsidiaries.

At face value, the notion of mindset connotes something that is set or fixed. But discussions suggest that, in practice, mindset is more aptly seen as a dynamic construct. So studies must examine how mindsets evolve, how individuals and groups learn, and what conditions undergird this learning process and what consequences can be expected. One must expect shifts in individual and collective mindsets as employees live through new experiences, new challenges, and new personal interactions with actors in different parts of the world.

References

Bowen, D. E. and Inkpen, A. C. (2009) "Exploring the role of 'global mindset' in leading change in international contexts", *Journal of Applied Behavioral Science*, vol. 45, no. 2, pp. 239–260.

Earley, P. C. and Ang, S. (2003) *Cultural Intelligence: Individual Interactions Across Cultures*. (Palo Alto: Stanford University Press).

Hofstede, G. (1980) *Culture's Consequences: International Differences in Work-Related Values*. (Beverly Hills, CA: Sage Publications).

Javidan, M. and Walker, J. L. (2012) "A whole new global mindset for leadership", *People and Strategy*, vol. 35, no. 2, pp. 36–41.

Johanson, J. and Vahlne, J.-E. (2009) "The Uppsala internationalization process model revisited: From liability of foreignness to liability of outsidership", *Journal of International Business Studies*, vol. 40, no. 9, pp. 1411–1431.

Kedia, B. L. and Mukherji, A. (1999) "Global managers: Developing a mindset for global competitiveness", *Journal of World Business*, vol. 34, no. 3, pp. 230–251.

Kuada, J. (2015) *Private Enterprise-Led Economic Development in Sub-Saharan Africa: The Human Side of Growth*. (London: Palgrave Macmillan).

Levy, O., Beechler, S., Taylor, S. and Boyacigiller, N. A. (2007) "What we talk about when we talk about 'global mindset': Managerial cognition in multinational corporations", *Journal of International Business Studies*, vol. 38, no. 2, pp. 231–258.

Maitlis, S., & Sonenshein, S. (2010). Sensemaking in Crisis and Change: Inspiration and Insights From Weick (1988). Journal of Management Studies, vol. 47, no. 3, pp. 551–580.

Paul, H. (2000). "Creating a Mindset", *Thunderbird International Business Review*, vol. 42, no. 2, pp. 187–200.

Schein, E. H. (1992) *Organizational Culture and Leadership*, 2nd Ed. (San Francisco: Jossey-Bass).

Trompenaars, F. and Hampden-Turner, C. (1997) *Riding the Waves of Culture*. (London: Nicholas Brealey Publishing).

Zaheer, S. (1995) "Overcoming the liability of foreignness", *The Academy of Management Journal*, vol. 2, no. 38, pp. 341–363.

2 Two Decades of Global Mindset Research

Approaches and Issues

Andreea Ioana Bujac and John Kuada

Introduction

The last two decades have witnessed a growing awareness within the academic and practitioner literature of the importance of a global mindset for cultivating competitive advantages and improving the organizational outcomes of international companies operating in diverse geographical areas (Kedia and Mukherji, 1999; Gupta and Govindarajan, 2001; Koh, Gammoh and Okoroafo, 2014). This awareness is also a reflection of the challenges that the increasing complexity of the global business world generate for employees and managers. In 2007, Levy and her colleagues undertook a critical assessment of the global mindset literature with a view to providing an integrated framework on which future theoretical and empirical research could build. They grouped the studies reviewed into two perspectives: cultural and strategic perspectives. They then combined both perspectives to form a third perspective, which they labeled a multidimensional perspective. They also identified two constructs from the social sciences (cosmopolitanism and cognitive complexity) that underlie the perspectives found in the literature. They noted further that there were limited empirical investigations on the topic at that point in time. Since then, the number of empirical investigations has increased and several other authors have contributed to the field. However, no additional review has been conducted to provide researchers with an overview of the ways in which the field has evolved and the consequences of its evolution for the construct itself as well as the conceptual models and methods that researchers have adopted to provide additional insight into the field. Furthermore, Levy and her colleagues adopted what is commonly referred to as a conventional approach to selecting the literature included in their review—i.e., based on what the reviewers arbitrarily considered as relevant. This is in contrast to a systematic approach to literature review—an approach described by Jesson, Matheson, and Lacey (2011:104) as "fulfilling the scientific requirements for internal validity."

The present chapter builds on the earlier review done by Levy and her colleagues and seeks to make two contributions to the field. First, in contrast to Levy, Beechler, Taylor, and Boyacigiller (2007), we have undertaken a systematic review of the global mindset literature spanning nearly two decades (1995–2014) in order to provide a description of the contemporary research knowledge in the field. By adopting a systematic approach to this review, we also opted for an approach that can hold grounds against the possibility of being biased. Second, we draw attention to distinctive knowledge gaps in current research and identify opportunities for future research.

We have organized the discussions in the chapter as follows. Section 2 presents the methods used in selecting the literature that has been reviewed. This is followed by a summary of the findings, discussing issues such as the profiles of the authors, the citations and impact of the papers, the main topics addressed in the studies, their theoretical groundings, and the methods used in the investigations, as well as the main conclusions they arrived at. The remaining sections examine the knowledge gap that we see and suggest directions for future research.

Methodology

As noted above, we have opted for a systematic approach to select the papers that we have reviewed. This approach is characterized by being methodical, objective, standardized, structured, transparent, and replicable (Collins and Fauser, 2005). According to Jesson et al. (2011:104), a systematic literature review provides a "transparent means for gathering, synthesizing and appraising the findings of studies on a particular topic." This is in contrast to conventional approaches to literature selection, which are frequently characterized as being whimsical, subjective, variable, chaotic, and idiosyncratic. Petticrew and Roberts (2006) suggest the following seven stages for conducting a proper systematic literature review:

1. Clearly define the question that the review is setting out to answer.
2. Determine the types of studies that need to be located in order to answer your question.
3. Carry out a comprehensive literature search to locate those studies.
4. Screen the results of that search (that is, sift through the retrieved studies, deciding which ones look as if they fully meet the inclusion criteria).
5. Critically appraise the included literature.
6. Synthesize the studies and assess heterogeneity among the study findings.
7. Disseminate the findings of the review.

With regard to the first step, the present study seeks to provide answers to the following questions:

1. How many conceptual/empirical papers have been published on global mindset between 1995 and 2014?

2. What are the main issues covered in these studies?
3. What are the characteristics of the authors involved in this strand of research?
4. What methods of data collection and analysis have the researchers adopted?
5. What research gaps have they identified that still need to be addressed?

For the second and third steps, we undertook a systematic search of the database ABI/Inform, where the terms "global mindset" and "business" were used to identify the available published papers within the time range 1995–2014. The first hit showed a total of 194 journal articles from 80 journal publications within 19 research domains: business ethics and governance, general management, management development and education, international business and area studies, operations, technology and management, human resource management and employment studies, marketing, organization studies, entrepreneurship and small business management, public sector management, information management, tourism and hospitality management, psychology, innovation, economics, strategic management, business history, accountancy, and sector studies.

The next step into the data search was to identify all journals present on the Association of Business Schools (ABS) journal list (2010) within these areas. Journals are usually ranked from grade four (top) to grade one (bottom). According to the ABS journal ranking list (version 4, 2010), grade four journals publish the most original and best-executed research. Articles in grade one journals are described as having a "recognized standard." In addition to the ABS graded journals, we also included a number of influential articles through the backward snowballing technique, by identifying key articles and authors referenced in a number of selected papers. In total, 36 articles were found that either mentioned global mindset or actually discussed the concept. Table 2.1 provides an overview of the articles.

We then read all the abstracts and keywords of the 36 articles in order to exclude those articles that were not of interest to this investigation (step four in the Petticrew and Roberts's list). As an outcome of the review, 28 articles were found to be of interest and accepted as part of the literature review (see Table 2.2). A short summary, including author, year, purpose of the article, document type, country of affiliation of authors, sample, data collection method, scale measurement, and findings, is presented in Appendix 2.1.

A quick review of the years of publication of the articles indicates that academic interest in global mindset increased significantly after 2010, with an average of four papers being published in reputed international journals per year. This is in contrast to an average of one paper per year between 1995 and 2004 (with no papers appearing in 2005 and 2006).

Table 2.1 Overview of Identified Articles

Research Area	Publication Title	ABS Rating	Number of Identified Articles Per Journal
1. International Business and Area Studies	1. *Journal of International Business Studies*	4	1
	2. *Thunderbird International Business Review*	2	2
	3. *Journal of World Business*	3	1
2. Organization Studies	4. *Organizational Dynamics*	3	1
	5. *Journal of Applied Behavioral Science*	1	1
3. Entrepreneurship and Small Business Management	6. *International Entrepreneurship and Management Journal*	1	2
	7. *Journal of International Entrepreneurship*	1	1
4. General Management	8. *MIT Sloan Management Review*	3	1
		1	1
	9. *Management Decision*	2	1
	10. *Canadian Journal of Administrative Sciences*	2	1
	11. *European Management Journal*		1
	12. *International Journal of Management*		
6. Strategic Management	13. *Strategic Management Journal*	4	1
7. Human Resource Management and Employment Studies	14. *Human Resource Management*	4	1

(*Continued*)

Table 2.1 (Continued)

Research Area	Publication Title	ABS Rating	Number of Identified Articles Per Journal
8. Other Journals Not Included in ABS Journal Ranking	Contemporary Management Research	N/A	1
	EuroMed Journal of Business	N/A	1
	European Journal of Training and Development	N/A	1
	International Business Research	N/A	1
	International Journal of Business and Social Science	N/A	1
	Journal of Chinese Economic and Foreign Trade Studies	N/A	1
	Journal of International Business and Cultural Studies	N/A	1
	Journal of Leadership & Organizational Studies	N/A	2
	People and Strategy	N/A	1
	South Asian Journal of Global Business Research	N/A	1
	The Academy of Management Executive	N/A	1
Total Number of Articles Reviewed			28

Findings

Authorship, Characteristics of the Studies, and Impact

The 28 articles were written by 62 authors—with 25 of them co-authored (a reflection of increased research interest in the subject). The authors with the largest number of publications were Augusto Felício and Subramaniam Ananthram, who have written three papers each. This is followed by Story, Barbuto, Caldeirinha, Rodrigues, Javidan, Kyvik, and Bowen, who have written two papers each. Seven of the co-authored papers were written by scholars from the same institution, the rest representing collaborations of scholars across two or more institutions. The country of affiliation of the authors is presented in Table 2.2, along with the journals in which they were published. It shows that 15 articles were written by scholars attached

Table 2.2 Country of Affiliation of Authors by Publication Journal

Publication Title	Western Europe	Central Eastern Europe	U.S.	Australia
Journal of International Business Studies	1			
Thunderbird International Business Review	1			1
Journal of World Business			1	
Organizational Dynamics			1	
Journal of Applied Behavioral Science			1	
International Entrepreneurship and Management Journal	2			
Journal of International Entrepreneurship	1			
MIT Sloan Management Review			1	
Management Decision			1	
Canadian Journal of Administrative Sciences	1			
European Management Journal			1	
International Journal of Management				1
Strategic Management Journal			1	
Human Resource Management	1			
Contemporary Management Research				1
EuroMed Journal of Business		1		
European Journal of Training and Development			1	
International Business Research			1	
International Journal of Business and Social Science			1	
Journal of Chinese Economic and Foreign Trade Studies				1
Journal of International Business and Cultural Studies			1	
Journal of Leadership & Organizational Studies	1		1	
People and Strategy			1	
South Asian Journal of Global Business Research			1	
The Academy of Management Executive			1	
Total	8	1	15	4

to institutions in the U.S., nine are from authors based in Europe, and four are from Australia.

Seven of the articles were of a conceptual nature. These include those authored by Kedia and Mukherji (1999); Gupta and Govindarajan (2002); Story and Barbuto (2011); Javidan and Bowen (2013); Gaffney, Cooper, Kedia, and Clampit (2014). Nineteen were based on empirical investigations. These include articles written by Murtha, Lenway, and Bagozzi (1998); Begley and Boyd (2003); Nummela, Saarenketo, and Puumalainen (2004); Bowen and Inkpen (2009); Ananthram, Pearson and Chatterjee (2010); Paul, Meyskens, and Robbins (2011); Ananthram, Pick, and Issa (2012); Felício, Caldeirinha, and Rodrigues (2012); Javidan and Walker (2012); Cseh, Davis, and Khilji (2013); Felício, Caldeirinha, Rodrigues, and Kyvik (2013); Kyvik, Saris, Bonet, and Felício (2013); March (2013); Massingham (2013); Ananthram and Nankervis (2014); Koh et al. (2014), and Vogelgesang, Clapp-Smith, and Osland (2014). There was only one literature review during the period—i.e., that by Levy et al. (2007).

Thirteen of the empirical investigations were done using survey methods, and six used interviews. The data were collected in 10 different countries: the U.S. (11 studies), Portugal, Canada, and India (3 studies each), Australia (2 studies), Norway, Croatia, Finland, Brazil, Japan, and China (with one study each). The survey sample sizes ranged from 27 executives in a single country (Massingham, 2013) to 13,000 managers worldwide (Javidan and Walker, 2012). In the case of the studies done using interviews, the sample sizes ranged from one (March, 2013) where Mr. Surya Kant, president of Tata Consultancy Services, was interviewed, to 39 (Begley and Boyd, 2003), where HR executives in 32 publicly traded high-technology MNEs, or Multinational Enterprises, were surveyed.

Using the Web of Science Citation Count by Thomson Reuters, we conducted a citation count for the 28 global mindset articles. An overview of the citation count can be seen in Table 2.3. The analysis showed that the articles received a total of 560 citations. The study conducted by Gupta and Govindarajan (2002) received the highest citation count of 123 citations and seems to be the most influential in the field, followed by the literature review by Levy et al. (2007), which was cited 92 times. Murtha et al. (1998) and Kedia and Mukherji (1999) received 72 and 71 citations, respectively.

We have examined the thematic issues that the authors have studied in connection with a global mindset. The results are presented in Table 2.4. Seven of the studies discussed a global mindset in relation to the internationalization process of firms with a focus on issues such as the role of a global mindset in the successful internationalization of small and medium-sized companies and the influences of global mindsets on the development of emerging market multinationals (EMNEs). The twenty other papers have covered themes such as the development of a global mindset, a global mindset in a hypercompetitive environment, characteristics of managers associated

Table 2.3 Citation Counts of Papers (Web of Science Citations)

Authors	Year of publication	Citation Count
Murtha, Lenway, Bagozzi,	1998	71
Kedia and Mukherji	1999	72
Paul	2000	35
Harvey and Novicevic	2001	18
Gupta and Govindarajan	2002	123
Begley and Boyd	2003	40
Nummela, Saarenketand, and Puumalainen	2004	64
Levy, Beechler, Taylor, and Boyacigiller	2007	92
Bowen and Inkpen	2009	14
Subramaniam, Pearson, and Chatterjee	2010	3
Lovvorn and Chen	2011	11
Paul, Meyskens, and Robbins	2011	4
Story and Barbuto	2011	7
Ananthram, Pick, and Issa	2012	N/A
Miocevic and Crnjak-Karanovic	2012	N/A
Felício, Caldeirinha, and Rodrigues	2012	2
Javidan and Walker	2012	N/A
Cseh, Davis, and Khilji	2013	2
Felício, Caldeirinha, Rodrigues, and Kyvik	2013	0
Massingham	2013	N/A
Kyvik, Saris, Bonet, and Felício	2013	1
Javidan and Bowen	2013	1
March	2013	N/A
Gaffney, Cooper, Kedia, and Clampit	2014	0
Story, Barbuto, Luthans, and Bovaird	2014	0
Koh, Gammoh, and Okoroafo	2014	N/A
Vogelgesang, Clapp-Smith, and Osland	2014	N/A
Ananthram and Nankervis	2014	N/A

with a global mindset, cultural intelligence combined with a global business orientation, the relationship between an international assignment experience and the development of a global mindset, antecedents of a global mindset, comparison between a domestic mindset and a global mindset, relationship between positive psychological capital and a global mindset, and outcomes of a managerial global mindset.

Table 2.4 Research Themes in Global Mindset Articles Between 1995 and 2014

Research Themes	Issues Addressed	Authors
Global Mindset and Management	Creating a global mindset as a prerequisite for global strategies	Murtha et al. (1998); Kedia and Mukherji (1999); Gupta and Govindarajan (2002); Begley and Boyd (2003); Javidan and Walker (2012); Cseh et al. (2013); Javidan and Bowen (2013);
	Global mindset in a hypercompetitive environment	Harvey and Novicevic (2001)
	Characteristics of managers associated with a global mindset	Bowen and Inkpen (2009); Ananthram, Pearson, and Chatterjee (2010); Paul et al. (2011); March (2013)
	Cultural intelligence combined with a global business orientation	Story and Barbuto (2011)
	Relationship between an international assignment experience and the development of a global mindset	Lovvorn and Chen (2011)
	Antecedents of a global mindset	Ananthram et al. (2012); Story, Barbuto, Luthans, and Bovaird (2014)
	Comparison between a domestic mindset and a global mindset	Massingham (2013)
	Relationship between positive psychological capital and a global mindset	Vogelgesang et al. (2014)
	Outcomes of a managerial global mindset	Ananthram and Nankervis (2014)
Global Mindset and Internationalization	Role of a global mindset in the successful internationalization of small and medium-sized companies	Nummela, Saarenketand and Puumalainen (2204); Felício, Caldeirinha and Rodrigues (2012); Felício, Caldeirinha, Rodrigues and Kyvik (2013); Kyvik, Saris, Bonet and Felício (2013) Koh, Gammoh and Okoroafo (2014)
	Influences of global mindsets on the development of EMNEs outward foreign direct investment (FDI) decision-making	Gaffney et al. (2014)

Evolution of the Global Mindset Stream of Research

Levy et al. (2007) trace the roots of global mindset studies back to studies by Aharoni (1966), Kindleberger (1969), and Perlmutter (1969), who have argued that the cognitive capabilities of senior managers are important to the performance of multinational companies (MNCs). But recent studies that use the global mindset construct appear to start with the study by Murtha et al. (1998), who investigated attitudes that underlie international strategy processes and proposed that certain managerial patterns document a process of organizational learning that can link managers' mindsets with senior managers' intentions in the course of proactive international strategic changes. While surveying 370 managers in 13 country affiliates over a period of three years (1992–1995), they found that the global mindset of managers working in a single MNC evolved as the global strategy of the organization and resulted in the development of a more global mindset among the managers. At just about the same time, Kedia and Mukherji (1999) wrote a conceptual paper to underlie the mindsets of managers that are less useful in the global environment and how a global mindset can overcome the challenges in a competitive environment. They suggested that the creation of an appropriate environment to move managers from a relatively dysfunctional mindset to one that creates a global perspective could overcome some of the challenges that managers face when operating in multiple international business environments. These studies were followed by Paul (2000), who examined how a global mindset shapes management perception and helps them develop global strategies. The main thrust of his argument was that managers need to continuously adapt the business models of their firms to market conditions in order to succeed with their international business operations. Harvey and Novicevic (2001) reported a study in which they examined the impact of dimensions of time (what they referred to as "timescapes") on the development of a global mindset. In their view, managers should develop a clear understanding of the functional and social dimensions of time as well as modify the standard operating procedures of an organization in order to gain a competitive advantage. Gupta and Govindarajan (2002) introduced a conceptual framework that can guide organizations and managers to assess the extent to which they have a global mindset.

The general studies of a global mindset were followed by industry-specific studies. Begley and Boyd (2003) examined how a global mindset impacts the competitiveness of high-technology MNCs by interviewing 39 HR executives. The results of their interviews showed that these firms appeared to enhance their competitiveness by balancing global formalization with local flexibility, and global standardization with local customization. This means it is more rewarding for MNCs in high-tech sectors to strive towards a balance between global practices and local delegation.

Research interest in the subject appeared to have waned between 2004 and 2008, when very few papers were published. The period between 2009 and 2014 has, however, revealed a renewed interest in the topic, with 20 of the 28 papers we have identified being published in this period. This wave of studies started with Bowen and Inkpen's (2009) study, which examined what characteristics enabled executives to effectively manage change in cross-culturally complex situations. They did so by interviewing the managing director of Johnson & Johnson Consumer Products in Brazil. The results revealed that the executive's cognitive capabilities that enabled him to understand the accepted rules of behavior in the Brazilian cultural context have contributed immensely to his success. Ananthram et al. (2010) adopted constructs such as organizational strategy, technology intensity, and entrepreneurial orientation as predictors of managerial global mindset intensity in the Indian and Chinese service industry. By surveying 239 Indian and 210 Chinese indigenous managers, they found that the service organizations in both India and China were highly technology intensive, and that technological intensity and entrepreneurial orientation were indeed significant determinants of managerial global mindset intensity. Paul et al. (2011) based their study on the premise that managers working in an international environment must balance competing expectations of maintaining the corporation's social and ethical norms while being open to and adaptive to diverse cultural expectations. They labeled the two divergent expectations as corporate social performance (ECSP) and cross-cultural sensitivity (CCS). The results of the study showed that ECSP and CCS were positively related, suggesting that companies whose managers have a global mindset are sensitive to both corporate social performance standards and cultural values and norms. Lovvorn and Chen (2011) argue that cultural intelligence plays a key role in transforming international experiences into a global mindset. With this understanding, they developed a model that sees the international experience of managers as a key antecedent for a global mindset and with cultural intelligence as a moderating factor. Story and Barbuto (2011) see cultural intelligence as a key antecedent in global mindset formation. They argue that a culturally intelligent person has the cognitive capacity to think and understand a new cultural environment and also to acquire behaviors that are needed in this environment. Building on Earley and Ang's (2003) study, they suggested the cultural intelligence construct can be decomposed into the following three sub-constructs: *cognitive*, *motivational*, and *metacognitive* intelligence. The *cognitive* component describes how individuals use the knowledge available to them, the *motivational* component describes the motivation of managers to adapt their behavior to new cultural contexts, and the *metacognitive* component describes managers' capacity to acquire new behaviors. The focus of their study was to explore the relationship between the global mindset of managers and outcome variables, including employees' trust in their leaders and organizational commitment. They present "complexity of global role" and "leader distance" as variables that moderate the relationship.

Based on an extensive research project with data from more than 13,000 managers from companies around the world, Javidan and Walker (2012) studied the critical importance of a global mindset orientation for leaders.

They argued that global mindset development entails intellectual capital (global business savvy, cognitive complexity, and cosmopolitan outlook), psychological capital (passion for diversity, quest for adventure, and self-assurance), and social capital (intercultural empathy, interpersonal communication skills, and diplomacy). Ananthram et al. (2012) identified six antecedents as potentially impacting global mindset development among Chinese, Indian, and Japanese executives. These were: knowledge and information, skills and abilities, risk tolerance, global identity, boundary-spanning activities, and international experience. Their empirical investigation revealed four of them to have statistically significant connections to the global mindset of the executives: knowledge and information at the managerial level, risk tolerance, boundary-spanning activities, and level of international experience. Similarly, Story et al. (2014) tested some theory-driven antecedents of a global mindset by surveying 136 global leaders of a well-known MNC in the U.S. The results showed that personal, psychological, and role complexity antecedents were related to the participants' level of global mindset. The relationship between positive psychological capital and a global mindset was also tested by Vogelgesang et al. (2014) on 176 students as part of a global leadership course. They found that positive psychological capital mediates the relationship between a global mindset and three relevant global leader competencies: non-judgmentalness, inquisitiveness, and performance.

As noted above, interviews were used in some of the empirical investigations to provide insights into the importance of a global mindset in international management decisions. Massingham (2013) compared domestic and global mindsets of managers in FDI decisions by interviewing executives at 27 of Australia's top 100 companies. The results showed that domestic mindsets tended to oversimplify FDI decisions, resulting in cognitive mistakes (e.g., in relation to making or buying decisions). He concluded that FDI decisions require global mindsets that reflect the complexities in identifying multiple variables that must be taken into account in making decisions that could enhance corporate performance. Cseh et al. (2013) also interviewed 24 global leaders in order to explore the requirements of leading in a global environment. The results showed the following factors as necessary for success within global environments: "transcendence, plasticity of the mind, mindfulness, curiosity, and humility" (p.493). They define plasticity of mind to include flexibility, thinking differently, rebalancing, openness, and having multiple frames of reference. Ananthram and Nankervis (2014) examined the outcomes and benefits of a managerial global mindset by interviewing 56 senior executives of MNCs in the U.S., Canada, and India. The findings suggested that there were similarities between the North American and Indian senior managers in terms of the outcomes and benefits of a managerial global mindset. Five dimensions and their outcomes of global mindsets were derived from the analysis. These are global identity, global strategy, flexibility, sustainable approaches to business, and diversity appreciation.

We have also noted that most of the researchers have not explicitly articulated the root assumptions underlying their discussions of global mindset. But, those adopting quantitative methods in their research appear to see organizational structures as key drivers of global mindset formation and tend to emphasize the impact of corporate mindsets on organizational goal attainment. Although they see individuals as executors of mindset through their behaviors and actions, they tend to do this on behalf of their organizations.

Global Mindset and Internationalization

The second research theme identified in our review is the relationship between global mindset orientation and internationalization process. The focus of most of the studies in this stream of research is on the impact that global mindset has on the internationalization process of small and medium-sized enterprises (SMEs). Nummela et al. (2004) studied the role of a global mindset in the successful internationalization of 72 small and medium-sized Finnish companies in the field of information and communications technology. They found that international managerial experience and market characteristics were important drivers of the global mindset in these firms. Felício et al. (2012) also studied the factors that develop a global mindset orientation and their influence on the internationalization of 211 small Portuguese companies. The results showed that the global mindset of key managers of these firms had a positive influence on the internationalization process of the firms, with particular reference to their international networking activities. But the impact was moderated by the growth potential and satisfaction with the performance in the domestic market, as well as the level of education of the entrepreneurs. Kyvik et al. (2013) studied the relationship between the global mindset of 215 Norwegian and 257 Portuguese small-firm decision makers and their firms' internationalization behaviors. The findings showed that there was a strong relationship between the global mindset of the managers and firm's internationalization behavior. Again, in 2013, Felício et al. extended their 2012 study by undertaking a comparative study of the influence of a global mindset on the internationalization behavior of 354 Norwegian and Portuguese small firms. The results showed some differences. While a global mindset appeared to have a behavioral impact on Norwegian entrepreneurs (i.e., conditions their international business behavior and experience), it appeared mainly to have a cognitive impact on the Portuguese entrepreneurs (i.e., influencing their desire to acquire technical expertise). Global mindset and global orientation were found to have more positive effects on the internationalization behavior of Norwegian firms than that of Portuguese firms.

Similar studies were conducted by Miocevic and Crnjak-Karanovic (2012) as well as Koh et al. (2014). Miocevic and Crnjak-Karanovic (2012) found that a global mindset was a crucial cognitive driver of 121 Croatian SMEs' export performance and internationalization process in general. In the same vein, Koh et al. (2014) examined differences in firm characteristics, export marketing strategies, and export performance outcomes across global mindset (ethnocentric, polycentric, and geocentric) orientations. The study covered senior-level executives of Canadian and U.S. small and medium-sized firms. The findings suggested that a global mindset influenced export strategy and performance, but not firm characteristics.

A few scholars focused their research on the impact of global mindset on the development of EMNEs. Among them were Gaffney et al. (2014), who examined the influences of global mindsets on outward FDI decision-making, drawing on institutional and cultural theories to explain the relationships. They argued that an individual level of global mindset drives organizational-level strategic orientation and vice versa. Furthermore, they argued that the process of EMNE internationalization will lead to an institutional transition within the home country, as well as stimulate the mechanisms that influence a global mindset orientation at the individual level and strategic orientation at the organizational level.

Some Research Directions

The studies also draw attention to gaps in the literature that require further academic attention. First, some scholars have called for more emphasis on researching the antecedents of global mindsets in different contexts, including differences across industry sectors as well as across organizations at different stages of the globalization process (see Ananthram et al. 2012). In this regard, it has been suggested that possible antecedents such as personality, management education, and leadership styles could be studied to see if they lead to global mindset development (Story et al. 2014). Second, additional investigations into how multinationals deal with the challenges of attracting globally minded employees have also been suggested. For example, Paul et al. (2011) suggest testing the relationship between two components of a global mindset: sensitivity to corporate social performance (CSP) and cross cultural sensitivity (CCS) among employees posted abroad or returning from international assignments. The idea is to examine the manner in which these variables could influence managers' willingness to continue to work with their companies. Third, some scholars have also suggested that testing the impact of organizational behavior variables such as psychological capital, motivation, employee satisfaction, and employee performance on global mindset development will help improve our understanding of the extent to which employee dispositions shape global mindset development (see Ananthram and Nankervis, 2014). Fourth, the role of psychological capital in global leadership has also been suggested as a topic for future research. Vogelgesang et al. (2014) argue in favor of the creation of a psychometrically validated instrument of PsyCap for global leaders given the global context in which they work. Finally, with regard to global mindset and internationalization, Perlmutter's study (1969) suggested that most companies move from an ethnocentric view to a polycentric and then to a geocentric view as their organizations operate at a global level. Koh et al. (2014) therefore suggest that future studies should include longitudinal assessments of changes in the firm's internationalization stages and variations in activities over time. It has also been argued that the impact of global mindset on international performance outcomes requires the introduction of new variables, like the entrepreneurial orientation. The introduction of such a variable would amplify the importance of intangible resources and capabilities in the SME internationalization process (Miocevic and Crnjak-Karanovic, 2012).

Conclusion

In sum, the discussions above suggest that the field of global mindset has experienced significant progress over the last decade. The amount of empirical research in the field has increased and the published investigations have become increasingly rigorous, moving global mindset discourses from a more conceptual level into the empirical domain in a variety of countries and contexts. Surveys and interviews have been the main approaches to data collection, while qualitative investigations have been few. Most of the studies have been done by scholars attached to institutions in Western Europe and the U.S. The field therefore provides good opportunities for research by scholars in other regions of the world. The study has also drawn attention to a number of knowledge gaps that current scholars have identified as worth researchers' attention. For example, the emergence of third-world multinationals on the economic scene provides opportunities for testing the appropriateness of previous models of global mindset formation to the executives of these companies.

References

Aharoni, Y. (1966). *The foreign investment decision process*. Boston: Harvard Business School Press.

Ananthram, S. & Nankervis, A.R. 2014, "Outcomes and Benefits of a Managerial Global Mind-Set: An Exploratory Study with Senior Executives in North America and India", *Thunderbird International Business Review,* vol. 56, no. 2, pp. 193–209.

Ananthram, S., Pearson, C. & Chatterjee, S. 2010, "Do Organizational Reform Measures Impact on Global Mindset Intensity of Managers? Empirical Evidence from Indian and Chinese Service Industry Managers", *Journal of Chinese Economic and Foreign Trade Studies,* vol. 3, no. 2, pp. 146–168.

Ananthram, S., Pick, D. & Issa, T. 2012, "Antecedents of a Global Mindset: A Mixed Method Analysis of Indian, Chinese and Japanese Managers", *Contemporary Management Research,* vol. 8, no. 4, pp. 305–330.

Begley, T.M. & Boyd, D.P. 2003, "The Need for a Corporate Global Mind-Set", *MIT Sloan Management Review,* vol. 44, no. 2, pp. 25–32.

Bowen, D.E. & Inkpen, A.C. 2009, "Exploring the Role of 'Global Mindset' in Leading Change in International Contexts", *Journal of Applied Behavioral Science,* vol. 45, no. 2, pp. 239–260.

Collins, A.J. & Fauser, C.J.M.B. 2005, "Balancing the Strengths of Systematic and Narrative Reviews", *Human Reproduction Update,* vol. 11, no. 2, pp. 103–104.

Cseh, M., Davis, E.B. & Khilji, S.E. 2013, "Developing a Global Mindset: Learning of Global Leaders", *European Journal of Training and Development,* vol. 37, no. 5, pp. 489–499.

Earley, P.C. & Ang, S. (2003). *Cultural Intelligence: An Analysis of Individual Interactions Across Cultures.* Palo Alto, CA: Stanford University Press.

Felício, J.A., Caldeirinha, V.R. & Rodrigues, R. 2012, "Global Mindset and the Internationalization of Small Firms: The Importance of the Characteristics of Entrepreneurs", *International Entrepreneurship Management Journal,* vol. 8, pp. 467–485.

Felício, J.A., Caldeirinha, V.R., Rodrigues, R. & Kyvik, O. 2013, "Cross-Cultural Analysis of the Global Mindset and the Internationalization Behavior of Small Firms", *International Entrepreneurship Management Journal,* vol. 9, no. 4, pp. 641–654.

Gaffney, N., Cooper, D., Kedia, B. & Clampit, J. 2014, "Institutional Transitions, Global Mindset, and EMNE Internationalization", *European Management Journal,* vol. 32, pp. 383–391.

Govindarajan, V., & Gupta, A.K. (2001). *The Quest for Global Dominance.* San Francisco: Jossey-Bass/Wiley.

Gupta, A.K. & Govindarajan, V. 2002, "Cultivating a Global Mindset", *Academy of Management Executive,* vol. 16, no. 1, pp. 116–126.

Harvey, M. & Novicevic, M.M. 2001, "The Impact of Hypercompetitive 'Timescapes' on the Development of a Global Mindset", *Management Decision,* vol. 39, no. 5/6, pp. 448–460.

Javidan, M. & Bowen, D.E. 2013, "The 'Global Mindset' of Managers: What It Is, Why It Matters, and How to Develop It", *Organizational Dynamics,* vol. 42, pp. 145–155.

Javidan, M. & Walker, J.L. 2012, "A Whole New Global Mindset for Leadership", *People and Strategy,* vol. 35, no. 2, pp. 36–41.

Jesson, J.K., Matheson, L. & Lacey, F.M. 2011, *Doing Your Literature Review: Traditional and Systematic Techniques.* (London: SAGE Publications), ISBN: 978-1-84860-153-6.

Kedia, B.L. & Mukherji, A. 1999, "Global Managers: Developing a Mindset for Global Competitiveness", *Journal of World Business,* vol. 34, no. 3, pp. 230–251.

Kindleberger, C.P. (1969): "American Business Abroad", *The International Executive,* vol. 11, no.2, pp. 11–12.

Koh, A.C., Gammoh, B.S. & Okoroafo, S.C. 2014, "An Investigation of Export Practices and Performance across Global Mindset Orientations", *International Business Research,* vol. 7, no. 1, pp. 60–73.

Kyvik, O., Saris, W., Bonet, E. & Felício, J.A. 2013, "The Internationalization of Small Firms: The Relationship between the Global Mindset and Firms' Internationalization Behavior", *Journal of International Entrepreneurship,* vol. 11, pp. 172–195.

Levitt, T., 1983, "The Globalization of Markets", *Harvard Business Review,* vol. 61, Issue 3, pp. 92–102.

Levy, O., Beechler, S., Taylor, S. & Boyacigiller, N.A. 2007, "What We Talk about When We Talk about 'Global Mindset': Managerial Cognition in Multinational Corporations", *Journal of International Business Studies,* vol. 38, no. 2, pp. 231–258.

Lovvorn, A.S. & Chen, J. 2011, "Developing a Global Mindset: The Relationship between an International Assignment and Cultural Intelligence", *International Journal of Business and Social Science,* vol. 2, no. 9, pp. 275–283.

March, R. 2013, "Global Mindset, Global Success at Tata Consultancy Services", *South Asian Journal of Global Business Research,* vol. 2, no. 1, pp. 27–32.

Massingham, P. 2013, "Cognitive Complexity in Global Mindsets", *International Journal of Management,* vol. 30, no. 1, pp. 232–248.

Miocevic, D. & Crnjak-Karanovic, B. 2012, "Global Mindset—A Cognitive Driver of Small and Medium-Sized Enterprise Internationalization: The Case of Croatian Exporters", *EuroMed Journal of Business,* vol. 7, no. 2, pp. 142–160.

Murtha, T.P., Lenway, S.A. & Bagozzi, R.P. 1998, "Global Mindsets and Cognitive Shift in a Complex Multinational Corporation", *Strategic Management Journal,* vol. 19, pp. 97–114.

Nummela, N., Saarenketo, S. & Puumalainen, K. 2004, "A Global Mindset—A Prerequisite for Successful Internationalization?", *Canadian Journal of Administrative Sciences,* vol. 21, no. 1, pp. 51–64.

Paul, H. 2000, "Creating a Mindset", *Thunderbird International Business Review,* vol. 42, no. 2, pp. 187–200.

Paul, H., Meyskens, M. & Robbins, S. 2011, "Components of a Global Mindset: Corporate Social Responsibility and Cross-Cultural Sensitivity", *Journal of International Business and Cultural Studies,* vol. 5, pp. 1–13.

Perlmutter, H., 1969, "The Tortuous Evolution of the Multinational Corporation", *Columbia Journal of World Business,* 4(1), pp. 9–18.

Petticrew, M. & Roberts, H. 2006, *Systematic Reviews in the Social Sciences: A Practical Guide.* (Oxford: Blackwell Publishing).

Story, J.S.P. & Barbuto, J.E. 2011, "Global Mindset: A Construct Clarification and Framework", *Journal of Leadership & Organizational Studies,* vol. 18, no. 3, pp. 377–384.

Story, J.S.P., Barbuto, J.E., Luthans, F. & Bovaird, J.A. 2014, "Meeting the Challenges of Effective International HRM: Analysis of the Antecedents of Global Mindset", *Human Resource Management,* vol. 53, no. 1, pp. 135–155.

Vogelgesang, G., Clapp-Smith, R. & Osland, J. 2014, "The Relationship between Positive Psychological Capital and Global Mindset in the Context of Global Leadership", *Journal of Leadership & Organizational Studies,* vol. 21, no. 2, pp. 165–178.

Appendix 2.1 Summary of the Articles

Authors Year	Title	Purpose	Type of Study	Region of Affiliation of Authors	Method	Findings
Murtha et al. (1998)	Global mindsets and cognitive shift in a complex and multinational corporation	The article investigates attitudes that underlie the process of organizational learning that can link managers' mindsets with senior managers' intentions during a proactive international strategic change process.	Empirical	U.S.	Survey covering 370 managers in 13 country affiliates and the head office of a U.S.-based diversified multinational corporation	The findings suggest that the global strategy of the organization led to a more global mindset among the managers during a three-year period (1992–1995)
Kedia and Mukherji (1999)	Global managers: developing a mindset for global competitiveness	The purpose is to examine those mindsets that the authors feel are useful in overcoming the challenges that managers face in a global competitive environment.	Conceptual	U.S.	—	A global mindset tends to make a manager more competent and effective in dispersing his knowledge and skills throughout the organization.
Paul (2000)	Creating a global mindset	The study aims at examining how mindset shapes the perception of management and determines which strategies to pursue and how to implement them.	Conceptual	Germany	—	The creation of a global mindset for companies depends on managers' ability to continuously adapt the company's business model to the prevailing market conditions.

(*Continued*)

Appendix 2.1 (Continued)

Authors Year	Title	Purpose	Type of Study	Region of Affiliation of Authors	Method	Findings
Harvey and Novicevic (2001)	The impact of hypercompetitive "timescapes" on the development of a global mindset	The study introduces the concept of "timescapes" and seeks to capture the dimensions of time in hypercompetitive environments. The construct of timescape is captured by seven dimensions: time frame, tempo, temporality, synchronization, sequence, emerging pauses/gaps, and simultaneity.	Conceptual	U.S.	—	The authors argue that a time-oriented global mindset is needed in order to enhance and accelerate managers' decision-making capabilities within hypercompetitive timescapes.
Gupta and Govindarajan (2002)	Cultivating a global mindset	The paper discusses the concept of global mindset, why it matters, and what companies can do to cultivate it.	Conceptual	U.S.	Cases	The authors provide a framework for conceptualizing global mindset and discuss how it can guide companies and managers in systematically creating a global mindset.
Begley, Thomas M and Boyd, David P (2003)	The need for a corporate global mindset	The authors investigate global mindset at the corporate level in high-technology MNCs.	Empirical	U.S.	Semi-structured interviews comprising 39 HR executives in 32 publicly traded high-technology MNCs	The results confirm the need for managers to balance global formalization/ standardization and local flexibility/customization within a global operational environment.

Author (Year)	Title / Aim	Type	Country	Method / Sample	Findings
et al. (2004)	is a prerequisite for successful internationalization? the role of a global mindset in the successful internationalization of small and medium-sized companies.			72 small Finnish companies in the field of information and communications technology.	managerial experience and market characteristics are important drivers of the global mindset.
Levy et al. (2007)	What we talk about when we talk about "global mindset": managerial cognition in multinational corporations. The paper reviews the literature on a global mindset and identifies common themes across writers: cultural, strategic, and multidimensional.	Literature review	Israel	Traditional literature review.	The authors define global mindset as a multidimensional construct using a cognitive framework. They argue that past research on a global mindset falls into three perspectives: cultural, strategic, and multidimensional. They suggested further empirical research in the field.
Bowen and Inkpen (2009)	Exploring the role of the "global mindset" in leading change in international contexts. The article aims at introducing "global mindset" as an individual-level variable to help explain the effectiveness of managers in international contexts. With this study, the authors wanted to map out the key characteristics of managers associated with effectively leading change in cross-culturally complex situations.	Empirical	U.S.	Interviews with managers of Johnson & Johnson Consumer Products Brazil	The findings suggest that global leaders of change should start the change process with an understanding of cultural contexts (power distance, future orientation, and uncertainty avoidance).

(Continued)

Appendix 2.1 (Continued)

Authors Year	Title	Purpose	Type of Study	Region of Affiliation of Authors	Method	Findings
Ananthram et al. (2010)	Do organizational reform measures impact the global mindset intensity of managers?	The paper investigates the strength of organizational strategy, technology intensity, and entrepreneurial orientation as predictors of managerial global mindset intensity in the Indian and Chinese service industries.	Empirical	Australia	Survey covering 239 Indian and 210 Chinese indigenous managers in the service sector	The results of the investigation demonstrate that technological intensity and entrepreneurial orientation were significant determinants of managerial global mindset intensity.
Lovvorn and Chen (2011)	Developing a global mindset: the relationship between an international assignment and cultural intelligence	The study aims at presenting how an individual's cultural intelligence will affect the relationship between an international assignment experience and the development of a global mindset.	Conceptual	U.S.	—	The authors argue that an individual's cognitive, motivational, and behavioral propensities impact his or her ability to develop the attributes of a global mindset.
Paul et al. (2011)	Components of a global mindset: corporate social responsibility and cross-cultural sensitivity	The study aims at developing an instrument to measure the relationship between two components: ESCSP and CCS.	Empirical	U.S.	Survey covering 439 business students from two large public universities in the Southeastern United States.	The findings suggest that the ESCSP and CCS scales are positively related, suggesting that they are convergent rather than divergent mindsets.

Author (Year)	Title	Aim	Type	Country	Method	Findings
Story and Barbuto (2011)	Global mindset: A construct clarification and framework	The paper proposes a framework of a global mindset that combines cultural intelligence and global business orientation.	Conceptual	Portugal	—	Based on the framework, the authors make three propositions that ought to be subjected to future empirical studies.
Ananthram et al. (2012)	Antecedents of a global mindset: a mixed-methods analysis of Indian, Chinese, and Japanese managers	The aim is to examine the extent to which current understandings about the antecedents of global mindsets apply to Indian, Chinese, and Japanese organizations.	Empirical	Australia	Survey and interview data were collected from 504 managers and interviews with done with 36 executives and managers.	The findings suggest convergence in the three Asian contexts, but there were variations in how the managers interpret their environments.
Miocevic and Crnjak-Karanovic (2012)	Global mindset: a cognitive driver of small and medium-sized enterprise internationalization?	The study examines the extent to which a global mindset can be a crucial cognitive driver of the SME internationalization process.	Empirical	Croatia	Survey covering 121 exporting SMEs in Croatia	The findings suggest that a global mindset is positively and significantly related to the export performance.
Felício et al. (2012)	Global mindset and the internationalization of small firms: the importance of the characteristics of entrepreneurs	The paper aims at addressing the factors that constitute the global mindset and their influence on the internationalization of small companies.	Empirical	Portugal	Survey of 211 small-sized Portuguese companies	The results show that managers' satisfaction with their companies' performance in the domestic market and the potential for growth in the domestic market has some impact on the extent to which they develop global mindsets.

(Continued)

Appendix 2.1 (Continued)

Authors Year	Title	Purpose	Type of Study	Region of Affiliation of Authors	Method	Findings
Javidan and Walker (2012)	A whole new global mindset for leadership	The paper discusses the critical importance of global mindset development for leaders.	Empirical	U.S.	Survey covering over 13,000 managers worldwide	The results confirm earlier findings, that a global mindset plays a significant role in the management of individuals, groups, and organizations from diverse cultural, political, and institutional backgrounds.
Cseh et al. (2013)	Developing a global mindset: the learning journeys of global leaders	The purpose of the study is to explore the requirements of leading in a global environment.	Empirical	U.S.	In-depth interviews 24 global leaders	The authors used their findings to develop a model that seeks to capture global leaders' learning journeys, characterized by informal learning during everyday work and life experiences, including learning from mistakes, and from and with others. This learning process shapes their global mindset development.

Felício et al. (2013)	Cross-cultural analysis of the global mindset and the internationalization behavior of small firms	The study aims at analyzing the influence of a global mindset on the internationalization behavior of Norwegian and Portuguese small firms.	Empirical	Portugal	Survey of 354 small firms	The results show that the global mindset of Norwegian entrepreneurs conditions their behavior and international experience, while for Portuguese entrepreneurs, it affects the cognitive domain and their technical expertise.
Massingham (2013)	Cognitive complexity in global mindsets	The article examines the cognitive complexity of decisions associated with FDI.	Empirical	Australia	Interviews: Data were collected from executives at 27 of Australia's top 100 companies	The authors examined the information-processing abilities of managers and compared domestic mindset with global mindset. They found that the decision whether to make or buy necessary knowledge is an important cognitive capability.
Kyvik et al. (2013)	The internationalization of small firms: the relationship between the global mindset and firms' internationalization behavior	The article adopts a cognitive perspective on management and explores the formation of the global mindset and the relationship between the global mindset of small-firm decision makers and their firms' internationalization behavior.	Empirical	Spain	E-mail survey of small firms: 215 in Norway, and 257 in Portugal	The findings suggest that there is a strong relationship between the global mindset and firms' internationalization behavior.

(Continued)

Appendix 2.1 (Continued)

Authors Year	Title	Purpose	Type of Study	Region of Affiliation of Authors	Method	Findings
Javidan and Bowen (2013)	The "global mindset" of managers: what it is, why it matters, and how to develop it	The paper presents two approaches to the development of a global mindset within international organizations.	Conceptual	U.S.	—	The two approaches presented by the authors are: 1. "find it" in individuals or organizations, and 2. "grow it." The first approach suggests that attributes such as demographics and the educational backgrounds of individuals can predict their global mindset development potential. With the second approach, global mindset must be developed through leadership development programs and coaching.
March (2013)	Global mindset, global success at Tata Consultancy Services	The paper examines how the president of North American, UK, and European operations at Tata Consultancy Services leads and grows a complex global company by adopting and operationalizing a global mindset.	Empirical	U.S.	Interview with Mr. Surya Kant, president of Tata Consultancy Services	By employing an inductive approach, the author suggests that there is a close link among the theoretical constructs of global mindset, paradox theory, complexity, leadership, and global business, and their use and applicability in driving a global corporation.

Gaffney et al. (2014)	Institutional transitions, global mindset, and EMNE internationalization	The study examines the influences of the home country institutions and intra-organizational mindsets on the development of EMNEs' outward FDI decision-making.	Conceptual	U.S.	—	The authors develop a conceptual framework that adopts a multi-level perspective of global mindset as an antecedent of firm decision-making. Institutional transition is believed to be a macro-level antecedent of a global mindset.
Story et al. (2014)	Meeting the challenges of effective international HRM: analysis of the antecedents of global mindset	The study identifies and empirical tests and some theory-driven antecedents of a global mindset.	Empirical	U.S.	Survey covering 136 global leaders of a well-known multinational	The findings suggest that personal, psychological, and role complexity antecedents were related to the participants' level of global mindset.
Koh et al. (2014)	An investigation of export practices and performance across global mindset orientations	The study examines differences in firm characteristics, export marketing strategies, and export performance outcomes across ethnocentric, polycentric, and geocentric orientations.	Empirical	U.S.	Survey covering senior level executives of Canadian and U.S. small and medium-sized firms	The findings show that a global mindset influences export strategy and performance, but not firm characteristics.

(Continued)

Appendix 2.1 (Continued)

Authors Year	Title	Purpose	Type of Study	Region of Affiliation of Authors	Method	Findings
Vogelgesang et al. (2014)	The relationship between positive psychological capital and global mindset in the context of global leadership	The authors tested a model that provides evidence for the role of positivity in global leader competence.	Empirical	U.S.	Archival data set of 176 students as part of a global leadership course	The authors found that positive psychological capital mediates the relationship between global mindset and three relevant global leader competencies: non-judgmentalness, inquisitiveness, and performance.
Ananthram and Nankervis (2014)	Outcomes and benefits of a managerial global mind-set: an exploratory study with senior executives in North America and India	The article examines the outcomes and benefits of a managerial global mind-set.	Empirical	Australia	Semi-structured interviews covering 56 senior executives of multinational corporations in North America (the United States and Canada) and India	The findings show that five dimensions of global mindsets were derived through the analyses: global identity, global strategy, flexibility, sustainable approaches to business, and diversity appreciation. These dimensions and their outcomes have significant implications for MNCs in relation to management development.

3 Moving Toward a Global Mindset
An Exploratory Process Framework

Nancy K. Napier[1] and Kelsey Crow[2]

For some time, global mindset has been a hot topic for managers to incorporate in their organizations and for academic scholars to study. As a result of its popularity, diverse views have sprung up around everything from its definition to how it can be developed practically. In this chapter, we review selected literature on global mindset and propose a process that addresses practical issues managers may face when wrestling with this important, yet often ambiguous concept. For instance, the idea of a global mindset that many academic articles describe may be, in fact, an ideal, even unreachable state that organizational leaders are striving for. The academic descriptions often seem highly conceptual and perhaps hard for managers to bring into their daily operations. Why is that? For starters, there are at least two primary challenges regarding the ephemeral concept of a global mindset. First is the problem of a useable definition, or figuring out exactly what the notion of a global mindset means in the workplace and what the precedents and factors around it are. Second is the issue of uncovering practical ways of applying it to specific organizations, each with its own processes, culture, and leadership style. In light of the possible variations of global mindset across and within organizations, it may be that the discussion, which has been mostly from the academic and research side, has been too abstract for managers to easily absorb and apply. Yet these ambiguous situations are the likely places where in an organization's attempts at a global mindset are most likely to not match up with the intended outcomes.

This chapter has three main parts. First, we provide a literature review of the recent literature on a global mindset to further explore its importance in the international business world, its key discussion factors, and potential gaps in the literature. Next, we present an exploratory process framework that includes: (1) articulating a workable version of global mindset, (2) making that version concrete enough for employees to understand and do something with it, (3) communicating the version using multiple methods, (4) evaluating employees' ability to comprehend and execute the version, and (5) comparing actual outcomes and behaviors to intended ones. Last, we suggest areas for future global mindset research springing directly from our exploratory framework.

Literature Review

We have divided this literature review into five key questions that link to the literature, but also to practical concerns managers have regarding the concept of global mindset. Within each section, we review selected existing literature and point out where the research gaps are and also where research has not been very well articulated. This will shape readers' understanding of the exploratory framework presented in the next section.

Why Is a Global Mindset So Important?

From business school deans (Aggarwal, 2011) to scholars and managers (Cohen, 2010; Javidan, Walker and Bullough, 2013; Levy, Beechler, Taylor and Boyacigiller, 2007; Nummela, Saarenketo and Saarenketo, 2004; Vogelgesang, Clapp-Smith and Osland, 2014), it has long been argued that a "global" mindset is important because of a "globalized" world. The importance emerges in several levels of analysis, but in particular, at the level of the firm, the level of the organizational unit, and the level of the individual.

Global mindset has been viewed from many different perspectives, from the internationalization of small firms (Kyvik, Saris, Bonet and Felício, 2013), to firm performance (Nummela, Saarenketo and Puumalainen, 2004; Raman, Chadee, Roxas and Michailova, 2013), to formulating strategic direction within an organization (Dragoni and McAlpine, 2012). It also lends itself to understanding a firm's consumer base—very convenient in international business, where consumer bases are often culturally diverse (Suh and Smith, 2008). In addition, a global mindset is particularly important in the management of teams, especially virtual and/or multicultural ones (Zander, Mockaitis and Butler, 2012). A particular advantage of a global mindset is its enhancement of individual managers' performance. It helps build managers' interpersonal abilities to negotiate with multiple cultures, each with its own precedents (just like individual organizations) (Smith and Victorson, 2012). A global mindset can provide managers with a toolbox they can use to influence people from different cultures (Javidan and Walker, 2013); furthermore, recent research even suggests that a global mindset may dovetail into the areas of innovation, creativity, and sustainability (Cleaver, 2012; Waite, 2014).

By now, some might say that a global mindset is old news, the argument for its necessity having existed for years. It is likely that academics and managers who operate globally no longer question the importance of managers thinking more globally in their decision-making; however, less clear are the specific actions and behaviors that employees who are lower down in the organization (non-managers) should be exhibiting to reflect their so-called global thinking. Should organizations focus first on translating their concept of global mindset into concrete behaviors as the core of the issue, or should they first focus on communicating a broad understanding of the implications of global mindset? Much of the literature seems to make an assumption that understanding global mindset cognitively leads to action that reflects it. In other words, is there a gap between how far the theory of global mindset has come and how concrete it's going to need to become in order to be realistically incorporated by managers in their organizations? We think there is.

What Exactly Is a Global Mindset?

One of the longest-running challenges for the academic community has been defining global mindset in ways organizational members can grasp. It's an ambiguous concept. One classic article compared a global mindset to the also ambiguous concept of love by titling itself after Raymond Carver's collection of short stories: *What We Talk About When We Talk About Love* (the article's title is *What we talk about when we talk about 'global mindset:' Managerial cognition in multinational corporations*) (Levy et al., 2007). Levy et al. (2007: 246) summarize the descriptors of a global mindset as being cognitive, existentialist (as in a state of "being"), and behavioral (as in "propensity to engage . . . adapt," or being curious). Further, much of the literature focus has been primarily at the senior, strategic, or top management team level.

Lots of research has gone into understanding the factors driving global mindset—such as the personal, psychological, and role complexity variables contributing to the various levels within global mindset (Story, Barbuto, Luthans and Bovaird, 2014). Other researchers, such as Gaffney, Cooper, Kedia, and Clampit (2014), suggest that while a global mindset relates to the internationalization process, emerging market multinationals may not be able to move as quickly as they wish because institutional change isn't present in large enough quantities to support them. Others consider cultural intelligence as critical (Lovvorn and Chen, 2011), and some researchers argue for more context-specific research (Tsui, 2004), raising the question of whether a global mindset is truly universal, or whether it is more context-specific, or at least context-influenced.

While much of the academic literature focuses on understanding the factors that go into creating global mindset (Levy et al., 2007), few researchers have examined whether a global mindset can translate into action—and if so, how. Bird and Osland (2005) do offer a framework suggesting that leaders must understand another culture before acting, and they lay out a process of framing a situation involving cultural differences and making attributions to try to understand it, ending with the selection of a script before action is taken. Earley and Peterson (2004) suggest a focus on the ability of adaptation rather than on the study of behaviors intended for specific cultures. They aim to integrate cognitive, behavioral, and motivational aspects in formulating a leader's global mindset.

Some of the academic literature focuses on how managers understand a given situation before taking action. There is an expectation that combining attention to culture with the proper interpretation of a given culture will lead to the proper action. In other words, most research moves from the theoretical to the specific. Given that academics have their own mindset of approaching concepts, this makes sense: It's a question of cognitive assessment before action. However, research on adult learning (Gardner, 1999; Knowles, 1990; Kolb and Fry, 1975) suggests that leaders learn in the reverse of the academic pattern—they start in the concrete, and through individual experiences, they broaden out to a more general level. Managers, and other employees as well, may need to observe and act via trial and error before later understanding the concepts that drive their global mindsets. For them, the focus could be more on action rather than on preliminary understanding. The ability to translate the abstract into the concrete, therefore, must be something that leaders and managers are able to do, and yet there is little attention to that in research. Perhaps academics, who tend to go from the universal to the specific, have assumed the same works for managers and employees within organizations, who may be the opposite.

How Is a Global Mindset Spread Throughout an Organization?

The literature on instilling or spreading the notion of a global mindset seems to follow three tracks. First, several people argue for training students in international business programs to think globally. Second, there is discussion about curriculum suggestions (Witte, 2010), including building in cultural experiences (Smith, 2012) with deliberate reflection (Tuleja, 2014). Finally, some research focuses on "training the trainers"—whether the trainers are professors, human resource managers, or global managers themselves (Blaess, Hollywood and Grant, 2012; Cseh, Davis and Khilji, 2013; Javidan et al., 2013; Wilson, 2013). Much of the suggested training and experiences is fairly similar—such as reading, talking with leaders about global mindset, or going through a cultural experience. Interestingly, the research does not tackle in any deliberate way how organizational leaders can or do spread the ideas and behaviors relating to global mindset throughout their organizations. The focus in the research is more about how to get the idea out to teachers (or students), but not within organizations where it plays out, or should. So how do leaders help organizational members develop and act in ways that reflect an ability to be more globally aware, inclusive, and open?

Somewhat related to instilling a global perspective into employees' mindsets is the question of how managers can enhance the chances that a global mindset is carried out through actions. Very little literature addresses the ongoing application of global mindset, although Bird and Osland (2005) recognize the need for explicit action when conflict arises. Their approach of framing situations, making "why" attributions, and selecting scripts comes close to suggestions for action. Most of the other literature seems to focus on explaining factors that either lead to or inhibit a global mindset—rather than on the ongoing process of living it on a regular basis. From a managerial perspective, there is a dearth in methods of equipping leaders to follow through on specific behaviors and actions.

How Do Organizations Know if It's Working?

Literature on the impact of global mindset links back to why it is important, ranging from enhanced internationalization to the increased performance in managers' ability to interact with people from different cultures and resulting in an increased ability to be flexible and open (Kyvik et al., 2013; Nummela, Saarenketo and Puumalainen, 2004; Zander et al., 2012). But several questions are unanswered in the literature. For instance, how do organizational leaders know whether a global mindset exists within their organizations—or in which parts of the organization it exists—or how it manifests? How do they determine which global mindset-oriented actions are critical for the organization? How do they measure whether employees' mindsets are as global as they desire? Finally, how do they answer one other, very fundamental question: Is a global mindset necessary in the same way throughout the firm? As Chapter 2 of this book suggests, perhaps the degree and the nature of global mindset needs to vary across levels—functions—and/or locations of a given organization. Rather than being a blanket expectation, should it be more context-driven and executed?

To address the gaps we see in the literature, we propose an exploratory process framework in the next section that considers some of these issues and offers a practical way for managers—and academics—to consider how to deliberately encourage a more global mindset within organizations.

Exploratory Process Framework

In this section, we propose a framework as a sort of potential question-and-checkpoints that managers—and academics—could use to encourage a broader global mindset within their firms. For this chapter, we view global mindset as a range of concrete actions or behaviors that employees, even those below managerial ranks, could be expected to incorporate and that enhance the openness toward people from experiences and backgrounds different from their own.

The exploratory process includes: (1) articulating an organization's specific workable version of global mindset, (2) making that version concrete and explicit for employees, (3) communicating the version using multiple methods, (4) evaluating employees' ability to comprehend and execute the version, and (5) comparing actual outcomes and behaviors to intended ones.

This framework is based on factors that we see and do not see in the literature and in practice, and we offer it as a way that leaders may consider instilling a global mindset in their organizations. We assume there is no single best way, place, or format for developing a global mindset. Rather, we expect that leaders within the units and locations of organizations will have their own view on what, how, and why they wish to encourage a more global way of thinking and behaving. In that vein, we lay out the exploratory framework as a process and series of checks that managers can use to implement their specific organization's plans for a global mindset.

Articulating the "Best-Case Scenario Global Mindset"

In visits and interviews with various leaders on global mindset, we frequently receive vague answers to the question, "What would the best-case scenario global mindset be in your organization?" Many leaders make comments like, "employees think beyond their units," "employees realize we source from and sell to people outside our country," "we need to hire people who are different than we are," or "we want employees to be able to work with people from other cultures." So, one of the first challenges for leaders at any level of an organization is to realize their part in the challenge of global mindset's ambiguity.

A similar situation exists when leaders discuss the values in their organizations and how those values may or may not translate into the current culture of the firm. For example, many organizations hold similarly stated values like respect, integrity, teamwork, or "doing the right thing." But even though the values sound similar, the ways they are manifested or shown in action can vary widely. In one firm, "respect" could mean executives and employees call each other out for interrupting or ignoring one another in meetings or discussions. In another organization, the concept of respect may involve saying "please and thank you" on a regular basis, or celebrating babies or holidays. So the ways values translate into actions can vary.

But even with all this variety, it is important across organizations for values (and global mindset is an example of a value) to be articulated by organizational leaders. In this exploratory framework, we focus on how to make that value set clear even to employees who are not leaders of the organization. As a result, for this chapter, we view global mindset as a range of concrete actions or behaviors that employees, even those below managerial ranks, could be expected to incorporate and that enhance the openness toward people from experiences and backgrounds different from their own. In some ways, this is a common value of respect or inclusiveness, regardless of the extent to which a firm might be engaged in global activity. Yet, we suggest that leaders and managers consider what the value(s) is (are) behind their understanding of global mindset and make those clear. Whether global mindset is articulated as, "thinking globally in terms of marketing, hiring, and supply sources," or whether it is explained as, "being open to views from outside the home country," these verbalizations need to be expressed and clarified so employees can become clearer about these otherwise ambiguous values.

Translating Abstract Values Into Concrete Actions

This step decodes the abstract ideas of what global mindset means and turns them into a sort of blueprint informing employees on how to act. The process of making the abstract concept of a global mindset concrete requires managers to clarify the specific behaviors that managers have decided exhibit a global mindset. For example, being inclusive to others from backgrounds not their own might mean very simple actions, such as explicitly asking for input from people from other units, backgrounds, or cultures. It could mean something as basic as not interrupting when people from different backgrounds and cultures are speaking. The key is that leaders and managers, along with employees, may need to come up with concrete examples of acceptable and non-acceptable behaviors and actions that illustrate the abstract value of "inclusiveness." Interestingly, in the literature, much of the assumption is that only the senior levels in an organization need global mindsets. But perhaps there are, and this is a question and checkpoint for leaders and managers to consider, certain behaviors that are applicable at all levels within an organization and that exemplify some of the global mindset basics that are critical.

The idea is similar to the ways that organizations translate generic values into behaviors. Within any given organization that espouses certain values, those abstract notions eventually need to become concrete actions or behaviors, which may vary by employee job but still are important to articulate. For example, a potential "checklist" of behaviors for a receptionist to exhibit the abstract concept of "a good attitude" might include: (1) looking up to greet someone, (2) listening to the request and then repeating it back to be sure it is clear on both sides, (3) answering a phone within three rings, and (4) asking colleagues if they need any assistance. Some leaders insist, when they think about values and culture, that employees must understand the values before they can affirm them in specific action. Others argue that it is sufficient for employees to behave in the ways expected of them, even if they don't understand or buy into the values they are expressing with their actions. For example, in a firm that values respect for all, employees will know racist or sexist language is unacceptable; even if they personally hold conflicting views, as long as they refrain from unacceptable language, that is all that managers can ask for or control. Behavior over time may or may not lead to change in attitude, but initially it may be more feasible to demand certain behaviors than to demand certain attitudes. In the same way, employees who are expected to behave in ways that affirm the value of global mindset may need to attempt to do so, at least initially, even if they do not fully understand (or perhaps fully agree with) the values underlying the behaviors.

Questions surface like: "How will top leaders communicate to the organization at large what global mindset means to them?" and "Will that look different in a given country?" and "How are employees within a given section of a firm—whether in marketing, finance, supply chain, or manufacturing—expected to behave?" This last question is tricky, because within each of those subunits, the need for and nature of what global mind-set means could vary. For instance, Vietnamese employees working for a German firm manufacturing sports shoes may have little need to understand the challenges German executives face when they consider selling in the North American market. Those employees may need only to understand how to operate a machine and get their work quota done. So is global mind-set an important concept for them? Perhaps not, although it could be if they seek to advance within the firm, if they see other possibilities for business within their country, or if they're considering additional education so they can work beyond their village or country.

Communicating Using Various Methods

Organizational leaders must begin to assess the implications of several variables of change—things like changing demographics, a world increasingly connected through social media, and the impact of information overload on employees. Some leaders are recognizing the need to be deliberately systematic in their communication of ideas inside and outside of their organizations. In the past, employees may have taken on and completed tasks because their bosses told them to. In the past, leaders may have been able to use simple forms of communication: telling people in large meetings or sending a memo. But the end of those days is fast approaching, if it is not already here. Now employees want to know WHY they're being told—or asked—to do something. They want to be empowered with knowledge and autonomy, to know what various actions will mean for them personally, how they might benefit from the actions, and how their actions will impact the organization as a whole.

This increased emphasis on the individual should be matched by an increased emphasis on individuals' varying modes of learning. It may have been assumed in the past that people absorbed information given to them only once or twice, but now it's increasingly clear that information must be given multiple times in part to overcome other distractions—even healthy distractions. Advertising confirms that many people need to hear and see an ad seven times before it registers at all, let alone before it works its way into a person's head for future consumer decision-making. Instead of communication methods being tailored to the main demographic of an organization's home country (for instance, the American workforce in the 1960s of white, English-speaking males), increasing diversity demands multiple forms of communication and getting information to people so they can absorb it.

To cater to more diverse, empowered, and autonomous learners, organizational leaders must be deliberate in choosing which types of communication to use, as well as how and when to use them. Research (Gardner, 2000) suggests that no single approach works for everyone, and people aren't as simple as their single favored learning approach. People learn best when they encounter multiple learning approaches. Several approaches are available and in the next section, we suggest three modes with short names: hear it, see it, and do it or experience it.

"Hear it" means that leaders take responsibility for spreading the notion of mindset through words so employees can receive the information in words, whether in meetings, one-on-one interaction, or through written words like documents and posters. "See it" refers to using visual means to convey an abstract concept like global mindset. This idea is already taking hold in organizations that seek to convey their values through visual ways. For example, leaders in an organization that highly values both stability and innovation use a piece of sculpture called Relentless Innovation. The eight-meter- high sculpture is a solid post that goes deep into the ground, suggesting long-term stability and the consistency of values of the organization. At the top of the post is a windmill, which moves when the wind moves and changes direction as well. The windmill suggests that the organization needs to be prepared to adjust to the environment, which can be quite volatile, even while holding strong to its key values. Likewise, firms that seek to convey the importance of global mindset use a range of means, from artwork from across the world, to rotating key meetings to different places in the world, to using different types of materials in its buildings.

"Do it" refers to the ways leaders might model a global mindset through their own behaviors. For example, if speaking English as the company language is expected, then leaders must do that even within their own cultural group, whether they are at headquarters or across borders. Another example that is becoming more common is appointing board members from markedly different backgrounds or cultures to illustrate the need for and importance of diversity in its employees and/or clients. Similarly, if a global mindset means bringing more diversity into the management ranks, then a leader must develop talent and promote employees in a way that reflects the organization's emphasis on a global mindset.

In a classic interview with Percy Barnevik, then CEO of Asea Brown Boveri, about the firm's attempt to become more global, he described the firm's requirement that managers use English and admitted that even he had trouble reminding himself of its implications (Taylor, 1991). He was rushing through an airport one day and took a call from a German manager, whose English was not strong. At one point, Barnevik asked him to speed things up and speak more quickly. There was silence at the other end of the line, and then the manager said he was doing the best he could in a language that was not easy for him. Barnevik realized he had violated a cardinal rule. He was trying to encourage his employees to be more global, but he forgot that not everyone was on the same level of ability as he was when he lost his patience.

Is Global Mindset Working?

Leaders are expected to do a good job conveying information, but employees also need to put in good effort to receive and implement the information.

Balancing the two "sides" of the equation—the sending and receiving of information—is critical. This ties directly back to the amount and variety of repetition people need to absorb information, which ties back to ways of learning (Gardner, 2000; Kolb and Fry, 1975).

This all leads to the necessity of employees having the ability to behave in ways that reflect a global mindset. This may be where training or "teaching" by other employees comes into play. Peer-to-peer support, in addition to more formal training, could help to instill and cement the behaviors and ultimately the habit or routine of a global mindset. Once armed with how to implement a global mindset as a set of behaviors, employees need the skills and knowledge to do so—ranging from things like language skills to cultural training. Furthermore, organizational leaders need to consider at least three other elements that can help make global mindset a habit of action, rather than something that is merely pulled out of the hat when necessary. Several means exist to try and make global mindset a part of the organization's ongoing way of operating, but initially, even they may require more deliberate effort and process.

First, it is helpful to hire candidates who already know how or try to act in ways that embody a global mindset. This can go a long way in helping to spread and sustain the presence of a global mindset in an organization. Deliberately building questions or experiences into the hiring process that test an individual's openness and ability to grasp a global mindset could be critical.

In addition, giving employees plenty of opportunity to practice (at their individual levels, locations, and jobs) the concrete actions that link to global mindset is fundamental. Equally important as the notion of using different communication approaches for different individuals is the idea of practicing small and specific behaviors. The simple, and easy to forget, idea of rotating times for global conference calls reinforces the idea of a global company. Not requiring certain groups of employees in selected geographic areas to be the ones awake in the middle of the night for a conference call on a regular basis shows consideration of the different time zones and experiences of employees in different areas. Rotating who leads the call also gives employees from different regions a chance to learn alternative approaches to holding remote meetings. But as intuitive as these ideas sound, they require repeated opportunities for practice in order to become sustainable, second-nature habits within an organization. Leaders at all levels must understand that even small behavioral changes take time and effort to bring about.

Finally, as much as we might not want to admit it, assessing how well ingrained a new mindset is within an organization might only be possible when something goes wrong. Barnevik's response to the slow English-speaking German manager ("Can you speak any faster?") showed how easy it is to slip into familiar patterns of behavior and to forget what global mindset means at a basic, person-to-person level. Being conscious and open about discussing mistakes when they arise—because they will—and learning how to refocus is crucial for sustaining a global mindset long term.

Future Research Directions

Although our focus has been somewhat more practical and leader focused than academic, we nevertheless end our discussion with more questions than answers (if there are any to be had, of course). As previously stated, global mindset is a very complex and ambiguous concept for even the most abstract and intuitive people, yet it is very much worth understanding and applying. The need for global mindset is not likely to decline, whether in large or small business organizations, in educational or governmental institutions, or in communities and countries. Thus, finding ways to bring it down from the clouds and repackage it into something concrete and clear is imperative—for leaders, managers and employees, students, and government officials alike. Going forward then, several areas could be especially useful for researchers to examine. We propose four general areas.

How to Assess and Measure Desired Global Mindset

Measuring concepts like global mindset is notoriously unsatisfying. Metrics such as (1) the percentage of an organization's members who speak a common business language like English, (2) the number of board members from countries outside the home base, or (3) numbers of successful expatriate transfers tell little of the true story. Yet if leaders are serious about enhancing or increasing the level of global mindset, they probably should attend to the idea of finding some way to track whether their organizations or units are moving in a desirable direction. The proliferation of anecdotes demonstrating both success and failure may a starting point, but what other means might leaders use to assess how globally oriented employees are? Also, how can current situations be assessed before something goes wrong? If leaders and academics could begin to develop such measures, it may become possible in the future to find out where the "overlaps" between desired and actual states of global mindset within an organization are.

How to Translate a Global Mindset Into Concrete Action

If a "global mindset" (or other ambiguous buzz phrases like "organizational culture" or "innovation") is to become real and actionable for organizations, these concepts must be divided and packaged into specific, concrete behaviors. One leader of a large governmental agency acknowledged that governmental organizations typically focus on "process"—holding meetings, establishing policies, or hiring people. But what they don't typically focus on are the outcomes that reflect the culture, goals, and mission statement of the organization—just as important to the life force of an organization as day-to-day bureaucratic procedures. While the organization may have values like integrity, teamwork, having a "good attitude," or "doing the right thing," such generic values are not concrete. Across various industry backgrounds, cultures, and perspectives, a "good attitude" could trigger very different types of behaviors. With all this variability, leaders must deliberately ask employees for specific behaviors instead of relying on a common consensus of understanding. As Chapter 2 suggests, a global mindset will also vary depending upon the organizational level (e.g., unit, division, headquarters) and numbers of people involved (individual, multiple, collective, or full corporate). A global mindset "checklist" would then need to vary depending on different localities of different organizational problems and procedures.

How Is a Global Mindset Best Conveyed Across Organizational Levels, Locations, and Types of Employees?

It is clear a one-size-fits-all approach to issues of management, leadership, and communication is impractical, and the same holds for global mindset. Should a deliveryman on a bicycle in Hanoi, Vietnam, have the same level and nature of global mindset as the senior manager who runs a global firm based in Munich, Germany? Of course not. So the question of how much an individual or group within a unit incorporates global thinking will vary. It is important to recognize the nature of what people in different areas and levels will need could potentially change over time. How we track such needs and changes, and how we develop effective means for encouraging a global mindset where it is required is an important and challenging question for business practitioners and academics alike. At this stage, we have almost no guidelines of what has worked, if anything, let alone what frameworks we need to use going forward. In the future, leaders will need to ask whether certain approaches need to vary over time with various groups of employees.

How Will Leaders Know if Global Mindset Works?

Finally, how do we know if organizations acquire enough, or the right type, of mindsets? How do we know if a global mindset is working within and across organizations? While some research considers the success of individual managers working in different cultures as a good indicator of a global mindset, how can that translated to their organizations at large? Performance, at least of smaller firms, has been one possible measure, but we likely need more consistent ways of assessing whether a global mindset exists, and how well it functions, within an organization.

Notes

1. Distinguished Professor, College of Business and Economics, Boise State University Boise, U.S., and Adjunct Professor, Aalborg University, Aalborg, Denmark
2. College of Business and Economics, Boise State University Boise, U.S.

References

Aggarwal, R. (2011). Developing a Global Mindset: Integrating Demographics, Sustainability, Technology, and Globalization. *Journal of Teaching in International Business*. 22, 51–69.

Allan, B., & Osland, J. S. (2005). Making Sense of Intercultural Collaboration. *International Studies of Management and Organization*. 35, 115–132.

Blaess, D. A., Hollywood, K. G., & Grant, C. (2012). Preparing the Professoriate to Prepare Globally Competent Leaders. *Journal of Leadership Studies*. 6, 88–94.

Cleaver, W. (2012). Najafi Global Mindset Institute Summit: Developing Leaders for Global Roles. *People & Strategy*. 35, 22–23.

Cohen, S. L. (2010). Effective Global Leadership Requires a Global Mindset. *Industrial and Commercial Training*. 42, 3–10.

Cseh, M., Davis, E. B., & Khilji, S. E. (2013). Developing a Global Mindset: Learning of Global Leaders. *European Journal of Training and Development*. 37, 489–499.

Dragoni, L., & Mcalpine, K. (2012). Leading the Business: The Criticality of Global Leaders' Cognitive Complexity in Setting Strategic Directions. *Industrial and Organizational Psychology*. 5, 237–240.

Earley, P. C., & Peterson, R. S. (2004). The Elusive Cultural Chameleon: Cultural Intelligence as a New Approach to Intercultural Training for the Global Manager. *Academy of Management Learning & Education*. 3, 100–115.

Gaffney, N., Cooper, D., Kedia, B., & Clampit, J. (2014). Institutional Transitions, Global Mindset, and EMNE Internationalization. *European Management Journal*. 32(3), 383–391.

Gardner, H. (2000). *Intelligence reframed: Multiple intelligences for the 21st century*. New York, NY, Basic Books.

Javidan, M., & Walker, J. L. (2013). *Developing your global mindset: The handbook for successful global leaders*. Edina, MN: Beaver Pond Press.

Javidan, M., Walker, J. L., & Bullough, A. (2013). Behind the Global Curve. *People & Strategy*. 36, 42–47.

Knowles, M. S. (1990). *The adult learner: A neglected species*. Houston, Gulf Pub. Co.

Kolb, D. A., & Fry, R. E. (1975). *Toward an applied theory of experiential learning*. Cambridge, MA, M.I.T. Alfred P. Sloan School of Management.

KOLB, D. A., & FRY, R. E. (1975). *Toward an applied theory of experiential learning*. Cambridge, Mass, M.I.T. Alfred P. Sloan School of Management.

Kyvik, O., Saris, W., Bonet, E., & Felício, J. A. (2013). The Internationalization of Small Firms: The Relationship between the Global Mindset and Firms' Internationalization Behavior. *Journal of International Entrepreneurship*. 11, 172–195.

Levy, O., Beechler, S., Taylor, S., & Boyacigiller, N. A. (2007). What We Talk about When We Talk about 'Global Mindset': Managerial Cognition in Multinational Corporations. *Journal of International Business Studies*. 38, 231–258.

Lovvorn, A. S., & Jiun-Shiu, C. (2011). Developing a Global Mindset: The Relationship between an International Assignment and Cultural Intelligence. *International Journal of Business & Social Science*. 2, 275–283.

Nummela, N., Saarenketo, S., & Puumalainen, K. (2004). A Global Mindset—A Prerequisite for Successful Internationalization. *Canadian Journal of Administrative Sciences/Revue Canadienne des Sciences de l'Administration*. 21(1), 51–64.

Raman, R., Chadee, D., Roxas, B., & Michailova, S. (2013). Effects of Partnership Quality, Talent Management, and Global Mindset on Performance of Offshore IT Service Providers in India. *Journal of International Management*. 19, 333–346.

Smith, D. N. (2012). Facilitating the Development of a Global Mindset Through a Cultural Experience. *Journal of Leadership Studies*. 6, 110–115.

Smith, M., & Victorson, J. (2012). Developing a Global Mindset: Cross-Cultural Challenges and Best Practices for Assessing and Grooming High Potentials for Global Leadership. *People & Strategy*. 35, 42–51.

Story, J. S., Barbuto, J. E., Luthans, F., & Bovaird, J. A. (2014). Meeting the Challenges of Effective International HRM: Analysis of the Antecedents of Global Mindset. *Human Resource Management.* 53, 131–155.

Suh, T., & Smith, K. (2008). Attitude Toward Globalization and Country-of-Origin Evaluations: Toward a Dynamic Theory. *Journal of Global Marketing.* 21, 127–139.Taylor, W. (1991). The Logic of Global Business: An Interview with ABB's Percy Barnevik. *Harvard Business Review.* 69, 89–104.

Tsui, A. S. (2004). Contributing to Global Management Knowledge: A Case for High Quality Indigenous Research. *Asia Pacific Journal of Management.* 21, 491–513.

Tuleja, E. A. (2014). Developing Cultural Intelligence for Global Leadership through Mindfulness. *Journal of Teaching in International Business.* 25, 5–24.

Vogelgesang, G., Clapp-Smith, R., & Osland, J. (2014). The Relationship between Positive Psychological Capital and Global Mindset in the Context of Global Leadership. *Journal of Leadership & Organizational Studies.* 21, 165–178.

Waite, A. M. (2014). Leadership's Influence on Innovation and Sustainability: A Review of the Literature and Implications for HRD. *European Journal of Training and Development.* 38, 15–39.

Wilson, W. (2013). Coaching with a Global Mindset. *International Journal of Evidence Based Coaching & Mentoring.* 11, 33–52.

Witte, A. E. (2010). The Global Awareness Curriculum in International Business Programs: A Critical Perspective. *Journal of Teaching in International Business.* 21, 101–131.

Zander, L., Mockaitis, A. I., & Butler, C. L. (2012). Leading Global Teams. *Journal of World Business.* 47, 592–603.

4 Globalization, Regionalization, and Global Mindset

Shifting Perspectives in the 21st Century

Nigel J. Holden

First Thoughts

For the last thirty or so years, we have lived with the fiction that world business is globalized. The idea of globalization of the world economy is not new. It has been applied to the state of the world at the end of the 19th century. It has also been argued that "Rome in the first century AD dominated the economy of the known world and that Latin was, as it were, the English of its day—the incontestable global language of its era" (Holden, 2015). One of the many limiting features of the core term globalization is that it implies a running of the world order—in the widest sense of that expression—as if by its own volition and not through any kind of human intervention. If there is some truth in that observation, then it follows that the subtext is that globalization transcends nations and the people within them.

Yet, many of us shy away from that particular notion, preferring to see the world composed of much smaller entities. The one that comes to mind is that of the region, but as we shall see, the more we put that notion under the microscope, the more it proves to be slippery. However, at least with the word region, we are more aware that the within given geographic spaces, economic activities are pursued by people in, admittedly, an almost infinite variety of personal and corporate guises. For all these misgivings, there is validity to the concept of globalization, which is at the very least vouchsafed by the global spread of modern IT communication systems.

After all, we live in a world in which any electronically mediated message can in principle be simultaneously sent to and read by people on all five continents, and as a result of that ability, more people can be said to be in articulate communication with each other than ever before in human history: not just in quantitative terms, but in terms of the nominal geographical, political, cultural, and linguistic boundaries that are simultaneously crossed in the process. This daily experience of the transcendence of physical and metaphysical barriers for millions of people has given rise, as it were, to the concept of the global mindset. But, if, as we shall see, so much of the world's business is being conducted inter-regionally, do we need a region-oriented analogue to the global mindset?

In order to address that issue, this chapter will review that uneasy term globalization, outline approaches to the notion of the global mindset, and consider the related terms region and regionalization. We will then be in a position to explore the feasibility of a modified version of the global mindset for the increasingly regionalized business world.

Globalization

Globalization is, by common agreement, a contentious term. This chapter will not wade into the controversies. It is nonetheless important that I begin this chapter with the way in which globalization should be understood in the context of this chapter. A useful starting point is offered not by a business scholar, but by the eminent British historian Eric Hobsbawm, who described it as "a state of affairs, in which the globe is the essential unit of operation of some human activity, and where this activity is constructed in terms of a single, universal system of thought, techniques and modes of communication" (Hobsbawm, 2003: 1). The business world as represented by thousands and thousands of companies worldwide does seemingly readily identify with that point of view. For managers worldwide, the notion that the market is global is not in the least contentious, nor is the idea of seeing themselves as active participants in the globalized economy.

But for all that, the term globalization remains an extremely complex term from economic, political, technological, and cultural points of view. Regardless of what particular emphasis we place on the term globalization, it suggests activities, processes, and sets of assumptions about international business operations that are considered to be at the expense of national identity. Furthermore, there appears to be a specific assumption that globalization is a natural outcome of human progress and that no unreasonable fetters should prevent firms from engaging in the globalized business world on the (unproven) grounds that everyone benefits.

Curiously, it was Marx and Engels in *The Communist Manifesto* of 1848 who make a very clear idea of the borderless business world in which the protagonists are not nations or subsets of nations (for example, corporations), but a wily sublimation called "the bourgeoisie." In their words:

> The need of a constantly expanding market chases the bourgeoisie over the whole surface of the globe. It must nestle everywhere, settle everywhere, establish connexions everywhere.
>
> (Marx and Engels, 1967: 83)

We will not detain ourselves on a discussion of the term "bourgeoisie." Nevertheless, their perception of business as a kind of nation-free blind force operating "everywhere" is, I think, inbuilt into the everyday notion of globalization. The particular proposition gains some weight when we reflect that many of the world's biggest MNEs have turnovers that exceed the gross national product of several nations.

Over the last 20 years, as more countries pursued liberal trade and investment regimes both domestically and internationally, this has created a new playing field for corporations. Many adopt (so-called) global strategies. Such strategies comprise a global distribution of economic activities (spatial dimension) and require that the firms coordinate and gain synergies from the activities (governance dimension). The aim of these globally distributed but coordinated activities was and is to increase efficiency and effectiveness/innovativeness simultaneously:

1. Operations across countries/cultures at the same time
2. Operations within specific countries/cultures
3. All the resulting complexity and uncertainty in a global context.

While internationally operating concerns may see globalization as a positive force in human affairs ("opportunities"), for it invokes the so-called borderless world, which is always open for business, there is a negative dimension ("threats"). In some parts of the world, globalization is a mere code word for Westernization or Americanization. Even in Western countries there is disillusionment with the term, which connotes unpleasant, possibly dehumanizing uniformities, while some voices are saying that we are really in an era of "de-globalization." For their part, business schools are especially keen on globalization. Hundreds if not thousands of them run courses on global management, on global marketing, global HRM, and yet it seems that business educators have themselves problems in teaching global business in relevant ways to students who will experience business not at some ethereal level of higher consciousness, but at, as it were, the pavement level in any country (see Datar, Garvin, and Cullen, 2010: 84). In this connection, it has been observed that the business school education presents a view of the world in which "countries are stereotypes, their inhabitants' abstractions" (Holden and Glisby, 2010: 19). This is a highly perturbing state of affairs precisely because MNEs and indeed smaller firms are forever being encouraged to adopt global strategies.

In other words, the globalized business world is seemingly hard to apprehend intellectually. It is in response to this challenge that the notion of the global mindset has been developed. It has been argued that the global mindset, despite "the conceptual confusion surrounding the concept, has emerged as a key source of long-term competitive advantage in the global marketplace" (Levy, Beechler, Taylor, and Boyacigiller, 2006). The academic premier center in the world for developing and refining the concept is the Thunderbird School of Global Management in the U.S. According to Professor Mary B. Teagarden:

> Global Mindset is defined as a set of individual attributes that help a global leader better influence those who are different from them. A

Global Mindset profile comprises three capitals: Intellectual Capital, which refers to one's global savvy, cosmopolitan outlook, and cognitive complexity; Psychological Capital, which refers to one's passion for diversity, quest for adventure, and self-assurance; and Social Capital, which refers to one's intercultural empathy, interpersonal impact, and diplomacy.

"Leaders with high levels of Global Mindset have an enhanced ability to make sense of their context and behave appropriately as the context varies. Leaders with high levels of Global Mindset are more expert global leaders because of their ability to understand and interpret what is going on in a global situation. They can more effectively interpret verbal and nonverbal messages and signals from people from different cultures. In addition, these same expert global leaders demonstrate high levels of flexibility, which manifests as the ability to act differently in different situations and contexts. Finally, leaders with high levels of Global Mindset have the ability to choose the right behavior or approach in different circumstances or contexts."[1]

According to the experts at Thunderbird, the intellectual, psychological, and social capital that make up a "global mindset" are each comprised of three key attributes that can guarantee organizations that their assignees are ready and likely to succeed in an international assignment. These attributes are:

Intellectual Capital: Global business savvy, cognitive complexity and a cosmopolitan outlook.
Psychological Capital: Passion for diversity, thirst for adventure, and self-assurance.
Social Capital: Intercultural empathy, interpersonal impact and diplomacy.[2]

At first glance, the scheme developed by the scholars at Thunderbird looks serviceable at both the global and regional levels, at least for Americans or non-Americans with a lengthy familiarity with U.S. culture as students or in a professional capacity. If one can apply the key attributes subsumed under intellectual, cognitive, and psychological capital in order to effect a sensitive projection of leadership competence, then that is a manifestation of the global mindset. QED?

According to Levy et al. (2006), the global mindset is "a highly complex cognitive structure characterized by an openness to and articulation of multiple cultural and strategic realities on both global and local levels, and the cognitive ability to mediate and integrate across this multiplicity." As for what is mediated and integrated, the authors have in mind "ideals and actions." (Perhaps ideas would be a better choice of words than ideals). Ignoring the word "structure," which in this context may not have the support of every psychologist, we cannot miss the striking emphasis on the link between global mindset and cognition. It is, however, noteworthy that the authors have no place for human emotion in their definition. Levy and co-authors argue that the concept can be patterned into three "research perspectives," namely, cultural, strategic, and multidimensional. The cultural perspective acknowledges "the increased cultural diversity associated with diversity," the strategic perspective "the increased complexity generated by globalization," and the multidimensional supports the conviction that "people with global mindsets tend to drive for the bigger, broader picture and are, among other things, comfortable with surprises and ambiguity" (Levy et al., 2006). As with the Thunderbird approach, the idea is to break down the concept into isolatable units.

By contrast, the *Financial Times* (FT) web-based lexicon of key business and management terms describes the concept of the global mindset in "softer" tones, as follows:

> We would define global mindset as one that combines an openness to and awareness of diversity across cultures and markets with a propensity and ability to see common patterns across countries and markets.
>
> In a company with a global mindset, people view cultural and geographic diversity as opportunities to exploit and are prepared to adopt successful practices and good ideas wherever they come from.
>
> "The twin forces of ideological change and technology revolution are making globalization one of the most important issues facing companies today. As such, cultivating a global mindset is a prerequisite to becoming a global company."[3]

The Thunderbird and FT notions of the global mindset are not so far apart, but there is a subtle point of difference. For the former, the global mindset is the sine qua non of global leadership; for the latter, it is something to do with becoming a global company.

In their search for global efficiency and effectiveness, transnational corporations concomitantly create the need for a global mindset. It also follows that the global mindset is more than just "thinking globally." This is evident when we consider it is variously as:

1. A horizon-broadening or control mechanism
2. An antidote to ethnocentrism or "cross-cultural myopia"
3. A branch of American business thinking
4. An attitudinal disposition for global leadership.

In other words, the term "global mindset" has many interpretations. In this chapter, I am regarding the global mindset to be a bundle of dispositions and competences that are valid for individuals, but "a response for the need for a corporate climate that encourages staff to rise above their respective national levels in thought, attitude and behaviour" (Holden, Kuada, Napier,

Sørensen, and Tesar, 2011). The choice of the word response is important, because unlike the cognition-oriented notions of the global mindset, the word allows for the engagement of emotions.

Regions

So far, so good. But there is a big catch. For all the integration of the world's economy, business is not transacted globally. The reality of modern business life is that strictly speaking internationally, firms do not operate globally. Their so-called global strategy is fashioned with respect to—and implemented at—lower levels of aggregation, of which a key one is the region. We first consider that term in a generalized way and then in relation to internationally operating companies.

Regions in a more general way can variously be "global, continental, sub-continental, national, international, or local . . . [creating] . . . 'many overlapping geographic layers" (Kacowicz, 1998). One can also add the word "oceanic; mindful of the Pacific Rim in the refrain 'The Mediterranean is the ocean of the past, the Atlantic is the ocean of the present and the Pacific is the ocean of the future" (Economist, 2014). Provided that the big powers in the Pacific—i.e., China and the United States—can be "pragmatic, not dogmatic . . . the Pacific Age could create new rules and new institutions for the 21st century" (Economist, 2014). Regions are characterized by "clusters of states coexisting in geographical propinquity as interrelated units that sustain significant security, economic, and political relations, but there is also 'subjective perception of belonging to a distinctive community and having a regional identity" (Kacowicz, 1998). As such, regions—the European Union being a prime example—may establish supranational institutions and arrangements, although at the cost of some national independence and freedom of action, for the perceived common good.

The word 'region' does not imply the word "country" (i.e., in the sense of nation state); rather it suggests a multi-country cluster bound by, among other factors, geography. Yet, one can immediately call to mind (at least) five very prominent countries that are not readily associable with a region owing to their large populations, enormous resources, and their equally enormous territorial size: the U.S., Brazil, Russia, India, and China (i.e., the U.S. plus the four BRIC countries). Finally, there is another kind of region, although this may not be accepted by all economists: the notion of the city, as advocated by Jacobs (1969, 1984, 2000). Cities "possess unique characteristics that differentiate them from other units of 'place' such as countries, regions or provinces' provide cohesion 'as nodes for bringing together a diverse range of complex economic processes" (McDonald, 2014).

But whenever one tries to make generalizations about regions, there always seem to be tricky exceptions. For example, what the Western world conceives of, say, the Middle East or Asia may not evoke the equivalent sense of community and belonging among local people. Equally, it may not be out-landish to suggest that a contemporary Chinese view of Asia is one in which Japan is airbrushed out and to which the U.S., as a self-styled Pacific power, *cannot* belong. Thus, if regions are supposed to be characterized by some kind of cultural and social homogeneity as a consequence of long-standing historical interactions, the case of China and Japan shows that homogeneity should *not* be assumed to be tantamount to affinities. Furthermore, corpo-rations for their part take a future-oriented view of regions as their potential as hubs of profitability.

The key thing to appreciate is that in the business world, a region is not a country, however big. A region refers to "a limited number of states linked by a geographical relationship and by a degree of mutual interdependence" (Kacowicz, 1998: 8). The interdependencies are generally reinforced by for-mal agreements of a political and legal character between states to create supranational bodies and for mutual advantage, although often with the rec-ognition that any particular state will need to make certain concessions for the greater good—and the cohesion of the arrangements. Plainly, the most powerful region in this sense in today's world is the European Union. A strik-ing feature of the EU is a general sense among its member states is they all subscribe to a common European heritage. There is, though, one anomaly. The UK is reluctant to admit to sharing this heritage, even though its language, with its Germanic, Latin, and Norman French roots, is the de facto language of political, economic, social, and cultural interchange from Lisbon in the west to Tallinn in the east, and from Helsinki in the north to Nicosia in the south.

As we have noted, world business is strictly speaking conducted inter-regionally rather than globally. So, how then do regions look to major com-panies? As Ghemawat (2005) has pointed out, "If your company has a signif-icant international presence, it already has a regional strategy—even if that strategy has been arrived at by default,"[4] which implies that firms willy-nilly use region-focused strategies, and even that it is no longer a question of talking about "the globalization of markets" (a once-famous phrase) in pref-erence to the regionalization of markets.

Consider these data, which indicate how just three regions dominate the world's business, namely, the U.S., the EU, and Japan. For example, accord-ing to the *Financial Times* website,[5] the world's 500 largest firms, measured by revenues and/or assets, have averaged 77% of their sales and 81% of their assets in their home region over the last 10 years. Only a handful of these firms—over 20%—have significant operations in each of the three broad regions. Despite the globalization rhetoric, business is actually largely regional. The FT then cites as an example the case of Wal-Mart, the world's largest firm, by revenues:

"Its North American operations represent the lion's share of its activities. Europe is an interesting case for Walmart; the company does have some substantial operations in the U.K. through its acquisition of Asda, however it pulled out of Germany in 2006 leaving it essentially in only one European country. It also operates in China, Japan and India but this is the extent of its operations in Asia. Certainly, Walmart is a world leader in terms of size, but it operates in less than 20 countries."[6]

A more accurate picture is provided in these data, taken from the 2013 annual report of Wal-Mart, about the worldwide distribution of its retail units.[7] In the U.S., Wal-Mart has a grand total of 4,835 retail units. For international operations, the figure is 6,107. However, of this latter figure, Mexico with 2,199 units and Canada with 398—countries that border the U.S.—represent a total 2,588 or 42% of all international outlets. In the vaunted BRIC countries, the presence of Wal-Mart is presented in Table 4.1:

Table 4.1 Wal-Mart's Presence in BRIC Countries

Country	No. of retail outlets
Brazil	556
Russia	0
India	405
China	20
	Grand total: 981

A lot of people reading that may well conclude that for all the massive size of its international business operations, the world's largest firm does not really pass muster as a global firm! It might be argued that retailing can never be as globalized a business as the automotive sector. According to Rugman and Collinson (2012: 85), "the automotive sector is concentrated in he the three triad regions of the United States (North America), Europe and Japan (Asia). Referring to what they call 'the world's regional automotive industry, these authors contend—citing 2001 data in their textbook published in 2012—that only one car maker could be called global, namely Mazda, in that it had at that time 'at least 20 percent of its sales in each of the three regions of the broad triad, adding that 60 of its sales are inter-regional."

At all events, "the leaders of successful companies seem to have grasped two important truths about the global economy. First, geographic and other distinctions haven't been submerged in the rising tide of globalization; in fact, such distinctions are arguably increasing in importance. Second, regionally focused strategies are not just a half-way house between local (country-focused) and global strategies that, used in conjunction with local and global initiatives, can significantly boost a company's performance" (Ghemawat, 2005).

It goes without saying that regions are never stable. They are affected by change brought about major economic and political shifts. At the time of writing, we can see very clearly how the very map of the Middle East is being redrawn with completely uncertain consequences for millions of people. Against that, in Eastern Europe, Russia is not just redrawing the "old" map of the Ukraine, but is seemingly redesigning itself as a region. Such moves appear to be motivated by what the Russians see as unwelcome encroachments of Western space. No one can be certain what "new" regions these actions will give rise to. Against this background it is now time to consider our next key term, regionalization.

Regionalization

In essence, regionalization refers to the process of dividing or sub-dividing a given territorial area into smaller units called regions for administrative purposes. One obvious example of this process is to consider modern states. Often, modern states are divided into smaller administrative units. By way of simplification: in the UK, the traditional administrative unit has been "the county," in the U.S. it is "the state," and in Japan, it is provinces (*ken*). Each such entity will have a capital city, under which other subdivisions are to be found, such as municipalities, boroughs, local councils, etc. In a strictly international sense, regionalization "refers to the proneness of the governments and people of two or more states to establish voluntary associations and pool together resources (material and nonmaterial to create common functional and institutional arrangements" (Kacowicz, 1998).

Like globalization, to which it may appear to be antithetical, the notion of regionalization is not entirely straightforward, but it is surely true to say that it is less controversial than globalization. If a problem with the term globalization is that it implies a vast unitariness underpinning all the world's business behavior, the challenge of regionalization is that this descriptor can allow the world to be broken down into an inconceivably vast number agglomerations of economic activity.

A recent IMF working paper found that "since the mid-1980s, the importance of regional factors has increased markedly in explain business flows especially in regions that experienced a sharp growth in intra-regional trade and financial flows. By contrast, the relative importance of the global factor has declined over the same period. In short, the recent period of globalization has witnessed the emergence of regional business factors" (Hirata, Kose, and Otrok, 2013). The authors of the working paper supply ample statistical data to substantiate their findings. If we can accept their position, then we are faced with a tricky question. Does the world of business, in which the bulk of economic activity is conducted on an intra- and inter-regional basis, require a modified version of the global mindset? If so, how is this to be achieved?

All this suggests is that the notion of the region from a world business perspective is not a straightforward term at all. Earlier, we suggested that the global mindset is an intellectual response to globalization. Do we need a corresponding concept for apprehending regionalization?

The Region-Oriented Mindset

Let us go back to the concept of the global mindset. Once, though, we accept that the world is full of regions, this calls for a shift in that mindset. There is, of course, no such thing as the "regional mindset," but it can be instructive to give attention to the academic field of area studies.

Areas studies in universities are interdisciplinary, bringing together subjects such as history, foreign languages, literature, political science, sociology, economics, and cultural studies. As implied by this list, areas studies embrace the humanities and social sciences. Area studies can even break away from "traditional areas" to include topics such as diaspora, human migration, and even terrorism. Some branches of area studies do not focus on the contemporary world at all: think of, say, classical studies, Egyptology, Byzantine studies, and so forth. Area studies are designed to produce "the area specialist." Ironically, such a person is either probably too specialized for most corporations and consultancies, but better suited to government organizations such as departments of foreign affairs and the security services or bodies such as think tanks and international charities. No doubt several graduates in area studies end up pursuing an academic career. They may feel better appreciated by the university world. Against that, there may be two regions in today's world about which corporations value area studies input: the EU and China.

What is perfectly clear is that academic classifications of area studies may not correspond well with corporate classifications. In the academic world, Burmese studies may be deemed to have, in principle, equal value as Russian studies, just as the Koranic world is on a par with the civilization of Ancient Greece, and just as the study of the languages and cultures of Polynesia cannot be said to be superior to the studies of Romance languages and cultures—in each case, intellectually speaking. What this implies is that area studies are in principle inclusive. The corporate classifications are exclusive and based on pragmatic assumptions about today and tomorrow. As examples, Toyota groups countries by existing and expected free trade areas, whereas the huge Mexican concern Cemex "created the so-called ring of gray gold: developing markets that fell mostly in a band circling the globe just north of the equator, forming a geographically contiguous but dispersed region" (Ghemawat, 2005).

The idea of a regional analogue of the global mindset is hard to imagine simply because, as we have seen, the region can assume a vast number of different forms and also different validities. A case in point is Toyota, which we have just mentioned. Their regionalization strategy, based on current and anticipated free trade areas, makes sense from their point of view, but for another industry sector, such a segmentation principle could well be viewed as idiosyncratic and downright unworkable. However, Toyota in its own way provides a valuable insight. First, the choice of free trade area was but one of several regionalization options available to the company.

They selected the free trade area after studying very considerable amounts of economic data, including projections. Oddly enough, notions of the global mindset either tend to neglect economic realities—except the big one, that the world economy is globalized—or suspend them as givens to be appropriated as and when necessary.

Second, Toyota as a Japanese company will be highly adept at sharing company-specific knowledge about its three regions to relevant people—hundreds, if not thousands of them—for actual business operations. Why is this observation important? Because a weakness of the global mindset is that it tends to be treated as an attribute of individuals. In fact, the Thunderbird scheme specifies the individuals: global leaders. There is not much scope in their concept of the global mindset that emphasizes the desirability of sharing it as a form of company-specific tacit knowledge, whereas for the regional analogue of the global mindset to work, it automatically involves knowledge sharing across a myriad of boundaries. As a result, we can deduce that our notional analogue is facilitated by 1. "cross-cultural collaborative learning" (Bartholomew and Adler, 1996: 27), and 2. networking not as the "mere" creation and maintenance of business contacts, but as the corporate quest for tangible and intangible resources needed today and in the future.

The contrasting approaches of Toyota and Cemex would appear to have several attractions for other internationally firms, which find it hard to strike the right balance between (as they say) "thinking globally and acting locally." Often, the global is an unwieldy unit. It is simply too big and indeed variegated within itself to be readily made sense, while the local is too small a unit for firms that operate in terms of clusters of markets, which are often geographically clustered. Toyota used free trade areas as its lowest common denominator, while Cemex devised a geographical concept to suit its business, and certainly not one used by geographers! The message of these two companies that it is possible to select country clusters that provide an overview of related markets that share important communalities at that particular level of analysis, but avoid being subsumed into an overarching global entity, which limits practical merit. These communalities, which inform the region-oriented mindset, can range from marketing approaches, employment of local staff, or the use of promotional tools. The critical challenge facing firms is to leverage valuable knowledge and experience and apply them judiciously to similar markets in the cluster, if they are to avoid reinventing the wheel.

Conclusion

The subject matter of this chapter has been wide ranging and the various themes do not necessarily lend themselves to straightforward integration. The leitmotif is that interpretations of the global mindset range from the very structured to the loose, and so the core concept lacks explanatory power. Perhaps, as implied in the preceding section, the very diversity of possibilities is a consequence of the global itself being unwieldy. However, these interpretations could not be lightly dismissed because after all, they form part of the thought world of both researchers and managers. The structured versions of the global mindset have been broken down into segments variously for theoretical, practical, and no doubt, pedagogical purposes. The looser versions are based on the formation of attitudes that derive from experience. Clearly, the validity and by extension usefulness of the concept depends on the degree to which its advocates are prepared to accept the fiction of a globalized world.

As for the region-oriented mindset, we readily conceded that this is also a tricky construct, if only for the incalculable ways we can construe the interactions of firms with regions of immense geographical spread, which in turn may be cohesive, yet undergirded with significant cultural and linguistic diversity (think of the EU). Despite those limitations, the region-oriented mindset has a very valuable advantage. The notion of the global mindset tends to focus the mind on very large companies, notably MNCs, whereas the former refers in principle to firms that have considerable international business operations, but are not "everywhere" with a substantial presence.

However, it does have the value of concentrating attention on reasonably well-delineated areas of economic activity that have relevance to companies and how they literally and metaphorically map the word. Instead of searching our brains for models and constructs to *theorize* about the region-oriented mindset, we—the academics—should consider creating them on the basis of corporate experience. Curiously, one may not even have to engage in lengthy and costly research projects. To put that in context: Once you know from a public source that Toyota's regionalization strategy is based on current and likely free trade zones, then you already have a potentially new and powerful way of thinking about the business world that is not beholden to any cherished academic notion.

Notes

1. http://www.thunderbird.edu/article/role-global-mindset-developing-global-leaders. Accessed on November 21, 2014.
2. http://www.thunderbird.edu/article/role-global-mindset-developing-global-leaders. Accessed on November 21, 2014.
3. http://lexicon.ft.com/Term?term=global-mindset. Accessed on November 21, 2014.
4. Ghemawat, P. (2005). Regional strategies for global leadership. Harvard Business Review online. Accessed at: https://hbr.org/2005/12/regional-strategies-for-global-leadership, December 1, 2014.
5. http://lexicon.ft.com/Term?term=regionalisation. Accessed on November 21, 2014.
6. Ibid.
7. http://cdn.corporate.walmart.com/66/e5/9ff9a87445949173fde56316ac5f/2014-annual-report.pdf

References

Bartholomew, S. and Adler, N. (1996). Building networks and crossing borders: The dynamics of knowledge generation in a transnational world. In: P. Joynt and M. Warner (eds.). *Managing Across Cultures: Issues and Perspectives*. London: International Thomson: 7–32.

Datar, S. M., Garvin, D. A. and Cullen, P. G. (2010). *Rethinking the MBA: Business Education at a Crossroads*. Boston, MA: Harvard Business Press.

Economist (2014). Special report: The pacific, 15 November.

Ghemawat, P. (2005). Regional strategies for global strategies. *Harvard Business Review* on-line. Available at: https://hbr.org/2005/12/regional-strategies-for-global-leadership. Accessed on 10 July 2015.

Hirata, H., Kose, M. A. and Otrok, C. (2013). Regionalization v. globalization. *IMT Working Paper WP/13/19*. Accessed at https://www.imf.org/external/pubs/ft/wp/2013/wp1319.pdf, 21 November 2014.

Hobsbawm, E. (2003). The nation and globalization. *Constellations*. Vol. 5, No. 1, pp. 1–9.

Holden, N. J. (2016). Economic exchange and the language of business in the Ancient World: An exploratory review. In: V. Ginsburgh and S. Weber (eds.). *The Palgrave Handbook of Economics and Language*. London: Palgrave Macmillan, pp. 290–311.

Holden, N. J. and Glisby, M. (2010). *Creating Knowledge Advantage: The Tacit Dimensions of International Competition and Cooperation*. Copenhagen: Copenhagen Business School Press.

Holden, N. J., Kuada, J., Napier, N. K., Sørensen, O. and Tesar, G. (2011). Grundfos: The quest for the global mindset. Aalborg University: Department of Business Studies (unpublished report).

Jacobs, J. (1969). *The Economy of Cities*. New York: Vintage.

Jacobs, J. (1984). *Cities and the Wealth of Nations*. New York: Random House.

Jacobs, J. (2000). *The Nature of Economics*. New York: Vintage.

Kacowicz, A. (1998). Regionalization, globalization, and nationalism: Convergent, divergent or overlapping? Working paper 262. The Helen Kellogg Institute for international Studies. Available at: http://kellogg.nd.edu/publications/working papers/WPS/262.pdf Accessed on 10 July 2015

Levy, O., Beechler, S., Taylor, S. and Boyacigiller, N. (2006). What we talk about when we talk about 'global mindset': Managerial cognition in multinational corporations. Discussion Paper Series of the Asia-Pacific Economic Cooperation, Columbia University.

Marx, K. and Engels, F. (1967; first published in 1888). *The Communist Manifesto*. London: Penguin Books.

McDonald, C. (2014). The impact of subnational heterogeneity on foreign direct investment location decisions and the performance of foreign affiliates: The case of multinational enterprises in China. Unpublished PhD thesis, University of Leeds.

Rugman, A. and Collinson, S. (2012). *International Business*. Harlow, UK: Pearson.

5 Global Mindset

From Strategic Choice to Situational Capability

Olav Jull Sørensen

Introduction

Global mindset (GM) has emerged as an important concept both in the academic world and as part of managerial discussions and practices. It has emerged alongside the globalization of the economy, where we have seen more and more companies moving from the domestic market via multi-domestic activities to the integration of globally distributed units for sales, production, and R&D.

It is in these new encounters and having to deal with global diversity that companies are in need of a GM. It is not enough to choose between various organizational structures (hierarchy, matrix organization, network organization) or managerial behaviors (adaptation, negotiation tactics, etc.) to perform globally. There is a need to go deeper and start with the way people think about business reality, and in this case, the reality of global business. The mindset is, admittedly, important in a domestic context, but here people are among people who think the same way, and thus the diversity is small. Expatriates staying in one particular country for a longer period gradually learn the dominant mindset in this country and can adapt their mindset to the business culture they are in. When working in a global company with multiple units in multiple countries, employees find *themselves* in a more complex situation where they need a more flexible mindset to be able to understand the situation and take advantage of the diversity they meet. It is this flexibility of the mindset concepts that this study will conceptualize.

However, the concept of global mindset is an elusive one. Literally, mindset means "way of thinking" (Paul 2000; Dweck 2006), and a global mindset is thus a way of thinking about the globalization and its processes that we have been witnessing in these years (Levy, Beechler, Taylor, and Boyacigiller 2007). The definition of mindset in dictionaries seems to agree that a mindset connotes a state of mind. *The Oxford Dictionary* defines a mindset as "a set of attitudes or fixed ideas that somebody has and that are often difficult to change." *The MacMillan Dictionary* is in line with *Oxford*. Mindset is "a way of thinking about things," and adds the example: "The company will have to change its whole mindset if it is to survive." This is in line with the conventional definition of culture (Hofstede 2001); here, cultural values are, if not permanent, then at least sticky and not easy to change.

Thus, a GM is something manifest and relatively stable. However, this is not completely the position we have in this study. We aim to widen the definition and understanding of GM in two ways, by arguing that people may have more than one mindset, i.e., the GM is context dependent, and by arguing for a more dynamic and process-oriented perspective on GM without falling in the trap of total relativism. For example, we do not think that people are completely opportunistic in the sense that they change mindsets according to any situation for selfish gains, but we will argue that a person may have more mindsets and that these mindsets reflect the typical situations the person is experiencing.

The overall aim of this study is to focus on the conceptualization of the GM construct by looking at the construct through different conceptual lenses, which in the end will bring us from seeing a GM as a manifest state of mind to seeing GM as a situational and dynamic capability that managers can use to make sense of the diversity they meet when they find themselves in different contexts and situations.

The chapter consists of five sections in addition to this introductory section. The second section defines the GM concept and discusses why a GM debate has emerged. The third section reviews the literature, focusing on its development and the main positions. In the fourth section, a revised conceptual framework is presented and discussed in greater detail, and this section is followed by a company case using the revised framework for discussion. Finally, the last section summarizes the chapter and points to the way forward.

Mindset Defined and the Emergence of a Global Mindset Debate

Global Mindset Defined

Mindset basically means a way of thinking and how people make sense of reality. It is a concept with a long history within cognitive psychology (Gupta and Govindarajan 2002), but in recent years, the concept has gained ground in organization and strategic management literature. Being a construct from cognitive psychology, it is a concept that sees people from the point of view of information and information processing. Human beings have limited ability to absorb and process information, i.e., we face human-bounded rationality (Simon 1972). Furthermore, we have filters, i.e. we are selective in what we absorb and how we interpret it. The filters "protect" our present mindset, but although a mindset may be relatively stable, it is also continuously changing due to new observations and experiences. Thus, a mindset can be seen as a mental construct consisting of knowledge-experience structures that we use to make sense of our environment and of the people with whom we interact. At the same time, the construct provides guidance for our actions.

Referring to the seminal literature review by Levy et al. (2007), it is clear that there is no agreed-upon GM definition. They found 25 different definitions and they grouped them along two dimensions of the global environment: 1. cultural and national diversity (the cultural dimension), and 2. strategic complexity associated with globalization (strategic perspective). They added a third category that combines the two.

Going through the many definitions, we notice that the authors try to convey the same message, although they may not use the exact same terms. The terms that appear more frequently are "being open-minded," "being attentive," "being adaptive," and "being proactive."

To serve the particular purpose of this study, we have looked at the definitions from a knowledge and cognition perspective and found that a number of definitions can be grouped into two categories, i.e., definitions that synthesize horizontally and vertically (laterally).

In the horizontal case, the definitions look for the common denominator across the global diversity, and in that sense, resemble the global orientation concept by Perlmutter (1969). Examples of the horizontal perspective are:

1. Gupta and Govindarajan (2002) define GM as "one that combines an openness to, and awareness of, diversity across cultures and markets with a propensity and ability to synthesize across this diversity."
2. Begley and Boyd (2003) define global mindset as "the ability to develop and interpret criteria for business performance that are not dependent on the assumption of a single country, culture or context and implement those criteria for business in different countries, cultures and contexts."

In the vertical case, the definitions use cognitive capability to move from concrete, local situations to a more abstract conceptualization of the diverse situations to synthesize the local and the global, i.e., finding a way where the local responsiveness benefits the global integration and vice versa. Examples of the vertical perspective are:

1. Kefalas (1998): "Global mindset is a mental model characterized by high levels of both conceptualization and contextualization."
2. Arora et al. (2004): "Global mindset is the ability to analyze concepts in a broad global array and the flexibility to adapt to local environment and be sensitive to context."

While the horizontal perspective builds on comprehensive knowledge and experience across the globe, the vertical perspective builds on cognitive reflection and conceptualizations to assure an interactive process between the concrete and the abstract levels.

One other dimension of some importance is whether the definitions see GM as something manifest and given, a state of mind, or as a process.

Javidan and Teagarden (2011) clearly sees the GM as a state of mind made up of the cognitive, the social, and the psychological capabilities. The more of the three there are, the higher a GM. Jeannet (2000) has a similar understanding: "Global mindset is a state of mind able to understand a business, an industry sector or a particular market on a global basis."

Turning to process views, there are none that reflect the dynamics that lead to a GM or that view GM as a continuous process of becoming. The closest we get is a definition by Story and Barbuto (2011): A person with a high cultural intelligence ". . . has the cognitive capacity to think and understand a new cultural environment and also to acquire behavior that is needed in that environment."

It is important to stress that mindset is a concept at the individual level and that most studies are conducted at this level (Levy et al. 2007). It is the individual that has a specific mindset. To come to a collective or organizational mindset, we need interactive processes that gradually form a common and shared mindset at a group or corporate level. Thus, mindsets, both at the individual level and the collective level, are formed through interaction. Management may design what they see as a preferable corporate mindset, but they will have to go into each and every mind in the company to convince them (and furnish them with skills) of the appropriateness of this mindset.

From this account of GM definitions, three overall positions on GM can be noted:

1. GM as a "state of mind"—something manifest that individuals carry with them wherever they go (one mindset)
2. GM as a "capability"—something we can use in various circumstances (context and situations) to orient ourselves, to make sense of things, and to act (multiple mindsets)
3. GM as a "process"—something dynamic that emerges through interaction in multiple global contexts (dynamic mindset) with experience-learning processes as mediators.

We will argue that a global mindset is a capability that can be drawn upon in different situations, but at the same time, the mindset is not stable and can therefore change in accordance with experiences and learning, i.e., a GM is a dynamic capability that is constructed and reconstructed through interactive processes.

Why a Global Mindset Debate?

Global mindset means putting the mindset concept into a specific context: the global context. Compared to previous contexts, this new context is more diverse in terms of behavior, structures, and ways of thinking, and thus, managers need a mindset that can make sense of the diversity and support them when interacting with managers from many different countries. In a cognitive sense, companies have to unbind their present bounded rationality within the present mindset to be able to cope with this new and more diverse and also dynamic global situation.

Thus, the GM debate has emerged due to changes in the environment and in the associated strategies and practices of transnational companies (TNCs). Over the last 20–30 years, more and more countries have opted for a liberal trade and investment regime both domestically and in their relations with other countries. This has created a new playing field for the TNCs, which now can leave the multi-domestic strategy (Porter 1980) and adopt new and more global strategies. These new strategies are shaped by the global distribution of economic activities (spatial dimension) and at the same time, TNCs have tried to coordinate and gain synergies from the activities (governance dimension). Thus, the companies were in need of a mindset that could handle operations across countries/cultures (the global dimension), but at the same time, they should be able to handle operations within specific countries/cultures (the local dimension) (Dicken 2015). The search for a balance between global advantages and local responsiveness was put on the agenda without any obvious or clear-cut solution.

Furthermore, the global economy is highly dynamic, which implies that companies need to be very flexible and agile. This challenges the conventional structural thinking on how to organize globally distributed activities (Dicken 2015) and the culture-based thinking on how to behave in culturally new settings. With the concept of GM, we move one step deeper ". . . from historical concentration on the grand issues of strategy, structure and systems, to a focus on developing purpose and vision, processes and people" (Paul 2000, p. 194). Thus, with the concept of GM, we venture into a much more fluid part of management: how managers (should) think, and how managers should be able to manage on "the global go," meeting the global diversity and uncertainty head on.[1]

Given that a GM is the way of thinking about the global business reality, there is basically no limit to the perspectives we can use to perceive and understand the global reality. Only our own absorptive capacity (Cohen and Levinthal 1990), creativity (Byrge and Hansen 2014), bounded rationality (March 1991), cultural values (Gullestrup 2006), and learning and experience (Lundvall 1992) set the limits to and frame our views on the global reality. This is both a strength and weakness of the GM construct. It is a strength that you can come up with new (mental) perspectives that can underpin new business models, but it is a weakness that you may socially construct solutions that are dreams far from the reality.

Literature Review

The Early Debate

The early debate on global mindset is well captured by Levy et al. (2007). The early literature centered on the concepts of "management orientation," "convergence," and "adaptation." Already in 1969, Perlmutter launched a distinction between four management orientations, the so-called EPRG-framework, related to the management of international companies. Managers may have *an ethnocentric, a polycentric, a regiocentric,* or *a global mindset* (Perlmutter 1969). In the first instance, the basis for the management mindset is the culture of the home country. In the second case, the way of thinking depends on the context, i.e., management thinking is adapted to the particular context, normally a specific country/market context, and in the third and fourth instances, the manager looks across a set of cultures to identify the commonalities and pursue his or her business based on such a perceived "global" mental platform. The distinctions made by Perlmutter are included in and part and parcel of any textbook on international marketing and management, as it provides an easy way of understanding what international management requires. However, the concepts have never been unfolded to form the basis of a more elaborate theory of mindsets for international management.

Perhaps the constructs by Perlmutter were not unfolded due to the seminal article by Levitt (1983), who argued for a convergence thesis. The increasing interaction through trade and tourism would, he claimed, form the basis for the convergence of tastes and behavior among consumers across the globe. The TNC would thus face a homogeneous global demand for its market offers. This convergence process would be underpinned by the marketing campaigns by TNCs and by TNCs' exploitation of economies of scale and scope whereby they could offer good-standard products at a lower price to the global market. Economies of scale would be the primary competitive parameter. Thus, consumers across the globe would, according to Levitt (1983), gradually form and adopt a global mindset in the sense of having the same way of thinking and assessing products and market offers in general.

The third concept, "adaptation," is partly in opposition to Levitt's "convergence" concept. In this case, the TNCs are asked to take a careful look at the local context and adapt to its particularities if they want to be successful in a market. Today, "adaptation" is a key concept in almost all basic texts on international marketing (Hollensen 2014) and management (Bartlett, Ghoshal, and Birkinshaw 2004). It fits well into the dominant marketing concept, where you differentiate your market offers to adapt to differences in needs and demands. "Adaptation" corresponds to the concept of "polycentric" in Perlmutter's framework and, contrary to Levitt, divergence or diversity is seen as the normal state of affairs rather than convergence.

The presented frameworks seem, however, not to fully grasp—or at least they need to be further developed—the present globalization of the economy. Clearly, the global development has not proven Levitt to be right. We have elements of convergence, but not in a linear manner. Consumers learn from their visits to other cultures and they enjoy the local tastes when at the locality. Back home, the enjoyment often fades—not completely, however, but they integrate the experience into their own culture. In this way, the trend is not convergence, and it is also not diversity by adding more to the menus at home. It is also not diversity in the sense of creating new habits by orchestrating, for example, new meals based on ingredients from abroad and from home. Furthermore, consumers now demand customized products, and through co-design and co-production (Ramirez 1999; Hu and Sørensen 2011), they even take part in the very development and production of market offers. Similarly, economies of scale advantages have been undermined by more flexible technologies (Garud and Kotha 1994) that lower setup costs and that are able to be economically efficient even on a small scale.

The Present Debate

Global Mindset as a Set of Capitals

Javidan and Teagarden (2011) see GM as a set of three types of "capitals" that an individual possesses to a higher or lower degree. Based on extensive conceptualization and empirical studies, they have identified three such capitals:

1. Intellectual capital
2. Psychological capital
3. Social capital.

Global intellectual capital reflects people's business savvy, global outlook, and cognitive complexity. Basically, it is their knowledge and analytical capabilities. Psychological capital reflects an individual's enjoyment in exploring the world and quest for adventure, including his or her willingness to take risks and handle unpredictable and even uncomfortable situations. Social capital reflects people's ability to engage with other people, their network and ability to integrate diverse perspectives (this latter competence may also require your intellectual capital). Scales for measuring these capitals have been developed so that in fact we can calculate how much GM we have. Global managers should score high on all three dimensions in today's global world.

Javidan and Teagarden (2011), more than most others, focus on GM as a source of competitive advantage. The GM ". . . of key decision makers contribute to strategic sense-making capabilities . . . by enabling the decision maker to make sense of complex and volatile organizational and environments, which in turn can enhance or inhibit competitive advantage" (p 19).

Thus, for Javidan and Teagarden (2011), GM is a stock of three types of capitals, which can be built and used to influence others across the globe. It is clear that the construct of "diversity" has moved from being something to adapt to in the early literature on GM to being a resource to explore and exploit. Furthermore, Javidan and Teagarden (2011) view GM as a state of mind, while there is less focus on the GM processes and actions.

GM as a Balance Between Global Integration and Local Responsiveness

While Perlmutter (1969) and Porter (1980) saw the global orientation and global strategy, respectively, as the ultimate stage of corporate globalization, researchers and companies alike gradually discovered that this was a too simplistic view on management orientation and strategy. Doz and Prahalad (1991) were some of the first to conceptualize the frictions or equilibrium between global integration and local responsiveness.

Gupta and Govindarajan (2002) developed a mindset framework to capture the balancing act of the global integration and the local responsiveness. They operate with three mindsets:

1. A diffused mindset where the company adapts locally but is not able to capture the global synergies
2. A parochial mindset where the company capture the global synergies at the expense of local responsiveness
3. A global mindset where global integration and local responsiveness are balanced.

We have used the Gupta and Govindarajan (2002) framework but modified it to some extent. It is shown in Figure 5.1.

In this framework, we clearly see the Perlmutter (1969) view on global orientation and also Porter's (1980) idea of a global strategy (global standard mindset). The framework also reflects the ideas of a multi-centered orientation/strategy presented in the writings of Perlmutter and Porter. The new element in the figure is the strategy/mindset act of balancing the global and the local (Cell 4).

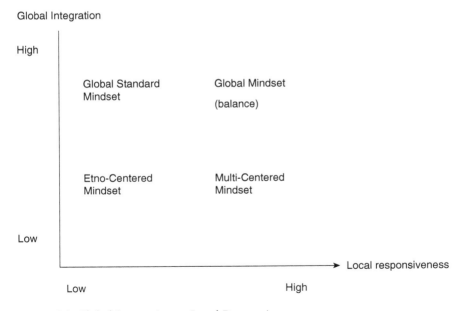

Figure 5.1 Global Integration or Local Responsiveness

However, the Gupta and Govindarajan (2002) framework seems not to fully reflect the theories and practices of today. The review of the literature has identified three positions on how global integration and local responsiveness are to be understood and thus what a GM should be able to accomplish. Firstly, Jeannet (2000) emphasizes the ability to identify (global) common denominators across space: "The executive with a global mindset has the ability to see multiple territories and focuses on commonalities across many markets rather than emphasizing the differences among countries" (p. 11). Thus, the GM is a construct based on the summary knowledge across market boundaries and defining the business model from the common denominators.

Secondly, others advocate that a GM enables a company to balance (Begley and Boyd 2003) or mediate the tensions between thinking globally and acting locally. Kefalas (1998) explains that the balancing act would require a mindset with an ability to conceptualize what is seen on the ground (i.e., take to the abstract) and also contextualize (i.e., respond to local demands). Based on the Kefalas framework, Arora et al. (2004) found in an empirical study of the textile industry in the U.S. that managers were better at thinking globally than thinking locally.

Thirdly, the strategy literature has not tried to handle the global-local dilemma from the point of view of the local platform. This would entail an ability on the part of the managers to sense local particularities with a global potential and lift the potentials to the global level by giving the local managers a global mandate to develop the locally developed product for the global market. The innovation literature seems to have sensed this source of competitiveness. The reverse innovation construct (Govindarajan and Trimble 2012) assumes that innovation starts locally (in the emerging market) and is then globalized. Furthermore, the general tendency by multinational companies to internationalize their R&D has many drivers, one of them being the search for local potentials that can be given a global mandate (Tidd and Bessant 2014).

Depending on which of the three ways you understand the global-local dichotomy, the GM will be in need of a different configuration of the three types of capitals that Javidan and Teagarden (2011) identified or will be in need of different interactive engagement and processes to accommodate each of the three perspectives.

Towards a Revised GM Conceptual Framework

The aim of this section is to create a GM framework that augments and synthesizes the previous frames by adding a process perspective. The frame encompasses both the more conventional state-of-mind inspired view and the process-and-interaction inspired one, i.e., seeing GM as a social construction that is continuously in a state of becoming through the interaction between global actors.

With this basic framework in place, a further deepening of the proposed framework will take place by discussing and including other concepts and theories of relevance to understand a global mindset in action. These additional elements are especially needed to develop Cell 4 in the framework, as this cell represents a GM in a process and dynamic perspective—a GM in action:

1. The Theory of Dynamic Capabilities: As GM is viewed as a capability apart from a state-of-mind, we will draw on the influential Theory of Dynamic Capabilities, the foundation that Teece, Pisano, and Shuen, (1997) created. With its focus on competences and resources, it may make the GM concept less elusive.
2. Combining Action and Reflection: GM as a cognitive concept naturally implies some reflections as part of the way of thinking. But from a process perspective, GM also implies actions followed by experience and reflections, and therefore we find it important to introduce action into the framework.
3. Combining Context and Situation: Managers in a global company will experience many contexts, for example, a new foreign country and many different situations, i.e., time, place and issues change continuously. If the context and situation are new, the GM capabilities will naturally have to be different from when the context and situation are familiar. A higher-level GM is required in the former case.
4. Place Matters: The cognitive and absorptive capacity of a global manager is important, but an interesting aspect of this is the agility of the global mindset. Is it—as the definition claims—a state of mind that we bring along and use in different places (context/situation), or is it an agile construct that can see things differently when abroad?

The Framework

The framework is a simple two-dimensional matrix with four cells. The two dimensions reflect the nature of the global mindset (a state of mind or a capability and process) and the organizational manifestations of GM (management defined or emerging).

The nature of GM, i.e., how GM is seen in reality, can be viewed as two extremes. As one extreme, GM is seen as a state of mind, i.e. as the way for the individual to think of global reality. In this case, there is only one mindset, one best way to think of global reality. The other extreme is a GM in a continuous state of becoming, i.e., a process view of GM. The other dimension is that the organizational manifestations of the GM is defined and driven by top management. Among all the possible GM structures, top management chooses the one that is most appropriate in their mind and implement it as THE way to think in their company. At the other extreme, we have the emerging mindset, i.e., a mindset that gradually emerges and that is different from one place or unit to another.

Combining the two dimensions, we get a four-cell matrix. Each cell will be discussed subsequently. The framework is shown in Figure 5.2.

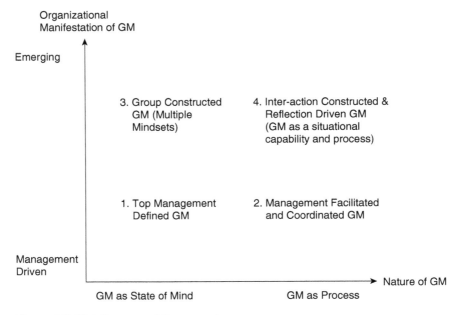

Figure 5.2 GM Conceptual Framework

Cell 1: Management-Driven Global Mindset

In Cell 1, we have the management-defined GM, which is rolled out in the global organization to all corners of the world. All are meant to have one and the same state of mind. The idea is that competitiveness and the achievement of common goals are better achieved if all think alike. In this case, the GM has much in common with the implanting of common corporate values in the global company.

Cell 2: Management-Facilitated Global Mindset

In Cell 2, we have a situation where management still plays a crucial role, but at the same time, it is realized that one corporate mindset is not possible or not even feasible, as all units and functions may not perform optimally based on the same GM. Thus, Cell 2 represents a situation where management takes the lead and facilitates and coordinates the GM processes and thus the GM capability development. The coordinating and facilitating mechanisms (Begley and Boyd 2003) could, for example, be arranging global meetings, establishing global networks, developing international career paths, etc.

The facilitation and coordination endeavors by management may be guided by the need to balance global integration and local responsiveness or, in general, the need to have an up-to-date way of thinking in a global sea of complexity, uncertainty, and diversity.

Thus, in Cell 2, management realizes the value of GMs, but puts more emphasis on a dynamic perspective, i.e., building capabilities and nursing a process so that the mindsets are developing alongside changes in the environment and the experiences and practices within the company.

Cell 3: Locally/Group-Constructed Mindset

In Cell 3, we have the GM as a specific state of mind, but it is different from one unit, group, or locality to another of the global company and it is not driven by top management. The GMs emerge in each and every unit in the company based on its experiences and practices. The unit may be a very local one, e.g., a production plant in a specific country, or a very global one, for example, a global R&D group. Cell 3 resembles the processes that create a "community of practice" (Wenger 2015). Thus, we have clearly defined but non-coordinated multiple GMs emerging from the experiences and practices on the ground.

Cell 4: Global Mindset as a Situational Capability

In Cell 4, we have a situation where the mindset is in a continuous mode of becoming. The nature of the GM is that of a capability and a process, i.e., the individuals have a capability to quickly sense a situation and engage in a process of interaction with others to construct a suitable mindset—"on the go," so to speak. The GM is not management driven. It is emerging based on capabilities and processes put into action by competent employees. Cell 4 reflects the situation of a highly dynamic world full of diversity. Cell 4 illustrates a situation where the GM is not just overcoming the constraints, but is able to see the opportunities, synthesize, and in the end construct a new mindset. In line with Rhinesmith (1992), the Cell 4 GM is comfortable with surprises and ambiguity and sees diversity as an opportunity rather than as a constraint, and finds a high degree of trust in organizational processes rather than structures. Perhaps what is most important is the ability to move between the concrete and the abstract levels—the ability to contextualize (as an entrepreneur) and conceptualize (as a researcher) according to Kefalas (1998). This would enable the company to both capture any "commonalities" across territories (to balance the global integration and the local responsiveness when needed), and also to give a global mandate to globally unfold local peculiarities.

It is a process of interaction where the process constructs new GMs continuously, as the situation is dynamic. The individuals are quick to sense the situation and act, and through the ensued interaction, the involved individuals construct a new GM. In Cell 4, the GM is an individual capability to sense the situation and act accordingly by creating a suitable GM.

As mentioned, to develop and understand this situational capability-endowed person in Figure 2, Cell 4, we need to elaborate the framework in several ways. First, we argue that the Theory of Dynamic Capabilities by Teece (1997, 2014) forms an appropriate theoretical foundation for Cell 4. Next, we elaborate by making a distinction between "reflection" and "action," and thirdly, we further elaborate by looking at the interplay between "context" and "situation," where situation connotes a specific time, a specific activity at a specific place.

GM as a Situational Capability and the Theory of Dynamic Capabilities

The "dynamic capability" theory (Teece 1997, 2014) has emerged as an influential theory. It contests the more structure- and strategy-based frameworks and builds on the resource-based theory. Teece (2009) defined dynamic capabilities as "the firm's ability to integrate, build and reconfigure internal and external competences to address rapidly changing environments," or as Tidd and Bessant (2014) phrase it, "a capacity to utilize resources to perform a task." Cell 4 seems to fit this definition: It is clearly associated with a "rapidly changing environment" through the globalization of the economy and the potential of multiple new technologies. Furthermore, it connotes a capability to integrate—and a process of integration, building, and/or reconfiguring competences and resources. Even so, there is no straightforward way to align dynamic capabilities theory with the GM theory. As clearly seen from a recent article by Teece (2014), the Theory of Dynamic Capabilities is at a stage of concepts and typologies of concepts. It has not yet moved to a stage integrating the concepts to frameworks, let alone a stage of operationalizing the frameworks.

Yet, as the most important issue in a dynamic world is to work with processes rather than structures, we may benefit from some of the discussions within the frame of the Theory of Dynamic Capabilities. One discussion is the sensing of opportunities and the seizing of resources to explore/exploit the opportunities (Teece 2014) or vice versa, indicating a GM as a way of thinking by focusing on linking and synthesizing the two. Another is that capability entails task performance, and thus dynamic capability could be linked to more action orientation rather than planning orientation. A third one is clearly the ability to reconfigure resources and competences to get new ideas or to implement new ideas. The Theory of Dynamic Capabilities is strong on reconfiguring or orchestrating resources, while the GM literature—through its focus on cognitive and other capitals—is strong on the iterative process between conceptualization and contextualization (Kefalas 1998) and on such core concepts as learning and experience. Capabilities are built on a strong learning platform, including high absorptive and dissemination capabilities (Cohen and Levinthal 1990). Thus, it is possible, but difficult, to align the more fluid mental construct of GM with the more hard-core resource concepts that dominate the literature on dynamic capabilities. Learning, organization, and management processes and mental constructs seem to be needed to make the Theory of Dynamic Capabilities really dynamic.

Combining Action and Reflection

When working internationally, the tasks and the task completion are crucial for performance. This entails a numbers of actions and interactions. By definition, these actions/interactions enhance the experience, which in turn can be reflected upon and used for new actions (and as indicated earlier, used to build a common understanding). This dynamic interplay is visualized in Figure 5.3, where action and reflection capability are measured on the horizontal and vertical axes, respectively. As indicated, if the cognitive capability is high but the action capability is low, we may produce good rapport, but it does not give rise to any action. In the opposite case, we will be good at getting things done and taking risks, as we have little insights but a high action capacity. If we are high in both dimensions, we will be able to build new realities.

This framework indicates that a GM includes a cognitive (intellectual) capability but in addition needs action capabilities to be successful.

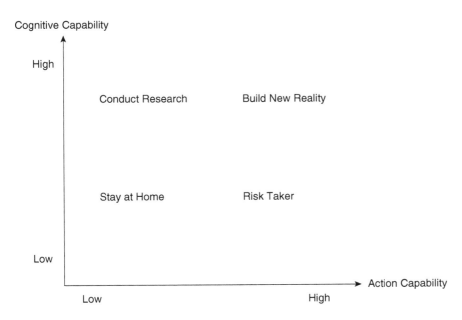

Figure 5.3 Combining Reflection and Action

Combing Context and Situation

We have discussed the nature of the GM and the organizational setting based on Figure 5.2. In this section, the setting of the GM will be elaborated. A distinction can be made between context and situation (see Figure 5.4).

The context is the global setting, for example, a country where the GM is activated. This setting may be known or unknown to the company and individual in question.

The situation is the more specific time, place, and activity for the activation of the GM. This could, for example, be August 2015 (time), in Beijing (place), where a new strategic alliance is discussed with a partner (activity). Again, the situation can be known or unknown, i.e., the persons in question may have been in a situation like this earlier or not, or it can be a follow-up meeting on the issue in question.

Combining the two dimensions of context and situation and assuming that the context/situation can be known or unknown for the person in question, we get four different settings. We have a setting where both the context and situation is known to the partners as one extreme, and as another extreme, we have a setting where neither the context nor the situation is known to the partners. Obviously, the latter case puts more pressure on the GM, i.e., a higher GM state of mind or capability is needed to cope with the challenge.

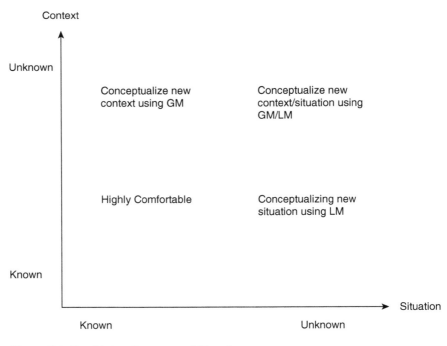

Figure 5.4 Combining Context and Situation

While the concept of context is well known and widely used in the literature, there is a need to take a closer look at the concept of situation. In common parlance, "situation" means something that happens in a specific time and a specific place.

In the literature, the concept of situation has not been used much. Some have seen it as more or less synonymous with the concept of "contingency" in the contingency theory. In a contingency perspective, the situation defines which GM is the most appropriate, and if the GM is inappropriate for the situation, people will perform poorly (Clegg, Kornberger, and Pitsis 2008, p. 136). It follows that it is useful to have a range of GMs to draw on in order to be able to cope with a variety of situations. As an alternative to a range of GMs, the GM of a person have may be adaptable and flexible so that it can adjust to different situations. From a contingency point of view, the GM is seen as a state of mind. Different states of mind suit different situations.

A contingency perspective on situations requires that we can define typical situations and from those derive the appropriate GM. In their analysis of leadership, Hersey et al. (1996) defined four situations and their appropriate leadership styles. A similar modeling of the relations between GM and situations has not been found, but we have already defined two extremes around whether the situation is familiar or not to a person. Another way of defining the situations could be by using the three types of GM capitals and define situations where the various capitals are needed or not. This would produce eight different situations.

The concept of situation has also been used in a methodological discussion. Clifford and Marcus (1986) argued for a "situational perspective," meaning that the researchers have special interest and ways of presenting and interpreting phenomena they have observed—an interpretation that those who were observed may not share. In other words, the researcher imposes his/her view of reality on others (= totalitarianism) (Hatch and Cunliffe 2013, p. 39). This understanding of the concept of situation illustrates a GM that is management defined and driven, i.e., the GM is imposed on the complete organization.

The situational perspective as described above together with other concepts leads to the concept of "reflexivity," which basically acknowledges that ". . . realities are incomplete and negotiated accounts open to multiple interpretations and meanings" (Hatch and Cunliffe 2013, p. 39). This view on situation, and how moldable a situation in reality is, fits well into the GM as a capability. Reflexivity is an essential mental activity when facing a new context and a new situation.

Finally, the concept of situation/situational context should also be contrasted with the concept of opportunism. Opportunism is defined as a change in behavior that suits one's own interests, irrespective of the harm you may cause to others. As our GM framework assumes sensitivity to different situations, it may be claimed that the framework is advocating opportunistic behavior. This, however, is not necessarily so, as the GM framework aims at close and long-term interactions and the construction of new realities in conjunction with others. Opportunism is normally shortsighted and short-lived, as those who have suffered from opportunistic behavior will cut off any further interaction with that person or company.

In conclusion, it is found that the introduction of the context/situation concepts is useful in defining which GM can be used in which setting. A state-of-mind GM may be sufficient when the context and situation are known, while a dynamic capability-based GM is needed when the context and situation are new.

Place Matters

We have made a distinction between context and situation, and place was part of both. Does place matter? Does it matter where we meet? We will argue that place matters in a mental sense.

Traditionally, the literature on culture and international marketing advises that if you want, for example, to export, you must adapt to the culture of the country to which you export (Usunier and Lee 2013; Hollensen 2014). The proposed GM framework is not denying the importance of adaptation (to existing realities), but puts more focus on the construction of new real-ities through the intensive interaction between partners. To argue for this construction view, we leave the national culture theories with their focus on comparison, and turn to the literature where interactions between people from different countries are in focus. We have earlier termed this interaction focus as "culture-in-action" (Kuada and Sørensen 2010). In an empirical study of GM among managers (Sørensen 2014), it was found that when peo-ple meet to strike a deal, they primarily focus on the tasks at hand and less on values. Furthermore, when in another culture, people are able to adapt, to some extent, as they are away from home with its routines, common values, and their interpretations, etc. In a new place, people can more freely think out of the box, reinterpret their values, be open-minded and learn and construct new solutions beneficial to both partners. The home trajectory is not forgotten, but it is reinterpreted.

This "opening up" is well-known from the creativity literature (Byrge and Hansen 2014), where creativity is on a platform (a kind of laboratory), and through exercises and procedures, it frees the mind and creates new ideas through defined tasks. Thus, place seems to matter for the GM in action, both in terms of freedom to reinterpret one's domestic GM and in terms of being more constructive in interaction with others and less adaptive.

Summing Up

The concept of GM is a fluid one. In this section, we have aimed at creating a conceptual framework for the understanding of the construct. A mindset is basically a way of thinking about reality, in this case, global business reality. In most definitions, GM is a specific state of mind that is not easily changed. This state of mind is used wherever you go to make sense of the surrounding reality. We challenged the usefulness of the concept in a global world of diversity and argued for a process view of a GM where GM is a dynamic capability to sense, interpret, and interact in new contexts and situations. This GM is a GM on the go, a GM in (inter)action, and a GM in a continuous state of becoming. Essential for this GM is the capability to move from the concrete/the local to the abstract/the global and vice versa, and thus a capability to synergize concrete facts and abstract thinking.

Thus, we have moved from a GM defined as a state of mind (made up, for example, of three types of capital) to a GM defined as follows: GM is a situational capability which through interaction is in a continuous state of becoming and which, in a given context and situation, enables us to make sense of the situation quickly, reflect constructively, and act purposefully.

Global Mindset in a Global Company—A Case Illustration

In their review of the GM literature, Levy et al. (2007) also reviewed the GM measures used in various studies. In this section, we will also operationalize the concept, not by measures to be used in a survey, but through a case, showing primarily the organizational manifestations of the GM in the case company and discussing whether the company sees GM as a state of mind or GM as a continuous process of becoming, and whether the GM is emerging from below or is top-management driven. The case is a Danish multinational company in the pump industry. The data were collected in 2011–12 by a team of researchers through deep interviews with 15 managers primarily from the headquarters (Grundfos, 2011).

Brief Description of the Case Company

The case company is a Danish multinational company within the pump industry. It produces more than 16 million pumps annually and is one of the world's leading pump manufacturers. The company was established in 1945 and from year one, the bottom line has shown black figures. In 1975, the company was established as an independent foundation, which owns almost 90% of the company. The turnover is above three billion euros and the number of employees is around 19,000 of which around 5,000 are working in Denmark (2011 figures).

For the purpose of the GM discussion, it should be noted that the case company has six values that are strongly communicated to all employees. It is a technical/engineering-oriented company with much focus on product/process innovation. It is in the midst of globalizing its R&D activities and defining centers of excellence. Apart from the corporate values, the company lives according to the slogan "be-think-innovate," which expresses both the purpose and the promise to contribute to global sustainability. In their own words, the company

> . . . is a global leader in advanced pump solutions and a trendsetter in water technology. We contribute to global sustainability by pioneering technologies that improve quality of life for people and care for the planet. It is our commitment to being responsible, thinking ahead and innovating that enables us to meet all our clients' needs on all levels (source: company website).

Formally, the case company has a hierarchical structure combined with a matrix-based structure for the sale and production side. However, the company has also features of network structures with numerous projects, groups, and teams established across the organizational units and borders. In the case company, there is room for things to emerge and be included on the agenda.

Organizational Manifestations of a GM: A Four-Level Model

Interviews and reports revealed that the company has four organizational levels much in line with the often-used distinction between the individual, group, unit, and corporate levels (Hatch and Cunliffe 2013). Figure 5.5 shows the four levels on the vertical axis to the left, and on the vertical axis to the right, the associated mindsets are identified.

The framework in Figure 5.5 helps to understand the intraorganizational structures and processes that lead to the creation of a mindset. On the vertical axis to the left, we have the organizational units that have a "mindset," starting with the individuals, moving on to the organizational units where individuals work together, and further up into what we call a "gray zone," i.e., an organizational zone where we see both hierarchical and matrix as well as network structures in a mix of organizational manifestations that are temporary or permanent, local or global, face to face or virtual, and that may be formed by people from the same level, i.e., horizontally or from different levels, i.e., vertically. They may be teams, networks, working groups, etc. Finally, at the fourth level, we have the corporate management and the corporate board. Thus, the company has basically a hierarchical structure, but it has also clearly marks of a matrix organization and networks criss-crossing units and borders.

The vertical axis to the right represents an increasingly formalized way of dealing with the GM. At the top, we have a GM defined and driven by management (level 4). Just below, we have a top-management or middle-management coordinated or facilitated GM (level 3). One step below, we have emerging, multiple mindsets in all the task-defined organizational units (level 2), and at the bottom, level 1, we have the mindset of the individual employees.

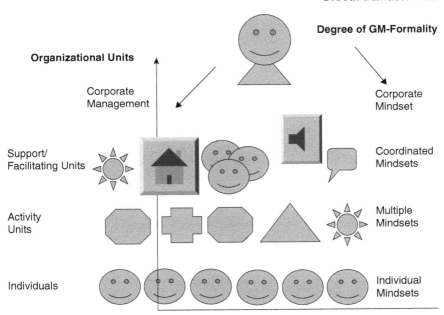

Degree of GM-Formality

Organizational Units

Corporate Management — Corporate Mindset

Support/Facilitating Units — Coordinated Mindsets

Activity Units — Multiple Mindsets

Individuals — Individual Mindsets

*Generalised from an actual company

Figure 5.5 The Global Mindset Framework

In the following section, we will present and discuss the organizational manifestations of the GM in our case company. It starts with the individual. It is the individual that has a mindset. The next step is to move from the individual employee to a shared mindset at the group or unit level. The third step is to take a broader view of the organization, and the final step is to discuss management-driven GMs.

Organizational Manifestations of the GM at Each Organizational Level in the Case Company

It All Begins With the Individual

Independent of the organizational level, the individual employee is important, as it is the individual who holds and use the mindset. An individual employee develops ways of perceiving and understanding the business reality around him/her. This constitutes his/her mindset. The mindset is thus shaped by the place/unit an individual is a member of and his/her tasks. The mindset of an employee in a small sales unit in country X is expected to be different from the mindset of a manager in the corporate sales division at headquarters.

As the theoretical discussion showed, it is not clear what it exactly means when we say that the individual has a GM. Does it mean that the individual has a lot of *knowledge* about the world, or much *experience* from working in various cultures, or a specific *orientation* (e.g., multi-centric or global orientation)? Or perhaps, the individual has a specific cap*ability* to act and interact with people across borders and build a common mindset through this interaction. Knowledge, experience, and orientation seem to be important constructs related to a GM as a state of mind, while for a GM in a continuous state of becoming, we also need the capabilities and processes of interaction to define what a GM is. From this, it is tempting to postulate that the more international knowledge, the more international experience, the "more" international orientation, and the higher the capabilities to act and interact, the more the individual has a GM. Even if it is not as simple as that, these are the elements that an individual employee brings to the other levels of the organization when GM is on the agenda. And this is what we will look at in our case company.

From the Individual to Basic Working Units

The many employees in the case company are organized into many different types of units, with a set of tasks to be performed by the members of the unit. These units may be located together or may be units composed of employees from across the organization. Inevitably, the unit develops some routines and some kind of mindset around the tasks they are challenged with, as shown in the literature on community of practice (Wenger 2015). This is a natural development from working together. The kind of mindset that will emerge depends on the context. That is, in a production unit, a common mindset suitable for production tasks will tend to emerge. The same holds true for sales units, R&D units, etc. Thus, from the actions and interactions within a unit, routines and best practices will emerge in the units, and they are both a practice and a mindset—a way of thinking about practice. In this way, we may see multiple mindsets emerge in a global company, as a global company has multiple and globally distributed organizational units.

Thus, at a general level, we can argue that the more isolated and fragmented organizational units are in a global company and the higher the task diversity is in the company, the more multiple mindsets one will expect to flourish, as different mindsets may be necessary to perform the tasks efficiently and effectively. For example, salespeople will have a more local mindset, as they have to respond to local demands, while production people may have a more global mindset, as they have their mind on economies of scale across units that are globally distributed.

Our case company is global, with numerous units abroad for production, sales, and R&D. As the units are at a physical, cultural, and functional distance, we expect to find multiple mindsets—unless management and others make sure that the units interact in various ways to create a common mindset. However, such attempts to create a common mindset across the units may cause friction and even conflicts at level 2 in our organization. To be locally responsive both in a cultural sense (locally responsive in a given market) and in a functional sense (sales, production, etc.), we need specific mindsets—not a common mindset. On the other hand, such multiple mindsets may not be in harmony and may thus jeopardize the overall goals of the company. This may give rise to having a GM defined and driven by management.

From Local to Global Mindset

Returning to Figure 5.5, we will discuss GM at level 3 and level 4, starting at level 4. Level 4 is the corporate level, where we have a management-defined and management-driven GM. It represents a top-down approach to the formation of a collective mindset. All units of the global company must adhere to this corporate way of thinking wherever their individual employees work (spatial/cultural dimension) and whatever they do (task dimension).

The case company has a set of six values, defined primarily on the basis of the virtues of the founding father of the company. The values have a cult status in the company and must be learned and adhered to by all employees. The same has not been the case with a GM, and this was not to be expected for several reasons identified during the interviews. Firstly, the concept is new and, as we showed earlier, it has neither a clear definition nor a clear operational formula. Secondly, the case company is in the midst of a debate on GM and thus is not ready to define the GM, and thirdly, the company culture is not strongly hierarchical. It is in many ways a networked company, especially related to its innovation and R&D units and activities. Although the owner has a strong will and personality, he also likes to have people with alternative views on reality around him as a way to be updated on trends and diversities.

The fact that we do not find a management-defined and-driven GM in the case company makes level 3 especially interesting, as this level is between the *purely corporate global mindset*, which is management defined and driven, and the *multiple mindsets* that emerged in each of the organizational units at level 2.

Level 3 comprises basic processes and structures that aim at directing/ controlling, integrating, facilitating, or coordinating the basic units at level 2 and of course in conjunction and harmony with the corporate level 4. In other words, level 3 comprises all units and initiatives that aim to promote interactions between employees, both horizontally and vertically, and thus also the units and processes that would be able to define and generate one or more GMs or a GM process.

There may be several reasons for promoting this interaction. One could be that the company wants to have a kind of GM (although not a purely corporate-defined one), and management assumes that intensive interaction will eventually produce a company-wide GM. Another could be that management believes in a great potential for improving performance and thus competitiveness through diversity management. A third could be that management finds it essential to balance the global integration with local responsiveness, and a fourth could be that management found it important to continuously host a debate that makes the employees feel part of a collective.

In the case company, we observed many initiatives within different organizational units at different levels aiming at debating and contributing to the creation of a GM. For example, the Corporate Academy of the case company aims, among others, to ensure the adoption of the case company corporate values and culture by all units of the company across the globe. Numerous other initiatives were taken and running rather independently of each other, including the company's expatriation policy, the establishment of cross-border technological teams within R&D, the GM project in R&D, the DNA project initiated by the HR department, the informal "club" where Danish and foreign employees meet (Rødgrød-med-Fløde-Club), the Expatriation Managers Initiative, etc. Each of these initiatives deserves to be discussed in more detail. However, the point in this chapter is not the individual initiative, but to show in general the organizational manifestations of a GM.

Two other observations from the case study are worth mentioning. The first is that the GM debates were mostly linked to actual activities, i.e., the units debated the value of a GM in relation to the actual activities they undertook. Secondly, the GM debate was in the main an HQ debate while, according to our informants, this was much less a debate at the subsidiary level.

In summary, the case company was, at the time of the interviews, in the midst of a debate of GM. This debate primarily took place in the HQ and at many levels and in many units, but nobody knew if they would find a GM, or if they did find one, would it then be one specific GM, more GMs, or GM as an organizational process in a dynamic market. Furthermore, the debate was fragmented and not coordinated by corporate management. The facilitators were the single units like the HR department, the R&D department, etc.

Referring to our conceptual framework (Figure 5.2), it is no easy task to unambiguously position the case company in the matrix. The company is in the midst of a debate, and initiatives have a number of different organizational manifestations. In that sense, we face an emerging GM on the organizational manifestation dimension, but the nature of the final GM is not yet clear. Will it be a process or a state-of-mind type of GM? In the interviews, we mostly met a state-of-mind type of thinking, perhaps as a reflection of the much-promoted set of corporate values of the company. However, the case company is very much network based and oriented, which may indicate a process- oriented GM, i.e., a GM in a continuous state of becoming. Thus, it can be expected that the company will never adopt a management-driven state-of-mind GM, but eventually will adopt a GM as a situational capability and a process, i.e., a GM in a continuous state of becoming through a continuous changing set of networks.

Summary and Conclusion

The starting point for this chapter was the dynamics and diversity of the global economy and how global companies can respond to such dynamics and diversity. The development of a global mindset was seen as a potential management tool for doing so. It was pointed out that adopting a global mindset as a way to stay competitive under the conditions of global dynamics and diversity indicated a need to focus more on the way of thinking (mindset), the processes, and the people in contrast to the dominant focus on global organizational structures and strategic positioning (Paul 2000, p. 194). In this sense, a global mindset approach to global management has much in common with the Theory of Dynamic Capabilities (Teece 2014).

The review of the literature identified the three main positions of the GM, i.e., the GM as a state of mind, the GM as a capability, and the GM as an organizational process. To cope with global dynamics and diversity, we combined the constructs of capability and process and focused on building or constructing ways of thinking through interaction processes. This way, a GM is in a continuous state of becoming and being constructed and reconstructed to align with global diversity. Furthermore, we acknowledged the crucial relationship between global integration and local responsiveness, and identified three positions in the literature. The first was the search across spaces for commonalities that could underpin a global strategy; the second, an attempt to balance the two; and a third and emerging one, especially in the innovation literature, was where local particularities are given a global mandate.

These observations informed a revised conceptual framework for capturing the diversity of the GM literature. A distinction was made between the nature of the GM (a state of mind or a capability and process) and the organizational manifestations of the GM (management driven or emerging). The two dimensions were related in a matrix with the following four cells:

Cell 1: A top-management-defined-and-driven global mindset.

Cell 2: A management-facilitated-and-coordinated global mindset construction process.

Cell 3: A set of emerging but uncoordinated global mindsets within units, groups, etc. of the global company.

Cell 4: A situational-capability-based global mindset construction process.

A case was presented to illustrate how the framework could capture the realities of a multinational company. By way of interviews with managers, an attempt was made to reveal the organizational manifestations of GM. To this end, a four-level model of the organization was used (individual, unit, gray zone, and top management). It was found that the company was in the midst of a discussion of the global mindset of the company. The debate was somewhat fragmented and more pronounced in the headquarters than in the multiple subsidiaries. The debates took place partly in the individual units and partly in the gray zone between the single units and corporate management. The number of initiatives was relatively high and seemingly independent of each other. Initiatives could be found at all organizational levels, which is in line with the fact that the company has a tradition for not being highly top-down managed. Things emerge from top and bottom in a not-always-transparent way. In that sense, you could find GM elements from all four cells in our framework. However, there seems to be a tendency towards Cell 4, i.e., an emerging GM based on strong capabilities and organizational processes. The GM is in a continuous state of becoming and is able to take part in both adapting to and framing the global dynamics.

The discussions and reflections on the theories as well as on the case company led to the following more elaborate but admittedly also more complex definition and understanding of the GM. In this chapter, we have moved from a GM defined as a state of mind (made up, for example, of three types of capital) to a GM defined as follows: GM is a situational capability which is in a continuous state of becoming (learning) through interaction (task performance), and which in a given context and situation makes you sense quickly, reflect constructively, and act purposefully (conceptualization-contextualization).

Note

1. In this chapter, we will focus on GM, but the organization literature also attempts to cope with this more fluid construct through constructs such as "ambidextrous organizations" (Hatch and Cunliffe 2013).

References

Arora, A. Jaju, A., Asterios G., Kefalas, A.G. and Perenich, T. (2004): An Explorative Analysis of Global Managerial Mindsets: A Case of US Textile and Apparale Industry. *Journal of International Management,* 10(3): 393–411.

Bartlett, C.A., Ghoshal, S. and Birkinshaw, J. (2004): *Transnational Management.* Boston: McGraw-Hill.

Begley, T.M. and Boyd, D.P. (2003): The Need for a Corporate Global Mind-Set. *MIT Sloan Management Review,* 44(2): 25–32.

Brown, J.S. and Duguid, P. (1996): Organizational Learning and Communities of Practice: Towards a unified view of working, learning and innovation. (in) *Organizational Learning,* eds Cohen, M.D. and Sproull, L.S., London: Sage Publications, 58–82.

Byrge, C. and Hansen, S. (2014): *Enhancing Creativity for Individuals, Groups and Organizations—Creativity as the Unlimited Application of Knowledge.* Frydenlund: Aarhus.

Clegg, S., Kornberger, M. and Pitsis, T. (2008): *Managing and Organizations.* London: Sage.

Clifford, J. and Marcus, G.E., eds. (1986): *Writing Cultures: The Poetics and Politics of Ethnography.* Los Angeles: University of California Press.

Cohen, W. and Levinthal, D. (1990): Absorptive Capacity: A New Perspective on Learning and Innovation. *Administrative Science Quarterly,* 35(1): 128–152.

Dicken, P. (2015): *Global Shift,* 7th Ed. Los Angeles: Sage.

Doz, Y.L. and Prahalad, C.K. (1991): Managing DMNCs: A Search for a New Paradigm. *Strategic Management Journal,* 12: 145–164.

Dweck, C. (2006): *Mindset: The New Psychology of Success.* New York: Random House Publishing.

Garud, R. and Kotha, S. (1994): Using the Brian Metaphor to Model Flexible Production Systems. *Academy of Management Review,* 19(4): 671–698.

Govindarajan, V. and Trimble, C. (2012): *Reverse Innovation: Create Far From Home, Win Everywhere.* Cambridge, MA: Harvard Business Review Press.

Grundfos: The quest for the global mindset (2011): Report prepared by the International Business Centre, Aalborg University.

Gullestrup, H. (2006): *Cultural Analysis: Towards Cross-Cultural Understanding.* Copenhagen: Copenhagen Business School Press.

Gupta, A.K. and Govindarajan, V. (2002): Cultivating a Global Mindset. *Academy of Management Executive,* 16(1): 116–126.

Hatch, J.H. and Cunliffe, A.L. (2013): *Organization Theory: Modern, Symbolic, and Postmodern Perspectives,* 3rd Ed. Oxford: Oxford University Press.

Hersey, P., Blanchard, K.H., and Johnson, D.E., et al (1996): *Management of Organizational Behavior: Leading Utilizing Human Resources.* New Jersey: Prentice Hall. Hofstede, G. (2001): *Culture's Consequences.* London: Sage Publications.

Hollensen, S. (2014): *Global Marketing,* 6th Ed. Pearson: London.

Hu, Y. and Sørensen, O.J. (2011): Innovation in Virtual Networks: Evidence from the Chinese online Game Industry. *Journal of Science and Technology Policy in China,* 3(3): 198–215.

Javidan, M. and Teagarden, M. (2011): Conceptualizing and Measuring Global Mindset. *Advances in Global Leadership,* 6: 13–39.

Jeannet, J.-P. (2000): *Managing with a Global Mindset.* London: Financial Times/ Prentice Hall.

Kefalas, A. (1998): Think Globally, Act Locally. *Thunderbird International Business Review,* 40(6): 547–562.

Kuada, J. and Sørensen, O. J. (2010): Culture-in-Action and Creative Learning in Cross-border R&D Teams. (in) *Leadership and Creativity: A Cultural Perspective,* eds Kuada, J. and Sørensen, O.J. Harlow: Pearson Education Limited.

Levitt, T. (1983): The Globalization of Markets. *Harvard Business Review,* 61(3): 92–102.

Levy, O., Beechler, S., Taylor, S. and Boyacigiller, N.A. (2007): What We Talk about When We Talk about 'Global Mindset': Managerial Cognition in Multinational Corporations. *Journal of International Business Studies,* 38(2): 231–258.

Lundvall, B.Å. (1992): *National Systems of Innovation: Towards a Theory of Innovation and Interactive Learning.* London: Pinter Publishers.

March, J.G. (1991): Exploration and Exploitation in Organizational Learning. *Organization Science,* 2(1): 71–87.

Paul, H. (2000): Creating Mindsets. *Thunderbird International Business Review,* 42(2): 187–200.

Perlmutter, H. (1969): The Tortuous Evolution of the Multinational Corporation. *Columbia Journal of World Business,* 4(1): 9–18.

Porter, M.E. (1980): *Competitive Strategy—Techniques for Analysing Industries and Competitors.* New York: The Free Press.

Ramirez, R. (1999): Value Co-Production: Intellectual Origins and Implications for Practice and Resources. *Strategic Management Journal,* 20(1): 49–65.

Rhinesmith, S.H. (1992): Global Mindsets for Global Managers. *Training and Development,* 46(10): 63–68.

Simon, H.R. (1972): Theory of Bounded Rationality. (in) *Decisions and Organizations,* eds. By McGuire, C. B. and Rodmer, R. Amsterdam: North Holland Publishing House, 250–270.

Sørensen, J.B. (2002): The Strength of Corporate Culture and the Reliability of Firm Performance. *Administrative Science Quarterly,* 47(1): 70–91.

Sørensen, O.J. (2014): *Global Mindset as a Driver of Export and Internationalization.* SMV-Panel Publication. International Business Centre, Aalborg University.

Story, J.S.P. and Barbuto, J.E. Jr. (2011): Global Mindset: A Construct Clarification and Framework. *Journal of Leadership & Organizational Studies,* 18(3): 377–384.

Teece, D.J. (2009): *Dynamic Capabilities and Strategic Management.* Oxford: Oxford University Press.

Teece, D.J. (2014): A Dynamic Capabilities-Based Entrepreneurial Theory of the Multinational Enterprise. *Journal of International Business Studies,* 45(1): 8–37.

Teece, D.J., Pisano, G. and Shuen, A. (1997): Dynamic Capabilities and Strategic Management. *Strategic Management Journal,* 18(7): 537–553.

Tidd, J. and Bessant, J. (2014): *Strategic Innovation Management.* Wiley: West Sussex.

Usunier, J.-C. and Lee, J.A. (2013): *Marketing Across Cultures,* 6th Ed. London: Pearson.

6 Incipiency of Global Mindsets Among Smaller Manufacturing Enterprises

George Tesar and Hamid Moini

Introduction

The purpose of this chapter is to explore the incipiency of the "global mindset" as a construct in international management among smaller manufacturing enterprises (SMEs). More specifically, this chapter attempts to formulate a conceptual model for research that could potentially lead to the detection of managerial activities that evolve as incipient global mindsets. The initial managerial activities among early stages of SMEs' exporting operations provide a unique opportunity to introduce a suitable platform for detecting and defining a global mindset as an operational construct in international management. The detection and definition of the construct among SMEs may potentially contribute to an understanding of their subsequent international activities.

The emergence of global mindset as a construct in international management literature is originally attributed to Perlmutter (1969) in his discussion of the evolution of multinational corporations. Global mindset as a research construct from the beginning was difficult to define and use in scientifically based research studies. Over the years, a number of case studies appeared in management literature without pointing to any statistically meaningful conclusions, or to a relatively common conceptual definition (Kyvik, Saris, Bonet and Felício, 2013). Based on a review of the number of corporate cases studies available, it can be concluded that global mindset as a research construct is more important to academic researchers than to practicing managers. Interested researchers need to develop a suitable internally consistent conceptual model and clearly define its meaning and intent.

When the notion of the early stages of exporting among SMEs is examined from the perspective of initiating international operations, individual SMEs provide an interesting dilemma. Studies suggest that export operations among SMEs may be undertaken with minimal knowledge of international environments (Tesar, Moini, Kuada and Sørensen, 2010). Any implied relationships between initial stages of export operations among SMEs and their potential foreign markets, clients, or customers may be imaginary at best. Case research suggests that, in the early stages of exporting, SMEs have opportunities to export their products through existing infrastructures or sales and distribution channels without being directly involved with the strategic or operations aspects of foreign environments. However, more competitive and market-aggressive SMEs initiate their export strategies and operations early in their development with full consideration of international environments (Bilkey and Tesar, 1977).

Many SMEs today tend to have latent international resources available to them. Most professional employees, managers, and engineers have been exposed to international dimensions in their undergraduate or graduate studies; they may have taken courses with international content or participated in internships or studies abroad. Although all these resources may be relevant to the potential internationalization of SMEs, they are not generally utilized until they are strategically or operationally relevant. And yet, they provide a tentative foundation for the incipiency of a global mindset.

The awareness of international environments among SMEs in their early stages of export operations is theoretically important. However, mostly due to the options of export engagement available to SMEs, some feel that awareness of international environments is only marginally important. This is primarily due to relationships between manufacturing and sales functions and their attitudes towards foreign markets, customers, and even consumers. If a sales organization is capable of selling its products with minimal changes or modifications through its domestic sales channels, it will do so.

In reality, SMEs' export strategies and operations need a great deal of knowledge from foreign environments, clients, and especially customers, but the sales organizations are generally not capable of soliciting that knowledge internally, and even obtaining sufficient information about foreign environments and markets may be too difficult. This is primarily because SMEs tend to deploy sales activities prior to having well-integrated marketing strategies. In order for SMEs to export their products successfully, they need to have some minimal level of understanding of international environments and fundamental marketing activities.

SMEs and International Activities

Researchers typically suggest that there are imposed mandates that motivate SMEs to initiate export operations: They enter international, multinational, or global markets out of competitive necessity and survival instincts. Others point out that some SMEs initiate export operations internally due to market demand for their products. And finally, some research findings indicate that SMEs tend to only respond to valid export orders and solicit information about foreign environments only when they need it (Tesar et al., 2010).

Some of the efforts to understand foreign markets are imposed on SMEs by outside groups such as federal or state agencies, trade organizations, or professional organizations. Both federal and state governments operate departments intended to promote, stimulate, and develop export activities among SMEs. Other government agencies attempt to provide targeted SMEs with specific export orders, organize trade missions led by top government officials, or provide direct assistance to facilitate export orders. The governments behind these efforts hope to stabilize their economies, create more job opportunities, and increase tax revenues.

In a number of countries, college and universities operate business development centers, centers for entrepreneurship, or centers for international education and tend to cooperate with SMEs and assist them in developing international perspectives through seminars, workshops, or one-on-one counseling. Many of these efforts are successful in the initial stages of exporting.

The global mindset, as a construct in the internationalization process of SMEs, is complex. The reluctance of SMEs to seek information about foreign environments early in their attempts to export their products suggests that the global mindset may not be important in the initial stages of export operations. SMEs, as individual entities, may have a number of global mindsets advocated by individuals within them. The global mindset, as generally defined, is individualistic. Nevertheless, at the beginning of their international activities, regardless how they are defined—exports or others—SMEs tend to have a composite global mindset that consists of inputs from a variety of professionals.

At this point in time, the global mindset consists of individual experiences, beliefs, perceptions, and opinions of what foreign environments represent to the individuals involved with initial internationalization activity. In reality, this composite global mindset may have little impact on the initial internationalization activities of an SME. However, the composite incipient global mindset eventually expands into a unique mindset reflecting the needs and preferences of experienced SMEs with highly structured export operations, leading to higher levels of international or global operations.

Although global mindset as a theoretical and conceptual construct has been explored in managerial literature, it has never been clearly defined and remains subject to speculation, especially among SMEs' management. Some researchers have attempted to define the construct based on information gathered through research cases, while others have constructed conceptual models based on input from the social sciences, especially sociology and psychology. These approaches both tend to produce unstable results providing marginal input into decision-making concerning SMEs' issues of understanding international activities, identity, and marketing performance.

In an effort to define and make the global mindset operational, applied researchers have attempted to design complex approaches based on a limited understanding of what the construct represents in the cognitive maps of individual managers within an SME. Management consultants constructed elaborate documents consisting of a series of questions leading to attempts to develop global mindset profiles of SME managers. The global mindset construct continues to be an elusive concept that may not be subject to specification by a series of randomly assembled questions.

For the global mindset construct to be defined and scientifically tested, an empirically based scientific foundation with a conceptual framework is needed. The conceptual model developed in this chapter (see Figure 6.1) is

Figure 6.1[1] Marketing Options Faced by Smaller Manufacturing Enterprises in Initial Stages of International Operations

	International Marketing Options									
	International marketing options with a domestic base						International marketing options with foreign bases			Internet-based international options (born global)
	Export marketing options with domestic entry modes—export structures			Export marketing options with foreign entry modes—import structures						
Smaller manufacturing enterprises (SMEs)	1. Export merchants	2. Export agents	3. Export buyers	1. Import merchants	2. Import representatives	3. Consumer-owned import establishments	1. Export entry modes	2. Contractual entry modes	3. Investment entry modes	
SME (1)			X							
SME (2)		X			X					
SME (3)			X							
...										
SME (n)										

Export marketing options with domestic entry modes—export structures

Export merchants: (1) export houses, (2) export trading companies, (3) pure traders.
Export agents: (1) selling agents, (2) manufacturer's agents, (3) export management companies, (4) international brokers.
Export buyers: (1) commission houses, (2) resident buyers.

Export marketing options with foreign entry modes—import structures

Import merchants: (1) import houses, (2) import trading companies.
Import representatives: (1) commission houses, (2) resident representatives of foreign exporters.
Consumer/customer-owned import establishments: (1) manufacturers, (2) retailers, (3) cooperative buying groups.

International marketing options with foreign bases

Export entry modes: (1) indirect, (2) direct agent/distributor, (3) direct branch/subsidiary.
Contractual entry modes: (1) licensing, (2) franchising, (3) technical agreements, (4) service contracts, (5) management contracts, (6) construction/turnkey contracts, (7) contract manufacturing, (8) co-production agreements.
Investment modes: (1) sole venture—new establishment, (2) sole venture—acquisition, (3) joint venture—new establishment/acquisition.

based on an international marketing framework that attempts to introduce such an approach. Both conceptually and theoretically, the global mindset as a construct should be one of the factors included in the development of international marketing strategies and operations.

It is also essential to systematically identify a stable set of enterprises with potential marketing intentions to internationalize. SMEs that are in early stages of international marketing, or more specifically, SMEs that were recently introduced to export operations by mandate or by choice, provide such a research opportunity. SMEs that were export motivated by their internal need to expand their operations need to be examined just as much as those that export due to outside forces. It is conceptually and theoretically apparent that both types of exporting SMEs, as collective entities, function on the basis of an incipient global mindset.

SMEs and the Marketing Function

SMEs in the world economy provide a wide range of operations managed by a variety of managers. They are known for innovative approaches using high technology combined with high skill sets and dexterity. Most SMEs start out as small, one-product, fabrication shops that grow into larger manufacturing operations marketing uniquely competitive products to a variety of clients, customers, and consumers. They differ in technological sophistication, rate of growth, and employment. Some operate with low capital reserves, while others are well capitalized. Their propensities to operate in foreign markets are also highly diverse. Managers operating SMEs can be divided into three distinct types (Tesar et al., 2010).

Craftsman-operated-and-managed SMEs tend to fabricate parts, components, and equipment for a variety of clients. Some of them are highly innovative and technologically advanced, while others specialize in low-technology, one-of-a-kind products built by obsolete tools using passing skills. Although some craftsmen are highly educated and may hold advanced degrees in scientific fields, their awareness of international environments and markets for their products may be limited. They are more interested in their technical capabilities and fabrication skills than in their sale and marketing skills. They are generally not interested in export operations, unless they know the clients or customers personally.

Promoters are more interested in promoting their products and commercial activities than in managing them on a day-to-day basis. They tend to focus on sales activities mainly to reduce their inventory. Promoters as managers may not be as skilled as the craftsmen, but they tend to understand their operations and market dynamics, including competition. They have some understanding of international environments and when appropriate, they tend to respond to unsolicited export orders. When the need arises, they willingly cooperate with local or national export development agents and tend to be opportunistically passive exporters.

Rational managers typically are interested in the effective and efficient management of SMEs' resources—financial, physical, or human. They use their marketing and financial skills to produce competitively priced products based on market demand and subject to well-formulated marketing strategies and operations. Rational managers generally do not differentiate between domestic and foreign markets. They employ a variety of market entry strategies for their domestic and international marketing activities; they may include direct exporting strategies on the low end and well-designed multiple market entry portfolio-type approaches on the high end of their marketing strategies. Their knowledge of international environments and markets is relatively high and typically based on their personal experiences. Their contact with governmental agencies is limited.

When all three types of managers are examined from a marketing management perspective, it becomes obvious that they consciously or subconsciously employ different marketing management theories and techniques. The production function becomes the most important fundamental aspect of marketing management in craftsmen-managed SMEs. In SMEs with managers who actively promote their product and operations, distribution and sales are the most important marketing management functions; they conduct little research or gather marketing information and view foreign markets opportunistically, yet, they are willing to service foreign markets. Finally, rational managers manage SMEs for growth and a strong market position. This requires formulations of effective and efficient marketing strategies in domestic and foreign markets, and its close monitoring is essential.

In the world of international marketing, SMEs are important elements of highly changing, technologically motivated markets. SMEs tend to be innovative, flexible, and competitive. From an economic perspective, SMEs grow, create employments, and pay taxes. From a relatively narrow marketing perspective, SMEs are important partners in international value chains because they contribute new technologies, flexible sourcing options, and manufacturing innovations. Their products are sought after by clients, customers, and consumers internationally, even though some SMEs tend to have a strict local or regional orientation. Very few SMEs tend to have an extensive international orientation and a well-defined global mindset.

There is an additional tool that marketing managers have integrated into their marketing strategies and operations: the Internet. The Internet by its own nature is an international medium. SMEs that operate Internet-based web pages tend to respond to international activities faster and more competitively than those that are still reluctant to conduct any marketing activities over the Internet. These latter SMEs tend to be locally oriented and reluctant to venture into the global marketplace. Developing suitable global mindsets within this subset of SMEs depends very much on the personal profiles and managerial styles of top executives, in many cases, the owners. For many SMEs, the Internet is very much connected with their view of the world, and they need to develop a suitable global mindset to participate in it. These incipient global mindsets eventually expand into unique mindsets reflecting the needs and preferences of experienced SMEs with highly structured export operations, frequently as parts of their total international or global operations (Moini and Tesar, 2005).

Conceptual Approach to Global Mindset Incipiency

A conceptual framework that would provide a suitable foundation for understanding early developments of global mindsets among SMEs should consist of several established concepts and theories relating to (1) the structural characteristics of SMEs as individual entities and (2) the marketing options faced by SMEs. The marketing options are diverse and should include factors that, when employed, lead to international activities, and more specifically, to the evolution of a uniquely representative global mindset for each SME. Such a conceptual framework also needs to include specific international marketing options that directly represent marketing activities at times when the construct—global mindset—is emerging within the operations of an SME.

SMEs based in specific countries are faced with two international marketing options from their domestic bases: (1) export marketing options with domestic entry modes connected to export structures and (2) export marketing options with foreign entry modes connected to import structures. Both marketing options indicate that SMEs may participate in foreign marketing operations by only exercising domestic sales.

In the first instance, SMEs can sell their products in their domestic markets directly to: (1) export merchants, (2) export agents, or (3) export buyers, without making any decision directly related to foreign or international dimensions. In other words, the three entities complete commercial transactions in domestic markets by assuming any and all export activities. The only variable in these transactions may be the foreign technical requirements for the products.

In the second instance, SMEs can also sell their products in their domestic market to: (1) import merchants, (2) import representatives, or (3) consumer-owned import establishments, again without concerns related to foreign or international dimensions because the import entities assume all responsibilities for importing the products.

When the two international marketing options are examined from the perspectives of the SMEs exercising these options, it becomes apparent that they consider them strictly domestic transactions. If, in reality, they are domestic transactions, the respective SMEs are now aware of many of the international challenges on which the global mindset construct is based. It is only after some difficulties emerge from the technical aspects of the products, sales approaches, or negligence associated with product use in foreign environments that SMEs begin to consider the necessary differences between their domestic markets and problematic foreign markets.

The results of case studies suggest that when SMEs opt to export their products through either export structures or import structures based in their own domestic markets, they are not necessarily aware of the complexities faced by the intermediaries facilitating export operations for SMEs. It is only when the intermediaries confront major concerns that may jeopardize export operations, and they communicate these concerns to the responsible SMEs, that the SMEs begin to question these concerns and respond to them. These responses provide the necessary foundation for global mindset incipiency.

The evolutionary process of export expansion and eventual internationalization of their marketing operations also suggests that when SMEs begin to realize that they need to operate under some sort of an organized mission, strategy, or operational philosophy, they tend to modify their initial global mindset to reflect on expanding international activities. This evolutionary process may eventually result in expanding their marketing operations into additional foreign markets by using other market entry modes and creating foreign bases for their activities.

To illustrate how concerns of export- and import-related entities stimulate the development of global mindsets among SMEs, it is useful to present three short case studies. The names of the SMEs have been changed and modified to illustrate specific concepts related to this chapter.

Case 1: Northland Harness

Northland Harness (NH) is a small fabricator of aftermarket automobile electrical wire harnesses used in the restoration of antique automobiles. It is located in a small university town, where it employs a mostly local workforce, including students who work part time. At the suggestion of one of the students, NH recently placed a web page on the Internet. The owner, Mr. Scott, asked the student to take the responsibility for designing the web page. Once the web page was operating, orders started coming in from places such as Australia, Argentina, and Saudi Arabia, among others. Mr. Scott was surprised and decided to ignore the orders. After a long discussion with the student and his suggestion that the harnesses could be exported without any problems, he realized that he knew an individual who frequently visited and purchased harnesses from him for delivery to foreign customers.

Mr. Scott decided to call the individual; he subsequently learned that he was talking to an export buyer, and that he would be glad to work with NH in the future. The export buyer explained that when he receives orders from his customers aboard, he then places an order with a supplier such as NH and simply facilitates the shipments to his clients—Mr. Scott does not need to know anything about his customers. The wiring harnesses fabricated by NH are standard products subject to technical specifications and installed in known automobiles. It does not make any difference where the automobiles are being restored.

Case 2: Hardwood Processing Ltd.

Hardwood Processing Ltd. (HPL) is technically a sawmill processing hard-wood logs into standard- length boards for shipment to cabinet and fur-niture manufacturers. HPL purchases logs from various suppliers located in a heavily wooded region that spans an approximately one-hundred-mile radius. Each board is assigned a number and scanned into a computer using standard industry codes. Each board is inspected and its quality graded based on its general appearance. Customers place orders based on their current needs, and HPL tries to fill orders and ship them within two working days.

The state export development specialists recently visited HPL to inform them that there is a strong demand for hardwood abroad and that the state is organizing a trade mission to Japan and wanted to know if they could include HPL sales literature. Mr. Davis, the manager of operations, was sur-prised by their request, but agreed. When the catalog show in Japan was over, HPL received promising feedback: (1) An export agent located on the West Coast was interested in representing HPL in Japan and other markets in Southeast Asia, and (2) a Japanese import representative was interested in an exclusive agreement for the Japanese market.

HPL agreed to both offers, but was concerned about the details concern-ing packaging and shipping the boards to Japan. Mr. Davis met with the export agent to discuss all the details and finalize the agreement. During the meeting, he mentioned the offer from the Japanese import representative. The export agent told Mr. Davis that he knew the import representative and was willing to work with him. Mr. Davis agreed that the export agent should contact the import representative directly and agree on cooperation that would not directly involve HPL.

HPL's main concern was that it will not, in any way, get involved with foreign transactions of any kind—including collecting payments. The ship-ments intended for Japan will be picked up at the mill and shipped to a loca-tion specified by the export agent, where the shipment will be prepared for delivery in Japan. In reality, HPL considers these transactions to be strictly domestic sales.

Case 3: Verona Planting Equipment

Verona Planting Equipment (VPE) is an old, well-established, family-owned manufacturer of planting equipment. The equipment was originally designed for planting potatoes, tobacco, and rice. The planting equipment represents old technology, is labor intensive, and economical to use. In the United States, it was typically pulled by a horse or a small tractor. If necessary, it could easily be pulled by any domesticated animal. With the demise of tobacco growing and the automation of rice and potato growing in the United States, the market for such planters diminished and VPE was faced with financial losses and employee layoffs.

The top management of VPE looked for options. During a meeting of the local international trade association, one of the owners was introduced to an East African guest who was visiting companies in the area. As a representative of a consumer-owned import cooperative, his mission was to sign up several companies manufacturing "appropriate" agricultural equipment with the intention of distributing and servicing their equipment in his home country. The planters manufactured by VPE were ideal products to meet the needs of local small farmers.

After a short visit to VPE's lawyer, they signed an agreement to ship a specified number of planters each year to the consumer-owned import cooperative. The agreement also stipulated that if any changes would be necessary to the equipment, the cooperative would send a representative to explain the changes to VPE's engineers. After several years, the African agreement accounted for approximately 72% of VPE's sales revenue. Most of the remaining sales revenue resulted from domestic sales to small agricultural enterprises specializing in bio-agriculture. After several years and still operating under the African agreement, VPE was sold to a venture capital group in New York and was liquidated shortly after the sale.

Closing Remarks

Although in all three cases, the SMEs exported their products, they had not intentionally sought export opportunities. All three were uninterested in international markets and considered exports as unnecessary sales or marketing activities. They did not consider developing their own export operations, or perhaps in the future, entering foreign markets directly.

The development of global mindsets among SMEs requires some minimal level of interest in international environments or markets. SMEs typically generate sufficient revenue from local sources to satisfy their needs or the needs of their owner-managers. These attitudes are particularly apparent among SME managers who are classified as craftsmen. They have passive attitudes towards export operations, or any operations that reach across national borders. The more business-oriented promoters consider export operations in an opportunistic fashion and export their products only under favorable conditions.

Rational managers tend be aggressive exporters who, after gaining practical experience and sufficient knowledge, proceed beyond export operations and enter multinational or global markets. They tend to build a profitable foreign basis for their international operation and seek knowledge in order to become more effective and efficient in foreign markets.

The main research questions that need to be addressed not only deal with the issues of global mindset as a construct and its definition in management research, but also with the fundamental question of when the construct emerges among SMEs as an incipient construct and evolves into operational constructs or theories. We believe that the conceptual framework introduced in this chapter will provide a partial foundation or a platform for such research.

Note

1. This diagram was constructed by the authors based on research reported by Kolde (1982, p. 222), Root (1982, p. 67), and Tuller (1994, p. 204).

References

Bilkey, WJ and Tesar, G 1977, 'The Export Behavior of Smaller-Sized Wisconsin Manufacturing Firms', *Journal of International Business Studies*, vol. 8, no. 1, pp. 93–8.

Kolde, E-J 1982, *Environment of International Business*, Kent Publishing Company, Boston, MA.

Kyvik, O, Saris, W, Bonet, E and Felício, JA 2013, 'The Internationalization of Small Firms: The Relationship between the Global Mindset and Firm's Internationalization Behavior', *Journal of International Entrepreneurship*, vol. 11, pp. 172–95.

Moini, H and Tesar, G 2005, 'The Internet and Internationalization of Smaller Manufacturing Enterprises', *Journal of Global Marketing*, vol. 18, no. 3&4, pp. 79–94.

Perlmutter, HV 1969, 'A Drama in Three Acts . . . The Tortuous Evolution of the Multinational Corporation', *Columbia Journal of World Business*, vol. 4, no. January/February, pp. 9–18.

Root, FR 1982, *Foreign Market Entry Strategies*, AMACOM, New York.

Tesar, G, Moini, H, Kuada, J, and Sørensen, OJ 2010, *Smaller Manufacturing Enterprises in an International Context: A Longitudinal Exploration*, Imperial College Press, London.

Tuller, LW 1994, *Exporting, Importing, and Beyond*, Adams Media Corporation, Holbrook, MA.

7 Smaller Manufacturing Enterprises
Managers and Their Global Mindsets

George Tesar and Hamid Moini

Introduction

This chapter will compare the potential of the three types of top decision makers managing smaller manufacturing enterprises (SMEs) to form global mindsets, and to assess the motivations, or reasons, why decision makers develop global mindsets related to the needs of their unique SMEs. The key question is the relationship between different types of SMEs' managers and their individual propensity to develop a global mindset. This chapter also introduces the question of whether or not SMEs' managers make a conscious decision to form their own singular global mindset.

SMEs are unique among other types of small and medium-sized enterprises. SMEs tend to offer products or services that are innovative, sometimes lack specific technical applications, and are occasionally without market demand. All of these tendencies are initially driven by individuals who exhibit a variety of managerial, technological, and social characteristics that are frequently described as entrepreneurship. However, entrepreneurial propensities among top decision makers frequently describe start-up enterprises. Entrepreneurial propensities also exist among the more matured SMEs managed by experienced decision makers that are able to formulated more dynamic marketing strategies and operations, but are generally less emphasized. Nevertheless, SMEs are managed by a variety of managers with various degrees of educational background and professional experiences.

SMEs and Their Managers

A close examination of SMEs and their managers suggests that SMEs tend to be managed by three types of decision makers: (1) craftsmen, (2) promoters, and (3) rational managers. Although entrepreneurial tendencies (sometimes opportunistic) may be present in the decisions made by all three types of managers, most enterprises at the beginning are managed by craftsman-type managers. Research and case studies among SMEs suggests that they start with a specific product developed by the founder, who mainly focuses on fabrication with little interest in sales or distribution. If and when the product is accepted by the market, often a very specialized segment of the market, and the SME begins to grow, it reaches a point where the original manager may not be able to manage the SME strategically. The promoter-type manager may take over and manage the SME to the next stage of growth, where the rational-type manager is needed in order for the SME to survive (Tesar, Moini, Kuada and Sørensen, 2010).

Research findings also suggest that there might be differences between low- and high-technology SMEs. Low-technology SMEs are typically managed by technically educated and oriented managers with advanced fabrication skills and production capabilities. In contrast, high-technology managers tend to have more extensive educational experience; they may have a doctoral degree in science or engineering combined with a study abroad program or even an internship. All experiences contribute to managers' so-called global mindsets and influence how they manage and respond to foreign environments and market opportunities. In most cases today, because of highly diversified international or global markets, SMEs produce products that have broad appeal. A manager classified as a craftsman who manages a high-technology SME has a substantially different view of the world than a craftsman who manages a low-technology SME.

Low-technology SMEs that custom-fabricate products are managed differently than high- technology SMEs producing specialized products. The low-technology managers typically respond to orders for custom fabrication. Low-technology SMEs frequently wait for orders, while high-technology SMEs actively compete for orders in markets unless they have a unique product based on new technology. These differences are also reflected in how the SMEs view their markets and their customers—especially in international or global environments. Similar situations can be found among SME managers defined as promoters. Most low-technology promoters are mostly domestically oriented in their strategies and operations, while high-technology managers seek opportunities wherever they can. Managers classified as rational managers make rational decisions, tend to manage more competently both low- and high-technology SMEs, and have broader perspectives on international or global markets.

Global Mindset as a Research Construct

The three types of decision makers respond differently to events that shape their growth and market operations. SMEs' marketing strategies and operations are impacted by their active or passive involvement in international markets. Many SME managers believe that they have to think internationally or globally in order for their SMEs to survive in today's highly competitive markets (Story, Barbuto, Luthans and Bovaird, 2014). Thinking internationally or globally requires an individual understanding of the world and its social, economic, and technological dynamics (Kedia and Mukherji, 1999; Levy, Beechler, Taylor and Boyacigiller, 2007). Such understanding is not distributed equally among SME managers. Some researchers and academic consultants suggest that managers need a "global mindset," which is sometimes defined as individual experiences, beliefs, perceptions, and opinions of what foreign environments represent to the individuals involved with foreign, international, or global activities. Many SME managers differentiate among the three sets of activities (Javidan, Hough and Bullough, 2010). From a more practical perspective, the global mindset construct represents managers' abilities to make effective and efficient decisions across markets— foreign, international, or global (Gesteland, 1999).

There is only a limited number of studies concerning managerial styles of SMEs' top decision makers and their global mindsets. Although there is a shortage of statistically significant studies that explore the types of top decision makers among SMEs in Europe, there is sufficient evidence regarding this phenomenon among North America-based SMEs (Tesar et al., 2010). The global mindset construct is not well defined in the managerial literature and tends to represent only academic perspectives. If asked, most top managers believe that they have a sufficient global mindset and that it is the operating managers who need it.

SMEs in Europe and the United States seem to have dissimilar levels of awareness of the foreign markets around them. European SMEs tend to be much more sensitive to foreign markets than their United States counterparts (Mole, 1995). This is likely due to the geographic closeness of SMEs in Europe, while in the United States, "foreign" markets are geographically apart but psychologically close—Canada and Mexico especially. Many SMEs in the northern states of the United States generally feel that they do not "sell" to a foreign market if they "ship" their products to Canada. At the same time, SMEs from the southern states routinely "sell" their products to Mexico and seldom consider Mexico to be a foreign market. Although the issue of psychic distances has been introduced in international literature in earlier research, it tends to account only for the European SMEs in their propensities to seek new markets (Johanson and Vahlne, 1977).

Based on both academic and consulting experiences, it might be suggested that SMEs generally respond to the individual experiences of their top decision makers and their abilities to confront the dynamics of foreign markets. This generalization might be based on the extent of international or global experiences each individual experienced in his or her private or professional life. In any situation, the level of these experiences is clearly reflected in the top decision maker's global mindset, assuming that the global mindset may be articulated and applied both in theory and action. In fact, the overall global mindset of a given SME might be that of the top decision maker and not an aggregated global mindset of other professionals within the SME.

In order to fully understand how managers of SMEs arrive at their apparent global mindsets, it is necessary to examine their decision-making

Smaller Manufacturing Enterprises 103

propensities, especially the decision to formulate their own individual global mindset. Literature focusing on management and psychology suggests that the managers theoretically use similar decision-making processes—they define their problem, seek different ways of solving the problem, attempt to understand the ramifications of each possible way to solve the problem, deliberate about their level of commitment to a selected way of solving the problem, and adhere to the decision (Bickhard, 2003). Although this process is relatively simple and pervasive among managers, not all managers use it routinely and consistently—some managers are impulsive, lack necessary knowledge, or are too impatient to make sound, comprehensive decisions (Janis and Mann, 1977).

A Model of Research Complexities

The global mindset as a research construct is difficult to define (Bouquer and Birkinshaw, 2003). The construct presents a major dilemma for academic researchers primarily due to its research fluidity. In order to better understand the complexities of defining the basic concept—the global mindset—it is necessary to relate several dimensions, in a conceptual model, that lead to its strategic and operational aspects. The formulation of the model needs to include three essential dimensions: (1) the management styles of top decision makers in smaller manufacturing enterprises, (2) an approach to managerial decision-making, and (3) the aggregate conceptual information necessary to understand the relationship of each stage of managerial decision-making as related to the three types of managers found among SMEs.

This model is presented in diagram 7.1. The conceptual model examines five stages of managerial decision-making in the context of the decision-making theory: (1) appraisal of change, (2) survey of alternatives, (3) weighing of alternatives, (4) deliberation about commitment to decisions, and (5) adhering to a decision despite negative feedback (Janis and Mann, 1977). For research purposes, each stage in the decision-making process can be defined and its content specified, depending on the professional individuality of the decision maker. Specific factors can be identified through research and their meaning can be related to the decision-making process of individual decision makers as illustrated in the conceptual model (see Figure 7.1).

The second dimension of the conceptual model focuses on managerial styles among SMEs. It is important to recognize that SMEs constitute a discrete homogeneous group, a subset of the small and medium-sized enterprises typically found in research studies examining managerial concerns. The three types of managers presented in the conceptual models have been systematically defined through scientific research, including longitudinal and case studies. For research convenience, they have been previously assigned labels that are subsequently used as constructs in the conceptual model: (1) craftsman, (2) promoter, and (3) rational manger (Tesar et al., 2010).

Figure 7.1 Stages of Managerial Decision-Making and Management Styles of Smaller Manufacturing Enterprises Related to a Global Mindset Decision

Management styles among smaller manufacturing enterprises (SMEs)	Stages of managerial decision-making				
	Appraising the change	*Surveying alternatives*	*Weighing alternatives*	*Deliberating about commitment*	*Adhering despite negative feedback*
Craftsman	Low propensity to appraise change among low technology and higher propensity among high-technology craftsman. **Global mindset potentially appraised, but not considered.**	Limited ability to survey alternatives, focus is more on current state of nature among low-technology craftsman. High-technology craftsman look for alternatives related to technology.	Subjective assessment of alternatives using limited sources of information—somewhat higher among high-technology craftsman due to more education and technological sophistication.	Limited deliberation combined with personal denial of negative decision outcomes.	Relatively changeable attitude towards decisions, depending on the level of investments. High-technology craftsman may seek advice from professional sources.
Promoter	The propensity to appraise change might be normally distributed—seeking new opportunities occasionally. **Global mindset appraised and considered.**	Surveying alternatives opportunistically with intentions to increase their market exposure and market share. **Global mindset alternatives surveyed.**	Somewhat subjective assessment of alternatives occasionally supplemented with financial information, historical developments, and personal experiences. **Global mindset alternatives weighed—global mindset most likely rejected.**	Moderate deliberation combined with personal denial and shifting of blame for negative decision outcomes	Relatively changeable attitude towards decision—depending on the impact of the decision on the overall operation. Indicators of financial outcomes become important.

| Rational manager | Relatively high propensity to appraise change—constantly seeking new opportunities. **Global mindset appraised and considered.** | Surveying related alternatives with emphasis on resource management and market expansion. **Global mindset alternatives surveyed.** | Required assessment of alternatives, use of financial data and marketing information. Alternatives are frequently related to resources. **Global mindset alternatives weighed— global mindset most likely accepted.** | Systematic deliberation of commitments combined with review of both positive and negative decision outcomes. | Fixed, long-term attachment to rationally determined decisions. Success is measured by financial and marketing indicators. |

Notes: (1) The information presented above was obtained from research published in *Smaller Manufacturing Enterprises in an International Context: A Longitudinal Context* by George Tesar, Hamid Moini, John Kuada, and Olav Jull Sørensen (London: Imperial College Press, 2010).

(2) The stages of managerial decision-making are based on the seminal research of Irving L. Janis and Leon Mann, *Decision Making: A Psychological Analysis of Conflict, Choice, and Commitment* (New York: The Free Press, 1977).

The aggregated conceptual information contained in each cell, which forms the third dimension of the conceptual model, has also been generated from longitudinal and case studies. In some instances, it has been generated through series of interviews or in-depth discussions with SMEs managers over more than thirty years. The level of technology deployed by SMEs is one important factor that complicates the process of attempting to clearly specify the attitudes and propensities of managers towards the global mindset. Although attitudes and propensities may be normally distributed among the three types of decision makers, they may have a significant impact on how the global mindset as a construct that is defined in light of environmental and market changes and adversities. Decision makers managing high-technology SMEs may, because of the specific nature of their high technology, have a much broader view of the world and therefore the ability to understand the characteristics of a global mindset regardless of how each individual manager defines it.

An additional issue considered in the conceptual model is the probability that some SME managers may reach a point in their decision-making process where they will not be able to formulate a global mindset to deal with foreign challenges, adversities, or changing markets. In other words, some managers may never reach the point where their individual global mindset, if they have one at all, will be reflected in the decisions related to the foreign strategic and operations actions of their SME. For example, if a manager of a low-technology SME fabricating custom-designed products for a small number of clients identifies an opportunity abroad and subsequently decides that it is too challenging and expensive, does it mean that the manager is operating under a latent global mindset? The key issue is whether or not managers are born with a built-in global mindset, or if a global mindset is acquired through education, professional experience, or another behavior.

In order to define global mindset as a research construct, it might be necessary to differentiate between the decision stages of the three types of managers. A craftsman-type manager faced with challenges or adversities stemming from competitive changes in domestic and foreign markets needs to decide whether or not to enter foreign markets. Theoretically, the decision needs to be made based on fundamental perceptions of foreign markets in the context of a global mindset. The manager first needs to become aware of his or her latent global mindset and move it into the level of consciousness. In other words, there is an assumption that every manager has some sort of a latent global mindset. At that point in the decision process, a manager may potentially appraise his or her global mindset, but not consider it. By arriving at that conclusion, the SME that he or she manages may never enter a foreign market. Research among SMEs that are in early stages of exporting suggests that some SMEs export their products without having a minimal understanding of foreign markets and therefore have not formulated any notion of a global mindset.

SME managers classified as promoters approach the process of formulating a global mindset differently. They generally tend to feel that a global mindset might be an advantage. Given the emergence of international challenges and adversities, they consider formulating a global mindset and attempt to systematically identify and survey the alternatives leading to their own individualized global mindset. When they reach the point in the decision process where alternatives need to be objective and professionally evaluated, they may conclude that it is expedient to formulate a global mindset. The expediency of this decision may be distributed differently among the promoters. Some managers may formulate their own personal global mindset and successfully implement it, while others may not.

The rational manager types may approach the process of deciding to formulate a global mindset more systematically. They may appraise the coming changes and conclude that in order to profitably function in foreign, international, or global markets, they need a comprehensive global mindset. They survey appropriate alternatives, weigh each alternative, and select the optimal alternative as the basis for formulating their own global mindset. Once it is formulated and implemented, they may fine-tune it to their needs. If it does not reflect global reality, they will modify it.

Conclusion and Observations

SMEs pose a special research challenge for researchers trying to define what the global mindset as a research construct is, how it is defined, and how it works in practice. There is no single scientifically based definition of the construct that can be used uniformly in managerial research connected with the foreign, international, or global dimensions of SMEs. The lack of a scientifically derived definition limits the type of research studies that can be designed to study the global mindset phenomenon.

Some researchers suggest that the definition of a global mindset may be formulated based on responses to a series of questions based on a series of observations about how managers of SMEs respond in their decision-making to foreign, international, or global markets. However, managers of SMEs consider the global mindset construct as a series of attitudes, perceptions, and preferences necessary to their decision-making about foreign, international, or global markets. They also suggest that the construct as such is a creation of the academic community and has little value in practice.

It is conceptually apparent that SME managers need to decide about their own individual global mindset when confronted with foreign, international, or global market options. The definition of the global mindset construct for individual managers begins with the recognition of a problem, imminent change, challenge, dilemma, or a similar conflicting situation. If the potential solution to the situation necessitates defining a global mindset as a framework for solving the problem, it is essential for the manager to formulate a global mindset. This requires the application of the entire decision-making process.

Some managers managing SMEs suggest that a global mindset is in reality an operations philosophy according to which strategies and operations in foreign, international, or global markets are formulated. The equivalency between operational philosophy and the global mindset construct is important and potentially applicable in managerial research for generating a better understanding of the entire global mindset conundrum.

References

Bickhard, MH 2003, 'Mind as Process', working paper, Department of Philosophy, Lehigh University, retrieved 9 November 2014, from http://www.lehigh.edu/~mhb0/mhb0.html or mark.bickhard@lehigh.edu.

Bouquer, AM & Birkinshaw, J 2003, 'Determinants and Performance Implications of Global Mindset: An Attention Based Perspective', working paper, draft, University of Western Ontario, London, May, retrieved 10 November 2014, from cbouquet@ivey.uwo.ca.

Gesteland, RR 1999, *Cross-Cultural Business Behavior: Marketing, Negotiating, and Managing Across Cultures,* Copenhagen Business School Press, Copenhagen, Denmark.

Janis, IL & Mann, L 1977, *Decision Making: A Psychological Analysis of Conflict, Choice, and Commitment,* The Free Press, New York, NY.

Javidan, M, Hough, L, & Bullough, A 2010, *Conceptualizing and Measuring Global Mindset: Development of the Global Mindset Inventory,* A Technical Report, Thunderbird Global Mindset Institute, Thunderbird School of Management, Glendale, Arizona, retrieved 10 November 2014, from http://globalmindset.thunderbird.edu/sites/default/files/gmitechnicalreportexecutivesummary1–1.pdf.

Johanson, J & Vahlne, J-K 1977, 'The Internationalization Process of the Firm—A Model of Knowledge Development and Increasing Foreign Market Commitment', *Journal of International Business Studies,* vol. 8, no. 1, pp. 23–32.

Kedia, BL & Mukherji, A 1999, 'Global Managers: Developing a Mindset for Global Competitiveness', *Journal of World Business,* vol. 34, no. 3, pp. 230–51.

Levy, O, Beechler, S, Taylor, S, & Boyacigiller, NA 2007, 'What We Talk About When We Talk About "Global Mindset: Managerial Cognition in Multinational Corporations"', *Journal of International Business Studies,* vol. 38, no. 2, pp. 231–58.

Mole, J 1995, *Mind Your Manners: Managing Business Cultures in Europe,* Nicholas Brealey Publishing, London.

Story, JSP, Barbuto, JE Jr., Luthans, F, & Bovaird, JA 2014, 'Meeting the Challenges of Effective International HRM: Analysis of the Antecedents of Global Mindset', *Human Resource Management,* vol. 53, no. 1, pp. 131–55.

Tesar, G, Moini, H, Kuada, J, & Sørensen, OJ 2010, *Smaller Manufacturing Enterprises in an International Context: A Longitudinal Exploration,* Imperial College Press, London.

8 Global Mindset as the Integration of Emerging Socio-Cultural Values Through Mindsponge Processes

A Transition Economy Perspective[1]

Quan Hoang Vuong

1 Introduction

A flat (Friedman 2005) or spiky (Florida 2005) world does not matter, as globalization has passed the point of no return. Much of the international recognition for an emerging economy, therefore, rests with its cultural relevance to its economic partners worldwide. Active participation on the global scale has made acculturation more apparent and faster today, especially for managers working in multicultural environments (Gupta & Govindarajan 2002). In other words, managers with global mindsets are presumably more open in their thinking (Taylor 1991), which in turn enables them to make use of serendipity as a strategic advantage (Napier & Vuong 2013b).

Meanwhile, businesspeople are facing an emerging problem of getting so very many cultural values. A framework for assessing the values may help them improve their ability to respond not only faster, but also more efficiently to a new cultural setting. Last but not least, a fast-changing world renders it possible to make a proper values today inappropriate tomorrow and vice versa. It is, therefore, necessary to keep value evaluation as well as learning/unlearning processes continuous.

This chapter proposes the concept of the mindsponge and its underlying themes that explain why and how executives, managers, and corporations could replace waning values in their mindsets with those absorbed during their exposure to multicultural and global settings. One can think of a mindsponge as a metaphor of the mind as a sponge that squeezes out inappropriate values and absorbs new ones that fit or complement the context at hand.

This chapter first provides a brief literature review on global mindset and cultural values, which suggests that not only can a mindset be improved, but that its learning mechanism can also be developed. Then the chapter offers a conceptual framework, called the "mindsponge," which builds upon earlier works linking mindset to themes of multi-filtering (e.g., Vuong & Napier 2013, 2014). The process is proposed to help identify emerging values in the transition economy of Vietnam and also to reconfirm existing core values. Discussions about (i) serendipity as a method of innovation, (ii) pursuit of creative performance, and (iii) trust as a process of building confidence and reliability are illustrated by practical applications of the mindsponge and real-life business evidence provided by an inclusive corporate innovation survey (the i2Metrix).

2   Literature Review

There are several works—such as Berry (1983, 1997), Dweck (2006), Levy, Beechler, Taylor, & Boyacigilier (2007), and Maznevski & Lane (2007)—that suggest that not only a mindset but also its learning mechanism can be developed to meet business management's need for strengthening competitiveness while the world economy is entering an unchartered territory. When arguing for a global mindset—which consists of core cultural values that are appropriate to a global setting—it should be open to the replacement of waning values. Therefore, the authors also raise the need for learning more about the values. For this purpose, this section reviews selected related literature on improving a global mindset and the cultural values that emerge in the improvement process.

2.1   *Global Mindset*

Goldstein & Brooks (2007) define mindset as assumptions and expectations that people hold about themselves and others. That is, one's mindset consists of [cultural] values defining the individual. Although such a definition suggests a limited and stable set of values, many—for instance, Gupta & Govindarajan (2002), Dweck (2006), and Levy et al. (2007)—argue that a mindset can be changed and even grown in order to adapt to the changing environment. Dweck (2006) claims that a mindset can be either fixed and/or growth oriented, but does not say explicitly that one should separate one type of mindset from another. In other words, a mindset consists of fixed and growth areas. The former focuses on developing a certain ability, while the latter is interested in new abilities. Indeed, Dweck introduces practices to train a growth mindset but does not explain how the two mindsets may interact with and affect each other.

Gupta & Govindarajan (2002) regard global mindset as a crucial factor for success in exploiting opportunities in a dynamic world of globalization. Also, Boyd & Richerson (1985) suggest that confidence in a particular belief may grow if many others with whom the individual has come into contact also share such a belief. Inconsistent information is either rejected or may be a reason to initiate changes in the mindset.

Levy et al. (2007) offer two major approaches to the conceptualization of global mindset: (i) a cultural perspective that focuses on cultural diversity and distance, and (ii) a strategic perspective that focuses on [business] environmental complexity and strategic variety. Cosmopolitanism is the underlying theme of the former, while cognitive complexity characterizes the latter. A third approach, the multidimensional perspective, combines the two.

Among researchers who support the notion of information processing as being critical to building a global mindset, Rhinesmith (1992, 1993, 1996) takes a practitioner approach. He defines global mindset as the ability to scan the world (i.e., process information) from a broad perspective and to find unexpected trends and opportunities to achieve organizational as well as individual goals. The definition, therefore, incorporates not only the cultural and strategic perspectives, but also individual characteristics. Pisapia, Reyes-Guerra, & Coukos-Semmel (2005) argue that leaders need a strategic mindset, which can be developed by advanced cognitive processes. In addition, a global mindset can be improved by education (e.g., Maznevski & Lane 2007). Building knowledge and skills is critical, but Maznevski and Lane argue that the development of a global mindset incorporates: (i) building a comprehensive cognitive structure that guides the process of information selection and processing, and (ii) building a capability for constantly updating this cognitive structure once exposed to new experiences. Muzychenko (2007) also suggests that a global mindset can be enhanced through a formal education, especially for entrepreneurs to develop competencies that allow them to exploit opportunities presented by globalization.

From a cultural perspective, a global mindset consists of "self-awareness, openness to and understanding of other cultures, and selective incorporation of foreign values and practice" (Levy et al. 2007, p.6). The strategic perspective of a global mindset (Levy et al. 2007) has emerged in part because of the complexity of globalization itself. Several scholars argue that globalization is so complex that structural means and administrative mechanisms (Chandler 1962) are now insufficient for multinational corporations (MNCs) to mitigate environmental and organizational complexity (Prahalad & Bettis 1986; Doz & Prahalad 1991; Evans, Pucik & Barsoux 2002). In light of this, the strategic perspective suggests that MNCs need a global and strategic mindset to compete successfully (Bartlett & Ghoshal 1989; Caproni, Lenway & Murtha 1992).

While academics and managers are reaching a consensus on the pivotal role of a global mindset, the "flat world" of information challenges them. The competitive pressures of globalization raise the demand for a practicable and learnable method for improving such a global mindset. In addition, recommendations on emerging cultural values of a globalized business environment, which are spotted by the method, may not only provide "best practice" stories, but also encourage applications of conceptual frameworks in daily management. In the light of this, it is necessary to learn more about the cultural values that would be spotted and evaluated by a global mindset improvement method in the following section.

2.2   *Cultural Values*

Academics attempt to investigate not only how managers and institutions learn and unlearn cultural values—for instance, Berry (1983, 1997), Dweck (2006), Levy et al. (2007), and Vuong, Napier & Tran (2013)—but also their influence on business performance and even social issues (Bell 1973, 1976; Inglehart 1977, 1990, 1997; Hofstede 1983; Kitayama, Markus & Kurukawa 2000; Schwartz & Bardi 2001; Schwart 2006).

In the 1950s and 1960s, principles of sound management were considered universal—especially in Europe and the U.S.—and nationality was ignored. Based on his 1967–1978 research on 116,000 responses of international staff of the large multinational corporation IBM from 40 countries, Hofstede (1983) argues that national and regional values are important to management because of political, sociological, and psychological reasons. Moreover, these values are difficult to change (Hofstede 1983, p.76; Lipartito 1995; Schwartz & Bardi 2001). Hofstede first describes national cultures in four dimensions: (i) individualism vs. collectivism, (ii) large or small power distance, (iii) strong or weak uncertainty avoidance, and (iv) masculinity vs. femininity. Then, together with Michael Harris Bond and Michael Minkov, Hofstede adds long-term orientation (1991) and indulgence vs. restraint (2010) as the fifth and sixth dimensions.

By examining the relation between Hofstede's (1983) cultural dimensions and Lumpkin & Dess's (1996) five dimensions of entrepreneurial orientation, Lee & Peterson (2000) propose that "a society's propensity to generate autonomous, risk-taking, innovative, competitively aggressive, and proactive entrepreneurs and firms depends on its cultural foundation." Further, Vuong et al.'s (2013) investigation of 115 individual respondents into business successes in Vietnam reveals that creativity plays a critical role in the "entrepreneurial stage" of a business's life cycle, while traditional cultural values, to a large extent, adversely affect the entrepreneurial spirit of the community (Vuong & Tran 2009). The investigation also suggests a significant role for a multiple-filters information process of innovation.

Lipartito defines culture as "a system of values, ideas, and beliefs which constitute a mental apparatus for grasping reality" (1995, p.2). Therefore, business culture is "that set of limiting and organizing concepts that determine what is real or rational for management, principles that are often tacit or unconscious." When seeing the world in similar terms, sharing a common understanding of how markets operate, agreeing on what generates profits and where to invest earnings, managers may make the same decisions. In addition, corporate cultural values affect the way firms create, collect, and coordinate resources, especially knowledge and information (Nelson & Winter 1982). In light of this, Lipartito (1995) notes that entrepreneurs have no choice but to "remake culture" in order to improve competitive capacity, and often in unexpected ways.

Schwartz defines cultural values as "conceptions of the desirable that guide the way social actors (e.g. organizational leaders, policy-makers, individual persons) select actions, evaluate people and events, and explain their action and evaluation" (1999, p.24). Schwartz suggests that the three dimensions, (i) embeddedness vs. intellectual and affective autonomy, (ii) hierarchy vs. egalitarianism, and (iii) mastery vs. harmony help societies deal with three basic issues, namely (i) defining the nature of the relation between the individual and the group, (ii) guaranteeing responsible behavior that will preserve the social fabric, and (iii) the relation of mankind to the natural and social world. Schwartz notes that as certain cultural value orientations share assumptions, "it is easier to affirm and act on them simultaneously in a culture" (2006, p.141). He also claims that a coherent circular structure of relations among cultural values distinguishes his approach from others such as Hofstede (1983) and Inglehart (1997), who proposes tradition vs. secular-rational and survival vs. self-expression value dimensions.

While modernization theorists—including Karl Marx, who foresaw that industrialization would transform the world when publishing *Das Kapital* in 1867—argue that overwhelming economic and political forces drive cultural changes, their opposites assume that cultural values are relatively independent of economic condition (DiMaggio 1994). The former predicts that traditional values would be replaced by "modern" values. The latter emphasizes the persistence of traditional values. Indeed, industrialization leads to changes in gender roles, attitudes toward authority, and sexual norms, declining fertility rates, broader political participation, and a less susceptible populace. But cultural changes do not take such a simple linear path (Inglehart & Baker 2000). Many—including Dahrendorf (1959), Bell (1973, 1976), and Inglehart (1977, 1990, 1997)—suggest that economic development has given rise to two dimensions of cross-cultural differentiation: (i) early industrialization and the rise of the working class, and (ii) affluent conditions of advanced industrial society and the rise of the service and knowledge sectors. The shift from the first to the second dimension brought changes in people's daily experiences and even worldviews (Bell 1973; Inglehart 1997). In light of this, one may expect changes in values to happen gradually when human beings enter a post-industrial society as well as the next level of development.

In a process of moving from the "game against nature" of pre-industrial life (Bell 1976, p.147) to the "game against fabricated nature" of industrial life (Bell 1973, p.147), then to the "game between persons" of post-industrial life (Bell 1973, pp.148–149), Inglehart & Baker (2000, p.22) note that "less effort is focused on producing material objects, and more effort is focused on communicating and processing communication." In addition to Bell's (1973, 1976) notice of an increasingly important role of formal education and job experience in developing one's capability of "autonomous decision-making," Inglehart (1997) emphasizes the growing self-expression, especially that of service and knowledge workers. The existing cultural and traditional religious values influence the ways in which societies nurture or hinder the changing process (Weber [1904] 1958; Huntington 1993, 1996). Also, distinctive cultural traits endure over long periods of time and continue to shape a society's political and economic performance (Putnam 1993; Hamilton 1994; Fukuyama 1995; Inglehart & Baker 2000). Based on empirical evidence from 65 societies, Inglehart & Baker (2000) suggest that the emergence of new values is difficult because the values "can and do change but they continue to reflect a society's cultural heritage" (p.49). In other words, with the help of the appropriate methods, one can spot the emerging cultural values in a changing society. Naturally, cultures have huge influence to the choice of leadership, and both form a type of "ecosystem" in which subsequent processes such as innovation, resource allocation, and decision-making would later reinforce or reject the values embedded in it, in line with Kuada (2010, pp.12–13).

The acknowledgement of emerging cultural values often requires supporting evidence accumulated over long periods of time and covered by large number of countries and territories. For instance, it took Hofstede approximately 11 years (from 1967 to 1978) to collect responses from 40 countries before introducing his seminal work on four cultural dimensions in 1983. As for Schwartz (2006), it took him seven years (from 1999 with data from 49 countries to 2006 with data from 73 countries) to affirm his three dimensions of cultural values. Such practices are incredibly expensive to business-people. They tend to classify a cultural value into a known category. This way of classification, however, does not provide them with a framework for evaluation.

3   Integration of Emerging Socio-Cultural Values Through Mindsponge Processes

The above-mentioned literature review raises three research questions.

The first is, *how should executives, managers, and corporations improve their global mindsets in today's changing—even faster and deeper—world?* Although a mindset is rather a stable set of cultural values, it is possible to change it when its elements are removed or replaced. Indeed, people often change their minds, especially those who experience cross-cultural settings. Businesses request more than just a change: They ask for change that assures that core values and entities are strengthened while capturing emerging opportunities. In other words, the process of improving a mindset needs to be manageable. To this end, this section discusses Vuong et al.'s (2013) mindsponge as a mechanism for learning and unlearning values. The mindsponge divides consciousness into three zones based on different levels of appropriateness of values, from a nucleus of core values to a comfort zone and then to an environment of cultural values that one may respect.

The second research question is, *what are the challenges of learning and unlearning cultural values?* Cultural values are difficult to change and deeply rooted in mindsets. There are so many values surrounding individuals and institutions. Just a few are accepted as core values, which identify a person or an organization. This suggests the availability of a filtering process that extracts assumingly appropriate values. Still, it is not enough. The "checks and balances" principle requests that the extracted values construct a certain level of trust. Last but not least, the inductive attitude enforces such procedures for value filtering and trust examining, repeatedly and continuously.

The third research question is, *what emerging values, if any, can the mindsponge mechanism and the multi-filter information process spot in the economy of Vietnam?* In addition to contributing to an understanding of transition economies, the quest for answering this question provides business executives and managers with manageable tools and practical guidance for employing a conceptual framework to deal with daily business operations.

3.1 A Conceptual Framework Constructed by the Mindsponge and Its Underlying Theme Multi-Filter Information Process

The mindsponge mechanism (Vuong *et al.* 2013) and its underlying theme of a multi-filter information process (Vuong & Napier 2014) offer a conceptual framework to address the three research questions. Figure 8.1 divides the values that one mindset deals with into four groups.

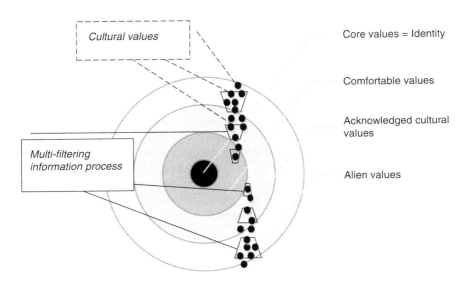

Figure 8.1 A Conceptual Framework for Spotting Values

Alien [cultural] values are plentiful in cross-culture workplaces in today's globalized world. People may ignore their presence until some effects are acknowledged, or sometimes just out of curiosity. Those who are eager to learn about something new kick off an *information multi-filtering process* for sorting positive-effect values. New cultural values may enter randomly and equally, but are not digested in the same way. Only people who desire to improve their mindset try to filter out inappropriate values. The remaining values are respectable and may cause some minor changes in responses to cultural difference.

Acknowledged values that bring benefits then keep being filtered and may become *comfortable values* as the multi-filtering process continuously affirms their appropriateness. Let's imagine that a manager first goes to a stadium for a football game because he acknowledges the willingness of his colleagues as an effort to build team spirit. Then he realizes that such a social activity brings him not only a better understanding of his team members, but also of potential business partners and clients who are also in the fan club. Now, shouting and cheering in public and drinking after the game would comfort him.

The dark solid circle in Figure 8.1 consists of *core values* identifying an individual (or an institution). As a value approaches the central circle, the filter becomes tougher. Not only is a cost-benefit analysis on the acceptance of the value conducted, but also its appropriateness is compared to the existing core values. Even if the value passes the hardest test to enter the central circle, that is, to become a core value, it cannot rest.

A well-functioning mindsponge suggests one should not take any new value to heart without a systematic testing and questioning process (Vuong et al. 2013). Moreover, whenever evidence shows that the value is not as certain as it seemed, the mindset is most likely to unlearn it. This is because the more "core" the value is, the larger the risk the mindset has to be willing to take if it trusts in a "wrong" one (Mayer, Davis & Schoorman 1995). To this end, the inductive mindsponge also conducts a reverse process for continuously testing, reconfirming, and even unlearning a value.

The mindsponge process offers businesspeople and corporations a practicable and doable framework to improve their global mindsets. Whenever they question a cultural value, the mindsponge helps them continuously evaluate it. Moreover, the mindsponge process, as a consistent analytical framework, builds their confidence in their evaluation and decision to learn or unlearn the value.

The mindsponge also suggests the most challenging thing one may face in learning and unlearning cultural values, namely, that it is a lengthy and tedious process. A new cultural value has to be acknowledged and then become comfortable before managing to enter the nucleus. The reverse is also true, as ejecting a value from the core nucleus is an equally painful process. Therefore, great patience and confidence built by the disciplined practice of an evaluation framework are necessary.

Indeed, the deployment of the mindsponge process helps spot three emerging values in the transition economy of Vietnam. The following section discusses the application of this conceptual framework in the Vietnamese economy, where different cultural values are struggling to find a certain place in the mindsets of people, corporations, and even society. Clashing with capitalist and Western culture provides the communist and Confucian Vietnamese with not only new values, but also opportunity for improving their global mindsets.

3.2 Three Emerging Values in the Transition Economy of Vietnam

The transition economy of Vietnam, which is rapidly being exposed to the global environment, is witnessing cultural changes (Napier & Vuong 2013a). The unequal relationship between student and teacher in a Confucian society is moving toward a student-centered education. Saving up as a traditional characteristic of Vietnamese people is being replaced by consumerism, especially by the youth. Communist corporate leaders welcome Western capitalists to be strategic partners. This circumstance raises an interest in exploring emerging values that exert great influence on the country's dynamic economy.

The employment of the mindsponge and its underlying multi-filter information process to investigate the transition economy of Vietnam unveils three emerging values. They first appear at the start of various change processes. Their appropriateness is tested and reaffirmed at different states, for instance, from a close, centrally planned (in the 1990s) to an open, market-oriented economy (2000s), and toward becoming a proactive player in the world value chain (2010s). While evaluating and re-evaluating the values, change processes—such as implementing economic renovation policies and building trust from performance and capability—not only validate but also carry them into society's nucleus of core cultural values. Last but not least, the values' influence is getting greater, as they are becoming core values. In other words, the values gradually enlarge their influential space. They first influence a group of people—for instance, the entrepreneurs—then an economic sector, and finally the majority of the society.

The three are (i) serendipity as a method of innovation, (ii) pursuing creative performance, and (iii) trust as a process of building confidence and reliability. Stories learned from entrepreneurial champions who participated in a survey on corporations, including innovation capacity (Vuong, Napier, Vu, Nguyen, & Tran 2014), help explain the concepts through real-life business experience.

Serendipity: From Loan-Seeking to a Method of Innovation

Relationship-based loan seeking is a typical Confucian behavior in Vietnam (Vuong & Tran 2009). Although relationships play a critical role in business development everywhere, its color in East Asian cultural settings is quite different from the West. Confucianism not only advocates a social hierarchy, but also imposes moral and cultural norms for guiding behaviors.

On financing business operations, for instance, the relationship between banks and entrepreneurs, even private businesses, is typically unequal. It is a popular notion that borrowing entrepreneurs are "asking for favors," for which bankers hold the overwhelming right to "giving decisions." In such circumstances, a decisive factor is bankers' knowing "who the entrepreneurs are" rather than "what capacity the entrepreneurs possess." This personal trust-based credit transaction, perhaps, shows the most apparent manifestation of the Confucian value of the unequal social relationship. The same holds true for credit transactions. It is common that when they have "good" relationships with the entrepreneurial borrowers, bankers can, on behalf of the borrowers, prepare loan documents. Both lenders and borrowers believe that this is part of the caretaking element in their trust-based relationship, partly reflecting the benevolence that has been highly advocated in Confucianism.

Loan seeking also results in the manipulation of interest groups and monopolists (Vuong 2014a). In the state-led economic model of Vietnam, corruption is rampant and accompanied by crony capitalism. For example, despite loss-making performances, poorly drafted projects, and paramount losses, state-run conglomerate Vinashin was able to borrow a multi-billion U.S. dollars loan to fund its operations and purchase broken ships from abroad at sky-high prices. The large differences in market price and reported price went into the pockets of the management. Vinashin was financed by ten local banks and international lenders. After its insolvency, the Vietnamese government guaranteed the issue of Vinashin bonds in Singapore to pay for its debt. In addition, the local bank HBB, which lost U.S. $200 million by lending to Vinashin, was allowed to be acquired by the Vietnamese privately run SHB. The acquisition was regarded as an alternative solution to clear Vinashin's debt with HBB.

The lack of genuine entrepreneurs results in mimicking investment concentration and business models—for instance, in the two years 2005 and 2007, 10 rural commercial banks were acquired by private traders, then upgraded to joint stock commercial banks, then expanded to include financial services such as securities and insurance. To escape from considering cost and benefit, verifying industry outlook, and examining management capability, the managers focused on increasing the chance of meeting serendipity by trying to enrich information inputs and quickly make decisions on any spotted opportunity. Here, it is noteworthy that valuable information is worthless when methods to digest it are absent. A systematic process is necessary to transform insights and creative ideas into new products, services, and solutions.

Also pursuing extraordinary, unintentional, or undiscovered business outcomes, entrepreneurs who tap serendipity, which is the ability to notice, evaluate, and take advantage of unexpected information better or faster than competitors, may build or develop this as an advantage. Napier & Vuong (2013b) argue that serendipity is not serendipitous. The former is a method of making creativity. The latter describes the unexpected exploration of an opportunity that seemingly appears out of the blue. Serendipity—as a method of creativity—offers innovation capacity improvement by increasing awareness of the existence of unlooked-for but valuable possibilities that can enhance the global mindset. For example, experiencing international distribution and learning from what people do in foreign countries help an entrepreneur realize an "idle" opportunity at home.

When the founders of Phu Le Wine Co. returned to their hometown, the winemaking couple planned some quiet time after their child's birth. During that time, they visited the village of Phu Le, famous for its traditional rice wine, and spotted an opportunity. Despite brand popularity and good quality, the Phu Le wine production was fragmented and unorganized. Almost every household in the village produced wine. Every producer claimed his/her wine to be the best. And the best wine producer was unable to make wine production commercially viable because of an unstable and insufficient supply. Phu Le Wine Company was founded to unite household wine producers and educate them on food safety awareness and standards. Four years later, Phu Le's sales reached U.S. $2 million. More importantly, more than 30% of the Phu Le commune population now works for the firm. By seeing a bigger picture, by thinking more "globally," or at least regionally, the couple was able to make a difference and help others see differently as well.

Exploiting serendipity works under certain conditions, as Figure 8.2 suggests. There is always an abundance of information suggesting chances of creating a new business in the economy and marketplaces. Also, there are available people who are capable of running a business. Only when the market prospect is appropriate for the person's preference and entrepreneurial orientation is a starting combination of some new business acknowledged.

Next, the combination goes into a multi-filtering process, which scans for the most useful insights in different disciplines, then tries to integrate various insightful dots into an innovation of a new product/service, new management process, or new business model. A "permanent bank"—which consists of understanding management theories, the global market situation, and experience of living and working in a multicultural environment, in conjunction with entrepreneurial alertness and risk tolerance, help entrepreneurs evaluate their readiness to move from the "observed" insights to a valuable innovation in the marketplace.

Then the mindsponge helps the entrepreneur evaluate the innovation and make a business decision. If the innovation is appropriate to the entrepreneur's core values, then the decision is "GO." It is noteworthy that the serendipity maker is able to see both value in the information and potential opportunity, but also to see and connect (odd) dots. The more dots the serendipity maker spots, the better he/she becomes at evaluating opportunities. The more efficiently he/she connects the dots, the better he/she is at detecting missing points.

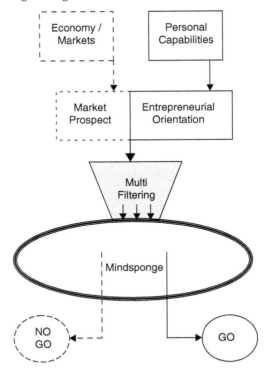

Figure 8.2 Information Process of Serendipity

Creative Performance: From Value Creation to Innovation

When economic renovation policies were introduced to the Vietnamese economy in the late 1980s, quality of goods and services were a strange concept, as arm's length transactions rarely occurred in a centrally planned economy. The voice of consumers, if any, had been very low when distribution and consumption targets were planned by the central government. Producers and manufacturers, therefore, had paid no attention to users, a word that better describes the circumstance than "consumers." The Renovation (famously known as "Doi Moi") did make changes, not only in economic performance, but also in the minds of the country's political figures (Heberer & Kohl 1999; Vuong, Dam, Van Houtte, & Tran 2011). Economic crisis and harsh reality were neither necessary nor sufficient conditions for such changes to take place. Heberer & Kohl (1999) point out that the changes in the structure of property rights, which resulted in an emergence of a new economic elite of private entrepreneurs, were accompanied by a change of the value system. Changing social and political values constituted a partial weakening of the economic and political power of the central government that then drove political change. Entrepreneurial elements—for instance, the willingness to create value—prompted consideration of structural changes and emerging opportunities, and then laid down cornerstones of policies and innovation (Vuong et al. 2011). It is noteworthy here that when the multi-filtering system sparked, the mindsponge started working.

In an exploratory survey of 40 firms about their innovative capacity (the i2Metrix, Vuong et al. 2014), the leaders of all of the surveyed firms reported experiencing major shifts in their cultural settings and beliefs due to changes in social ideologies, business modalities (e.g., moving from a market economy in the southern part of Vietnam during the American War to a purely socialist economy and then back to a more market-oriented one), or form of enterprise (e.g., moving from being a traditional state-owned enterprise to a privatized one). They were also able to give examples of the mindsponge process in their organizations, even though they were unfamiliar with the term. For instance, the corporate leaders acknowledged that they need to build subordinates' confidence in their leading competence, which is proved by improvements in business performance. Such effort—which is likely affected by Western leadership—is certainly not a norm in a Confucian hierarchy, where subordinates should obey superiors.

The concept of innovation, moreover, is developed further to include responsible creativity as a cultural value driving economic growth, as illustrated by the "Vietnamese Coffee King" Dang Le Nguyen Vu (Napier 2012; Schatz 2012). That is, pursuing innovation is not for corporate earnings, but to create harmony and sustainable prosperity. Meanwhile, Chairwoman Vu Thi Thuan of Traphaco (a pharmaceutical manufacturer) insisted that replacing hundreds of workers with automated production lines was not an innovation. Her firm must not only secure jobs for loyal workers, but also provide a stable income source to their families. Traphaco's innovation efforts, therefore, focus on smarter and friendlier marketing and distribution as the firm is serving special clients: the patients.

Trust: From Intuitive Awareness to Cost-Benefit Analysis and Multi-Filtering Process

Trust in the Confucian society of Vietnam means a relationship in which one can entrust their work to the hands of someone that he/she knows and is confident about (Vuong & Tran 2009, p.74). In other words, "who the guy is" outweighs "what the guy is doing and capable of." In this social setting, trust easily turns into a personal matter, even in institutional transactions. That is, if you do not accept an offer by your friend, then the friend will interpret your refusal to mean you do not trust your friend (to give you a good deal), and finally your friendship will most likely be broken. Such social pressure may lead to business mistakes.

Fortunately, entrepreneurs think differently in order to pursue creative performance. As the mindsponge suggests, a new value has to go through a process of information multi-filtering and trust evaluating, which may yield a better performance and higher profits. When receiving an idea for a new product or a proposal for a new business model, they make a decision to approve or refuse based on technological feasibility and commercial viability, not friendship, loyalty, or family relation (Vuong et al. 2014). Indeed, as cost-benefit analysis becomes popular—perhaps, as a result of increasing numbers of MBA graduates and lessons learned from the business practices of multinational corporations in Vietnam—the solidity of a business relation now depends on how benefits are allocated among business partners.

Lewicki & Bunker (1996) have developed a three-stage process of trust. The first stage is calculus based, assessing cost-benefit considerations. The second is knowledge-based trust that relies on information rather than deterrence, and develops over time with increasing interaction among individuals. The last stage is identification based, when trust matches or comes in sync with another person's desires and intentions. While there is significant overlap between the stages, an expectation of a continuous relationship suggests a high level of trust (Paliszkiewicz 2011).

4   Closing Remarks

The concept of mindsponge provides executives, managers, and organizations with not only a practical framework for improving their global mindset by identifying and strengthening core values, but also capturing emerging opportunities. In today's fast-changing world, globalization and the Internet revolution provide businesspeople with abundant information. The mindsponge and its underlying theme of multi-filtering help them overcome the challenge of the information flood by considering only appropriate values and worthy opportunities (Vuong & Napier 2014). Also, great patience should be acknowledged in any change process, as learning and unlearning cultural values are tedious, lengthy, and even painful.

In addition, a disciplined information process makes it possible to catch even short-lived ideas and opportunities—which are consequences of Friedman's (2005) "flat world"—with a serendipity-based method of creativity (Napier & Vuong 2013b). When approaching the mindset of core values or getting business decisions to move forward, the value or opportunity has to convince a trust guard whose inductive attitude is getting more suspicious of its "appropriateness" and "worth." A reverse flow is to eject a waning value existing in the mindset or to stop an ongoing business.

Efforts to introduce the mindsponge and its workhorse multi-filtering information process to the business community through the corporate inclusive innovation capacity survey resulted in uncovering three emerging values in the transition economy of Vietnam. The three are (i) seeking serendipity as a method of innovation, (ii) pursuing creative performance, and (iii) building trust with the multi-filtering process. Here, a well-functioning mindsponge plays the role of not only an explorer, but also a judge enforcing the "checks and balances" principle.

For instance, while entrepreneurs acknowledge that innovation capacity largely defines the destiny of entrepreneurial endeavors, most of them do not realize that only a small percentage of innovations have been adopted into industrial commercialization and of these, only a small percentage of adopted innovations have reaped financial payoffs. Firms should also beware of abusing innovation. Scrambling for innovation may cause an entrepreneurial curse of innovation (Maddock 2013). Innovation per se does not determine the success of an innovating firm. The market does. Overexcitement about innovation cannot replace an appropriate methodology of organizing the business process, disciplines for pursuing desired outcomes, and tools/techniques for measuring the efficiency as well as the effectiveness of such important, and oftentimes tricky, pursuits (Vuong 2014b).

Note

1. **Acknowledgement:** The author sincerely thanks Dr. Nancy K. Napier (Boise State University, Idaho, U.S.), Dr. Dolly E. Samson (Stamford International University, Bangkok, Thailand), and Tran Tri Dung (DHVP Research, Hanoi, Vietnam) for the insightful discussions and suggestions for improvements.

References

Bartlett, CA, & Ghoshal, S 1989, *Managing Across Borders: The Transnational Solution* (Vol. 1). Boston, MA: Harvard Business School Press.

Bell, D 1973, *The Coming of Post-Industrial Society*. New York: Basic Books.

Bell, D 1976, *The Cultural Contradictions of Capitalism*. New York: Basic Books.

Berry, JW 1983, 'Acculturation: A comparative analysis of alternative forms,' in Samuda, RJ & Woods, SL (Eds.), *Perspective in Immigrant and Minority Education* (pp.66–77). Lanham, MD: University Press of America.

Berry, JW 1997, 'Immigration, acculturation, and adaptation,' *Applied Psychology: An International Review*, vol.46, no.1, pp.5–68.

Boyd, R & Richerson, P 1985, *Culture and the Evolutionary Process*. Chicago, IL: University of Chicago Press.

Caproni, PJ, Lenway, SA & Murtha, TP 1992, *Multinational Mind Sets: Sense Making Capabilities as Strategic Resources in Multinational Firm*. Division of Research, School of Business Administration, University of Michigan. http://141.213.232.243/bitstream/handle/2027.42/35479/b1579411.0001.001.txt

Chandler, AD 1962, *Strategy and Structure*. Cambridge, MA: MIT Press.

Dahrendorf, R 1959, *Class and Class Conflict in Industrial Society*. Stanford, CA: Stanford University Press.

DiMaggio, P 1994, 'Culture and economy,' in Smelser, NJ & Swedberg, R (Eds.), *The Handbook of Economic Sociology*. Princeton, NJ: Princeton University Press, pp.27–57.

Doz, YL, & Prahalad, CK 1991, 'Managing DMNCs: A search for a new paradigm,' *Strategic Management Journal*, 12(S1), pp.145–164.

Dweck, CS 2006, *Mindset: The New Psychology of Success*. New York, NY: Random House.

Evans, P, Pucik, V, & Barsoux, JL 2002, *The Global Challenge: International Human Resource Management.* London, UK: McGraw-Hill.

Florida, R 2005, 'The world in number: The world is spiky,' *The Atlantic Monthly,* October, 296(3): pp.48–51.

Friedman, LT 2005, *The World Is Flat.* New York, NY: Farrar, Straus and Giroux.

Fukuyama, F 1995, *Trust: The Social Virtues and the Creation of Prosperity.* New York, NY: Free Press.

Goldstein, S & Brooks, R 2007, *Understanding and Managing Children's Classroom Behavior: Creating Sustainable, Resilient Schools.* New York, NY: John Wiley and Sons.

Gupta, AK & Govindarajan, V 2002, 'Cultivating a global mindset,' *Academy of Management Executive,* vol.16, no.1, pp.116–126.

Hamilton, GG 1994, 'Civilization and organization of economies,' in Smelser, NJ & Swedberg, R (Eds.), *The Handbook of Economic Sociology* (pp.183–205). Princeton, NJ: Princeton University Press.

Heberer, T & Kohl, A 1999, 'Private entrepreneurship and social change in transitional economies: The sociopolitical impact of private industry in Vietnam,' *The Private Economy in China and Vietnam and Its Economic, Social, and Political Consequences.*

Hofstede, G 1983, 'The cultural relativity of organizational practices and theories,' *Journal of International Business Studies,* vol.14, no.2, pp.75–89.

Hofstede, G, & Minkov, M 2010, 'Long-versus short-term orientation: new perspectives,' *Asia Pacific Business Review,* vol. 16, no. 4, pp.493–504.

Huntington, SP 1993, 'The clash of civilizations?' *Foreign Affairs,* vol.72, no.3, pp.22–49.

Huntington, SP 1996, *The Clash of Civilizations and the Remaking of World Order.* New York: Simon and Schuster.

Inglehart, R 1977, *The Silent Revolution: Changing Values and Political Styles in Advanced Industrial Society.* Princeton, NJ: Princeton University Press.

Inglehart, R 1990, *Culture Shift in Advanced Industrial Society.* Princeton, NJ: Princeton University Press.

Inglehart, R 1997, *Modernization and Post-Modernization: Cultural, Economic, and Political Change in 43 Societies.* Princeton, NJ: Princeton University Press.

Inglehart, R & Baker, EW 2000, 'Modernization, cultural change, and the persistence of traditional values,' *American Sociological Review,* vol.65, pp.19–51.

Kitayama, S, Markus, HR, & Kurokawa, M 2000, 'Culture, emotion, and well-being: Good feelings in Japan and the United States,' *Cognition & Emotion,* vol. 14. no. 1, pp. 93–124.

Kuada, J 2010, 'Culture and leadership in Africa: A conceptual model and research agenda,' *African Journal of Economic and Management Studies,* vol.1, no.1, pp.9–24.

Lee, MS & Peterson, JS 2000, 'Culture, entrepreneurial orientation, and global competitiveness,' *Journal of World Business,* vol.35, no.4, pp.401–416.

Levy, O, Beechler, S, Taylor, S & Boyacigiller, NA 2007, 'What we talk about when we talk about "global mindset": Managerial cognition in multinational corporations,' *Journal of International Business Studies,* vol.38, no.2, pp.231–258.

Lewicki, RJ & Bunker, BB 1996, 'Developing and maintaining trust in work relationships,' in Kramer, RM & Tyler, TR (Eds.), *Trust in Organizations, Frontiers of Theory and Research* (pp.114–139). Thousand Oaks, CA: Sage.

Lipartito, K 1995, 'Culture and the practice of business history,' *Business and Economic History,* vol.24, no.2, pp.1–41.

Lumpkin, GT, & Dess, GG 1996, 'Clarifying the entrepreneurial orientation construct and linking it to performance,' *Academy of Management Review,* vol. 21. no. 1, pp.135–172.

Maddock, M 2013, 'Invention: The entrepreneurial curse,' *Forbes*, May 15.
Mayer, RC, Davis, JH, & Schoorman, FD (1995). An integration model of organizational trust. *Academy of Management Review*, 20(3), pp.709–734.
Maznevski, M & Lane, H 2007, 'Shaping the global mindset: Designing educational experiences for effective global thinking and action,' in Muzychenko, O (Ed.), *Facilitating International Entrepreneurship through Developing a Global Mindset*. Glasgow, Scotland: Institute for Small Business and Entrepreneurship, pp.171–184.
Muzychenko, O 2007, *Facilitating International Entrepreneurship through Developing a Global Mindset*. Glasgow, Scotland: Institute for Small Business and Entrepreneurship.
Napier, NK 2012, 'What's small, tasty and may change the world? The yin and yang of responsible creativity,' *Psychology Today*, <http://www.psychologytoday.com/blog/creativity-without-borders/201205/whats-small-tasty-and-may-change-the-world>
Napier, NK & Vuong, QH 2013a, *What We See, Why We Worry, Why We Hope: Vietnam Going Forward*. Boise, ID: Boise State University CCI Press.
Napier, NK & Vuong, QH 2013b, 'Serendipity as a strategic advantage,' in Wilkinson, TJ (Ed.), *Strategic Management in the 21st Century; Volume 1: The Operational Environment* (pp.175–199). Westport, CT: Praeger/ABC-Clio.
Nelson, R & Winter, S 1982, *An Evolutionary Theory of Economic Change*. Cambridge, MA: Harvard University Press.
Paliszkiewicz, JO 2011, 'Trust management: Literature review,' *Management*, vol.6, no.4, pp.315–331.
Pisapia, J, Reyes-Guerra, D & Coukos-Semmel, E 2005, 'Developing the leader's strategic mindset: Establishing the measures,' *Leadership Review*, vol.5, no.1, pp.41–68.
Prahalad, CK & Bettis, RA 1986, 'The dominant logic: A new linkage between diversity and performance,' *Strategic Management Journal*, vol.7, pp.485–501.
Putnam, R 1993, *Making Democracy Work: Civic Traditions in Modern Italy*. Princeton, NJ: Princeton University Press.
Rhinesmith, SH 1992, 'Global mindsets for global managers,' *Training and Development*, vol.46, no.10, pp.63–69.
Rhinesmith, SH 1993, *Globalization: Six Keys to Success in a Changing World*. Alexandria, VA: The American Society for Training and Development.
Rhinesmith, SH 1996, *A Manager's Guide to Globalization: Six Skills for Success in a Changing World* (2nd Ed.). New York, NY: McGraw-Hill.
Schatz, R 2012, 'Culture and values as keys to economic growth,' *Vietnamica*, <http://www.vietnamica.net/culture-and-values-as-keys-to-economic-growth/>
Schwartz, SH 1999, 'A theory of cultural values and some implications for work,' *Applied Psychology: An International Review*, vol.48, no.1, pp.23–47.
Schwartz, SH 2006, 'A theory of cultural value orientations: Explication and applications,' *Comparative Sociology*, vol.5, no.2/3, pp.137–182.
Schwartz, SH & Bardi, A 2001, 'Value hierarchies across cultures: Taking a similarities perspective,' *The Journal of Cross Cultural Psychology*, vol.32, no.3, pp.268–290.
Taylor, WE 1991, 'The logic of global business: An interview with ABB's Percy Barnevik,' *Harvard Business Review*, vol.69, no.2, pp.93–105.
Vuong, QH 2014a, 'Vietnam's political economy: A discussion on the 1986–2016 period,' *Working Papers CEB*, N°14–010, Université Libre de Bruxelles.
Vuong, QH 2014b, 'The harsh reality of pursuing innovations: Emerging market perspectives,' *Proceedings of the 2nd National Conference on Management and Higher Education Trends & Strategies for Management and Administration*, Oct. 31–Nov. 1, Stamford International University, Bangkok, Thailand.

Vuong, QH, Dam, VN, Van Houtte, D & Tran, TD 2011, 'The entrepreneurial facets as precursor to Vietnam's economic renovation in 1986,' *The IUP Journal of Entrepreneurship Development*, vol.8, no.4, pp.6–47.

Vuong, QH, & Napier, NK 2013, 'Anatomy of the 3D innovation production with the Cobb-Douglas specification,' *Sociology Study*, vol. 3, no. 1, pp.69–78.

Vuong, QH & Napier, NK 2014, 'Making creativity: The value of multiple filters in the innovation process,' *International Journal of Transitions and Innovation Systems*, vol.3, no.4, pp.294–327.

Vuong, Q. H. & Napier, N. K. 2015, 'Acculturation and global mindsponge: An emerging market perspective,' *International Journal of Intercultural Relations*, 49, pp.354–367.

Vuong, QH, Napier, NK & Tran, TD 2013, 'A categorical data analysis on relationships between culture, creativity and business stage: The case of Vietnam,' *International Journal of Transitions and Innovation Systems*, vol.3, no.1, pp.4–24.

Vuong, QH, Napier, NK, Vu, KH, Nguyen, MC & Tran, TD 2014, 'Measuring corporate innovation capacity: Experience and implications from i2Metrix implementation in Vietnam,' *ASEAN Journal of Management and Innovation*, vol.1, no.1, pp.1–17.

Vuong, QH & Tran, TD 2009, 'The cultural dimensions of the Vietnamese private entrepreneurship,' *The IUP Journal of Entrepreneurship Development*, vol.6, no.3/4, pp.54–78.

Weber, M [1904] 1958, *The Protestant Ethic and the Spirit of Capitalism*. [Translated by Parsons, T.] Reprint, New York: Charles Scribner's Sons.

9 Mindsets, Culture, and Danish-Ghanaian Interfirm Collaborations

John Kuada

Introduction

Cross-border interfirm collaboration has been suggested as important policy and strategic tool for improving developing country firms' opportunities for growth (Mowery, Oxley and Silverman, 1996; Mathews, 2006). The central argument in support of this viewpoint is that collaboration provides developing country firms with access to both tangible resources, such as technology, and intangible resources, such as knowledge (Beamish, 1987; Driffield and Love, 2003). This helps the firms to undertake product, process, and functional upgrading at a faster pace than would otherwise have been the case (Pietrobelli and Rabellotti, 2011). It has, however, been noted that collaboratively induced access to intangible resources does not always translate smoothly into usage within the developing country firms. The reason is partly because such resources frequently encompass the crystallization of values, culturally prescribed rules of behavior, and tacitly endorsed organizational forms. Transferring them effectively, therefore, entails that the collaborative partners possess mindsets and relational competencies that enable them to appreciate the contextual peculiarities under which they should be applied. Furthermore, developing country firms are typically small, family-owned businesses with limited growth ambitions and absorptive capacities (Kuada and Sørensen, 2000; Kuada, 2002). This places additional demands on the competencies of the resource providers in the collaborative relationships.

Since the mid-1980s, development aid agencies have sponsored collaboration between firms in industrialized and developing countries as a means of facilitating enterprise development and poverty alleviation (Kuada, 2002; Kuada and Sørensen, 2005). This policy initiative has been adopted in response to the enormous difficulties that developing country firms face in attracting developed country partners due, in part, to their small sizes, as well as resource disadvantages and limited strategic importance within the global business environment (Kuada and Sørensen, 2000; Asiedu, 2002). There has, however, been limited academic interest in studying the nature and performance of these donor-sponsored collaborative relationships

(Kragelund, 2005). The few empirical investigations available have focused attention on structural, cultural, and resource-based weaknesses of developing country firms without exploring possible weaknesses that may be attributable to their collaborative partners from the developed countries. Some previous studies have suggested that factors such as power asymmetries, motives of collaboration, and leadership styles exhibited by developed country partners as well as the mindsets that guide their decisions and actions may significantly influence the relations and determine the degree to which the expectations of the developing country partners are fulfilled (see Hansen and Schaumburg-Müller, 2006). For example, cognitive bias (e.g., illusory superiority/inferiority tendencies among developed and developing country firms, respectively) can influence their relationship building process (Kuada and Sørensen, 2005). As many developing countries are emerging as new growth frontiers, business managers, consultants, and policy makers are in search of knowledge and guidelines on the appropriate relational modalities to adopt when operating in these countries or sponsoring enterprise development initiatives. The study reported in this chapter draws its justification from these considerations.

In terms of structure, the chapter continues with this introduction with a brief review of the theoretical arguments underlying cross-border interfirm collaborations and factors that influence their effective management. It then discusses the characteristics of firms in developing countries and the manner in which these characteristics shape their relationships with developed country firms. This is followed by a summary of the results of a series of investigations I conducted about Danish and Ghanaian interfirm collaborations between 2000 and 2008. The collaborations investigated were sponsored by Danida (the Danish bilateral aid agency) between 1993 and 2006. The final section of the chapter discusses the policy, strategy, and research implications of the issues presented.

Theoretical Rationale for Cross-Border Interfirm Collaborations

Most contributions to cross-border interfirm research have largely drawn on theoretical viewpoints such as transaction cost economics (Gander and Rieple, 2004), agency theories (Eisenhardt, 1989), the resource-based perspective on firms (Barney, 1991, 2001), competence-based perspectives (Prahalad and Hamel, 1990), knowledge-based perspectives (Nelson and Winter, 1982; Inkpen and Crossan, 1995), and global mindset perspectives (Beechler and Javidan, 2007; Clapp-Smith, 2009), as well as relationship management theories (Gulati, 1998). These theories have provided insights into the motives underlying collaborative arrangements, modes of partner selection, as well as the firm-level capabilities required to effectively manage the relationships.

Motives

Following the existing literature, economic considerations seem to underlie firms' decisions to enter cross-border collaborations (Gulati, 1998; Kotabe, Martin and Domoto, 2003; Reuer and Arino, 2007). Their motives may include the need to minimize the costs and risks of innovation (Mowery et al., 1996; Das and Teng, 2000), to enhance competitive advantage (Zinn and Parasuraman, 1997), to leverage financial resources and technology (Beamish, 1987; Wu, Rudolf, Sinkovics and Roath, 2007), to gain access to local markets (Stopford and Wells, 1972), and/or to meet government requirements for local ownership (Datta 1988; Wu et al., 2007). In addition to these motives, some scholars argue that companies may enter into relationships with firms in strategically less important markets in order to train their managers in international business operations and to improve their intercultural competencies (Beechler and Javidan, 2007; Clapp-Smith, 2009).

It has been noted that not all interfirm relationships are long lasting due to the different motives that may underlie their formation. The duration of the relationships appears to depend on (1) the strategic and/or operational importance of the resources exchanged, (2) the extent to which one of the partners has discretion over the resource, and (3) the extent to which there are limited alternatives (Pfeffer and Salancik, 1978). Where strategic requirements encourage partners to enter into a long-term relationship, they establish relational bonds (Lorenzoni and Lipparini, 1999). These bonds are manifested in practice through product and process adjustments, logistical coordination, and knowledge about counterparts. Other concepts used in the literature to describe such relational bonds include relational capability (Zaheer and Venkatraman, 1995) and relational strength (Capaldo, 2007).

Partner Selection and Relationship Formation Process

Having identified the need to collaborate, firms are expected to conduct a systematic search for appropriate partners. Building on agency analytical frameworks, it has been argued that firms in collaborative relationships face two types of vulnerability in their operations. The first is *adverse selection*, which describes the condition under which the firm cannot be certain that competencies that the partner claims to have are also those required to provide the inputs and resources that it needs for the optimal performance of its own value-adding activities. The second is what is referred to in agency theory as *moral hazards*. Moral hazard is the condition under which prospective collaborative parties cannot be sure if the partners have put forth maximal effort (Eisenhardt, 1989). Addressing these two issues requires careful partner selection and monitoring of the collaborative process. It is therefore normal for firms to develop "search properties" (i.e., attributes to be verified prior to the selection) in order to reduce the risk of choosing the wrong partner.

The literature advises firms to select partners with similar values, beliefs, and practices in order to minimize tensions during the process of collaboration (Weitz and Jap, 1995). The search process may therefore start with the partner-seeking firm making contacts with firms with which it already has some relationship. If they do not meet the selection attributes, they may hire consultants to identify appropriate prospective partners or rely on the recommendations of third parties who can vouch for prospective candidates' performance and trustworthiness.

Once a suitable candidate is identified and negotiations for relationships have been completed, partners begin to lay the groundwork for the relationship in the form of norm adoption for mutual conduct and "setting the ground rules for future exchanges" (Dwyer, Paul and Sejo, 1987: 17). In other words, they start building a common culture to speed up the social-bonding process that is critical for achieving mutual goals (Wilson, 1995). As Iyer (2002) observes, there emerges (towards the end of the phase) a systematic effort by the partners vicariously to learn deeply embedded knowledge, such as skills, processes, and routines. However, the relationship at this stage will be very fragile, with minimal investment and interdependence, leaving a very easy outlet for quick dissolution (Kuada and Sørensen, 2005).

When partners gain satisfactory insight into the institutionalized practices and procedures of each other and are convinced of sustaining the collaboration (with an acknowledgement of their interdependence and mutual vulnerability), they begin to share investments and technology as well as engage in an adaptation of processes of products/services to satisfy each other's requirements. Routines are also institutionalized at this stage. This helps lay the groundwork for an enduring relationship.

Relationship Management Process

Relationship management capabilities are seen as key prerequisites for collaborative performance. Kumar and Nti (1998) argue that an effective management of the collaborative process requires an awareness of the differences between factors relating to contributions made by the partners and factors concerning their psychological attachment to the relationship. The contributions here refer to the resources and efforts that partners make to build the relationship. The psychological dimensions of the relationships are evaluated in terms of *process discrepancies* in the relationship (i.e., differences between what is anticipated and what actually happens within any given time period). The contributions and the processes lead to the concrete outcomes of the relationship. Favorable process and outcome discrepancies engender further commitment to the relationship. Unfavorable discrepancies produce a reverse impact, i.e., low motivation of the partners to make the relationship work. The expectations and perceived contributions of resources from the partners therefore influence their willingness to build the capabilities required to manage the relationships effectively.

Relational capabilities are usually built over time and can involve cultural training as well as internalization of best practices and organizational routines. Hausman (2001) introduces the concept of "relationship strength" to reflect differences in the relational character of business relationships. She defines relationship strength as ties between relational partners, reflecting their ability to weather both internal and external challenges to the relationship. She argues then that relationship strength would depend on the levels of trust and commitment between focal business partners. Fukuyama (1995) defines trust as the expectation of regular, honest, and cooperative behavior based on commonly shared norms and values. Similarly, Anderson and Narus (1990: 45) define trust as "the firm's belief that another firm will perform actions that result in positive outcomes for the firm, as well as not take unexpected actions that would result in negative outcomes for the firm." Where trust exists between people in relations, they are willing to sacrifice their short-term, individual self-interests for the attainment of joint goals or longer-term objectives (Sabel, 1993). Thus, trust improves flexibility in dealing with relational conflicts between partners, lowers the cost of coordinating activities, and increases the level of knowledge transfer between them (Morgan and Hunt, 1994).

Past studies have shown that partners will increase mutual trust when they have demonstrated to each other that they will not betray the confidence placed in them by their partners and are committed to developing the relationship (Aulakh, Kotabe and Sahay, 1996; Inkpen, 1998). Morgan and Hunt (1994) have therefore suggested that *commitment* and *trust* should be considered the foundations of interfirm relationships. The committed party believes the relationship is worth working on and therefore actively contributes to its continuity. Commitment is built on trust, i.e., confidence in each other's reliability and integrity. Trust therefore leads to higher levels of loyalty. "When both commitment and trust—not just one or the other—are present," they argue, "they produce outcomes that promote efficiency, productivity and effectiveness" (Morgan and Hunt, 1994: 22).

Mindsets, Culture, and Collaborative Capabilities

Past studies have suggested that relational capabilities of managers are influenced by their personality traits, individual mindsets, and cultural sensitivity, as well as their degree of international exposure (Ket de Vries and Miller, 1985; Campbell, Rudich and Sedikides, 2002; Rosenthal and Pittinsky, 2006). Briefly considered, personality influences peoples' openness as well as the degree to which they are seen as "agreeable" (i.e., demonstrate empathy, courtesy, cooperative capability, and conflict avoidance in their relationships with others). People who are open-minded are also willing to learn from their mistakes and try new behaviors (Ket de Vries and Miller, 1985; Campbell et al., 2002). It has also been argued that some managers may have personalities that reflect narcissist tendencies—i.e., they are driven by their own egotistical needs for control, power, and self-importance even if they outwardly appear to champion the needs of others (Rosenthal and Pittinsky, 2006). Managers with such personality profiles tend to demonstrate a sense of superiority and vanity in their behavior and relationships with others. Mangers with these tendencies are described as demonstrating a weak ability to maintain relationships and never learning from their mistakes. They believe that they are superior in ability and competence to all others and are comfortable with building parental relationships with their followers—talking down to them as if they were children (Campbell et al., 2002). This perceived superiority is most often illusory rather than real. As psychologists argue, cognitive bias is the human tendency to draw incorrect conclusions in certain circumstances based on cognitive factors rather than evidence (Ket de Vries and Miller, 1985; Rosenthal and Pittinsky, 2006). Such biases are reflected in social attributions and unwarranted stereotypes and unconstructive behaviors.

Building on this perspective, it is tenable to speculate that developed country managers may nurture a sense of relative superiority in their relationships with their counterparts in developing countries. Developing country managers may also entertain a reverse cognitive bias—i.e., an illusory sense of inferiority that may constrain their ability to relate to developed country partners as equals. As long as partners remain prisoners of their existing mental models, they tend to create what Argyris (1993) refers to as "defensive routines," thereby exhibiting a general reluctance to leave old ways of thinking for new ones. This mindset constrains the emergence of mutual trust between them and therefore negatively impacts their relationships.

Following Earley (2002), an individual's capacity to adapt to unfamiliar cultural environments partly depends on that individual's cognitive disposition. Similarly, Gupta and Govindarajan (2002) see individuals with a global mindset as those who demonstrate a combination of awareness and openness to the diversity of cultures. Thus, persons with a global mindset are able to take advantage of their cognitive feedback mechanisms to expand and refine their mental schemas through their interactive experiences with others. In other words, when people interact with each other, they cultivate a sense of understanding that shapes the evolution of their relationships. The shared experiences allow them to form similar perceptions that they jointly reflect on. The experiences also encourage them to explore common solutions to the challenges that they face in their lifeworlds. Stated differently, the ability of managers to decipher others' values (Schein, 1985) and understand a new environment using situated knowledge structures (Shapiro, Ozanne and Saatcioglu, 2008) is an important tool for improving the chances of attaining collaborative objectives. Thus, the contemporary literature is replete with concepts such as cross-cultural sensitivity (Rodrigues, 1997), cultural adaptation (Andreason, 2003), and cultural intelligence (Earley and Ang, 2003) as tools for developing collaborative capabilities.

Previous studies have shown that because individuals and organizations are part of their societies, it is plausible to expect them to reflect their national culture in their thinking, practices, and values (Hofstede, 1980). Culture is usually described in the anthropological and sociological literature as a system of socially transmitted behavior patterns that serve to relate human communities to their environment as well as order relations among individuals (Kluckhohn and Strodtbeck, 1961; Geertz, 1973; Triandis, 1994; Harris, 1997; Trompenaars and Hampden-Turner, 1997; Gullestrup, 2006). The transmission mechanism is referred to as the process of socialization. Through socialization, individuals are taught the norms and values as well as the shared expectations of the community in which they live. The process starts from childhood. Each child is taught the customs and norms of "good behavior" of a particular sub-unit of its community in order to equip it with means of interacting sensibly and smoothly within its social structure.

The cultural factor is particularly important in this study, which focuses on the relationships between firms located in distinctly dissimilar cultures. In a previous study, I developed a classificatory model for small enterprises in Africa by grouping the triggering cues of African entrepreneurs into either *necessity-oriented* or *growth-oriented* entrepreneurs (see Kuada, 2015). The necessity-oriented businesses are usually established as a last resort source of livelihood rather than as a first choice for their owners (Beck, Demirguc-Kunt, Laeven and Levine, 2005). There is some evidence from past studies indicating that the growth potential of small enterprises in Africa seems to be constrained by cultural factors (Okpara, 2007; Kuada, 2015). For example, many family members tend to consume more and contribute less in terms of efforts and personal commitment to family businesses (Neshamba, 2006). Poverty and inequalities in income distribution in these societies further accentuate the need for relying on the traditional family structures and the acceptance of the moral obligations of family members to help their less advantaged siblings. Thus, owner-managers of small enterprises tend to use their resources to support the weaker members of their families at a rate that outpaces their capacity to recoup them for the survival and growth of their businesses. In worst cases, this behavior may lead to the collapse of the businesses.

The Collaborative Experiences of Danish-Ghanaian Firms

The empirical evidence discussed in this section is based on information drawn from a series of studies done on collaborations between Danish and Ghanaian firms sponsored by the Danish Development Agency (Danida) between 1993 and 2006 under its private sector development program

(PSDP). The program was established as an instrument for encouraging and facilitating long-term business links between Danish firms and those based in developing countries. Through these linkages, it was expected that the Danish firms would transfer technology and management skills to their developing country partners, thereby enhancing the latter's commercial capacities and performance. Fourteen pairs of such collaborative arrangements provided the empirical data for the study reported in this chapter. They consisted of six within the fishing and food processing sectors, four in wood treatment and furniture businesses, and one each in pharmaceuticals, textiles, solar energy, and road construction. Details of the investigations have been reported elsewhere (Kuada, 2002; Kuada and Sørensen, 2005). In addition, the discussions below have benefited from empirical research conducted by Kragelund in 2002 and 2003 (see Kragelund, 2005).

The research instrument adopted for the studies was semi-structured interviews, with each interview lasting between two and three hours. For each company, executive(s) who had been intimately involved in the collaborative process right from the formation stage were interviewed. The Ghanaian partners were interviewed in Ghana and the Danish partners in Denmark. Interviewing partners separately has facilitated an assessment of their perceptions of the relationship independently of each other.

The Collaborative Motives and Expectations

The Ghanaian companies engaged in the collaborations were owner-managed and relatively small, having between 10 and 250 employees. The Danish companies had similar profiles: owner-managed, small, and with limited international business experience. Their relatively small sizes explains their dependence on catalyst institutions for support in initiating and building their collaborations. The Ghanaian firms tended to enter the relationship for strategic reasons, i.e., to leverage external technology, skills, and finances. By upgrading their technologies and management skills, some hoped that their products could enter markets within the EU. The Danish firms' decisions to establish collaborative arrangements with the Ghanaian firms were based partly on a wish to contribute to poverty alleviation in Ghana through the transfer of superior technical and managerial knowledge to Ghanaian firms (i.e., an ideological motive). In this regard, there was some discrepancy in the partners' strategic orientations in relation to the collaborative relationships.

Danida's time frame for the collaborative arrangements did not offer the partners adequate time to get to know each other before the collaboration began. Once a prospective partner was identified with the help of Danida's project coordinator, arrangements were made for the managing directors of the prospective collaborating firms to meet and agree on the specific conditions for the relationship. The initial contacts, though short, provided the partners with opportunities to make promises and exchange expectations. But the firms indicated that there were discrepancies between what they believed they had agreed upon during their negotiations and the services delivered by their partners subsequently—an indication of some degree of communication breakdown during the negotiations. For example, some Danish partners were accused of delivering obsolete machinery when they had promised to deliver new or "fairly new" plants and equipment (Kuada, 2002). There were also indications that some of the Ghanaian partners exaggerated their financial capacities, and thus, in some cases, proved unable to raise funds that had been pledged. This resulted in the projects running into immediate financial difficulties. Added to this, some Ghanaian partners tended to focus on short-term financial gains from the project rather than growing their companies.

Partners admitted to having limited knowledge about each other's culture prior to the relationship, although their business cultures were admittedly different. But they did not see this weakness as critical to the success of their relationships. The collaborations were generally simple, i.e., low on both organizational and task complexity. Personnel from partner organizations interacted infrequently and the number of individuals involved in each case was generally small, limited usually to top management.

Challenges of Collaboration

Three categories of factors were found to impact the collaborative relationships (see Table 9.1). These are (1) the personal characteristics and context-specific knowledge of the Danish managers involved in the projects, (2) the degree of cultural sensitivity of the Danish partners, and (3) the willingness of the partner firms to commit resources to the projects. Personal characteristics such as openness, mutual respect, and sincerity were seen as promoting collaboration, while disrespect, poor communication, and excess complaints were listed among the factors that inhibited collaboration. Furthermore, the Danish partners did not have prior international business experience before engaging in the projects and did not take deliberate steps to gain context-specific knowledge that could prepare them effectively for their assignments. The Ghanaians felt the Danes made too many unnecessary complaints and ascribed them to culturally induced misunderstandings regarding attitude to time and work within the Ghanaian work culture in general. The Danes were reported of complaining that the Ghanaians have been unduly slow in making critical decisions and thereby delaying the implementation of the projects. The Danish partners' choice of words while communicating with the Ghanaians had also been interpreted by the Ghanaians as evidence of disrespect and poor communication style. These incidents of misunderstanding have, in several cases, posed serious challenges to the governance of the relations. They engendered mistrust and provided justifications for the establishment of rigorous control measures in some of the relationships.

Table 9.1 Factors Influencing Danish-Ghanaian Interfirm Collaboration

Factors	Positive	Negative
Personal Characteristics	Fairness and openness	Disrespect
	Mutual respect	Delays in communication
	Sincerity and frankness	Excessive complaints
	Friendliness	Naivety
	Personal initiative	
Professional Characteristics	Effective communication	Poor knowledge about the partners' mode of operation
	Decisiveness	
	Good technical and managerial knowledge	Lack of precisionDoubt about partner's capabilities
Resource Considerations	Business information, particularly on the EU market	Delivering sub-standard technology
	Financial commitment	Evidence of low commitment
	Transfer of high-quality technology	Misusing Ghanaian partners' dependency on the Danish partner
	Transfer of managerial skills and knowledge	

The results of the investigations also showed that some of Ghanaian partners were divided in their views on the extent to which the Danish partners should be involved in the management of the businesses. Some were against shared management if that implied Danish partners' full participation in top management decisions. Some were willing to accept shared management arrangements with their Danish partners, granting that the Danes made equity investments in the businesses. To them, the Danish partner's equity involvement would reflect a declaration of trust, commitment, and willingness to engage in a long-term relationship.

They were, therefore, disappointed when their Danish co-partners turned down their request for financial contributions.

Two Illustrative Cases

(Names of companies and persons in the two cases have been changed to preserve their anonymity.)

Case 1: The Fishing Net Producer

A Ghanaian entrepreneur, Mr. Allotey, who was born and raised in a fishing community in Accra, established Ghana Fishing Nets (GF) in 1979. Mr. Allotey had a limited formal education, and described himself as "a self-made businessman." His major investment as an entrepreneur started in 1960 when he bought two small fishing vessels for off-shore fishing and concurrently imported and distributed fresh fish from Europe and the USSR. In the mid-1960s, he extended his investment into cash crop farming (palm plantations) and served as an agent for the producers of hospital equipment in Switzerland and the Netherlands. In 1980, he decided to develop the fishing business within his local community by providing the fishermen with cheaper and better-quality fishing nets than those hitherto imported into the country.

He invested approximately 2 million U.S. dollars in the project. All equipment for the factory was imported from Japan and installed by the suppliers in 1980. But just as production was to begin, a new military regime came to power in Ghana and suspended the importation of raw materials of various kinds. With no raw materials and no immediate signs of change in the import policies of the new government, Mr. Allotey decided to close down the factory and retained a skeleton staff of technicians to maintain the machines. He left the country to reside in a European country for health reasons.

Inspired by a UNIDO market assessment report on the fishing sector and its recommendation that local fishing net facilities should be established in the country, the PSDP coordinator in Ghana and his local consultants approached GF with a proposal for revamping the business. Initial discussions were held with the production manager of GF (a nephew of Mr. Allotey). It was proposed that GF should inject additional capital into the business in the form of renovation of the factory and getting the machines ready for full-scale production. Such an investment was to be taken as evidence of GF's commitment to fishing net production after being out of business for over 12 years. In return, the PSDP would find a Danish firm to upgrade the skills of GF's staff and provide technical and management expertise until the company became fully resuscitated. All expenses regarding the technical assistance and knowledge transfer were to be paid for by the PSDP. In addition, Danida would undertake to provide a package of soft loans that could facilitate the purchase of raw materials and additional equipment. The initial discussions were communicated to Mr. Allotey for his approval. He was encouraged by the news and came down to Ghana to finalize the negotiations with the PSDP. In the interim, a Danish partner was identified and meetings were arranged between him and Mr. Allotey.

On the insistence of the PSDP officials and consultants, it was decided that GF should rebuild its management capacity by recruiting people for the following positions: a general manager, a marketing manager, an accountant, and a production engineer. The company was also required to conduct elaborate market research to determine the types and characteristics of fishing nets in demand. It was further agreed that production would commence in August 1998 concurrently with the training and technical services to be offered by the Danish partner.

Several follow-up meetings were held by the PSDP consultants with Mr. Allotey after the agreement was signed in 1997 to encourage him to recruit the required management staff. About nine months after the agreement had been signed, a general manager was appointed and Mr. Allotey's nephew (who was involved in the initial discussions) was confirmed as a production manager. The office was refurbished and computers were installed, but production did not start due to delays in ordering raw materials.

The Danish partner visited Ghana for two weeks to undertake an initial assessment of the knowledge needs of the Ghanaian staff. Because no production had taken place in the factory earlier, no experiential knowledge existed. Everything had to start from scratch. He suggested that the production manager should visit Denmark for a three-week training session, after which he could assist the Danish counterpart in training the Ghanaian production staff. These arrangements were approved by Mr. Allotey.

For nearly a year after these initial plans were made, Mr. Allotey refused to give a final go ahead for the implementation of the contents of the agreement. Subsequent enquiries revealed that he had all along been suspicious of the real intentions of the PSDP and the Danish partner. He could not believe that Europeans would help him develop the company and let him keep it, i.e., without finally taking over if it became a prosperous business venture. None of the co-partners (i.e., the PSDP officers as well as the Danish counterpart) was aware of this strong suspicion and therefore did nothing to allay his fears. The persistence of this suspicion led to the project being eventually abandoned.

Case 2: Dixcove Solar Project

Dixcove Engineering (a Ghanaian company) has been engaged in assembling solar water heating systems for the Ghanaian market since 1993. In 1996, Dixcove took the strategic decision to expand its product line to include solar electrical systems. The new product line was targeted at hospitals (serving their emergency lighting needs) and households, as well as infrastructural facilities such as street lighting and traffic lights. The implementation of this strategic decision entailed purchases of new equipment by Dixcove Engineering as well as upgrading the technical capacity within the company to be able to design, assemble, install, and service the solar electrical systems. The PSDP agreed to support the project. Jylland A/S (A Danish firm) was commissioned to collaborate with Dixcove Engineering to find the most suitable technology for the purpose and to help Dixcove acquire the requisite competencies for the implementation of the project. The choice of Jylland A/S for this task was based on the compatibility in the two companies' lines of business, the relatively superior technological capacities and capabilities of Jylland A/S, and its previous business experiences in Ghana and Zimbabwe. The technical assistance agreement specifically required Jylland A/S to upgrade Dixcove Engineering's technical capacity to "supply photovoltaic system solutions to energy requirements in Ghana." A successful transfer of skills and knowledge would enable Dixcove to assess the energy requirements of its prospective customers, determine the sizes and combinations of individual components of the electrical system (panels, inverters, batteries, cables, etc.) that would fulfill the needs, and provide the appropriate post-installation services to the customers. Jylland and Dixcove designed an elaborate plan for the technology transfer. Key activities in the plan included:

(1) Training of Dixcove's staff in both Ghana and Denmark. On-the-job and off-the-job training methods were to be used and the trainees were to receive accreditation and certification from the Danish Technical Institute, one of the leading technical institutions in Denmark.
(2) The design and production of marketing materials.
(3) The procurement and installation of demonstration units.

Out of a staff of 27 people at Dixcove Engineering, the training was limited to the general manager, the workshop manager, and a newly appointed engineer. The expectation was that the knowledge and skills acquired by these people would be effectively disseminated throughout the organization. When the trained managers were interviewed after the training, they maintained that the knowledge they acquired was not adequate for the effective accomplishment of the tasks that they were expected to undertake. That is, the post-training knowledge gap made it impossible for them to analyze the implications of differences in weather patterns and atmospheric conditions for the performance of the solar electrical systems they designed after the training, which was apparently due to the nature of the training methods used. Subsequent analysis of the training process indicated that the trainers in Denmark lacked an adequate understanding of the context within which the technology was to be used.

As such, they could not successfully transfer the core skills required to apply the imported technology. This led to the sub-optimal performance of the systems under weather conditions that were very different from those under which the systems were designed and tested in Denmark. Consequently, some of the Ghanaian customers were grossly dissatisfied with Dixcove Engineering because their lights did not work at all or worked intermittently. The situation was partially remedied when a local consultant was attached to the project to provide the Danes with insights into the Ghanaian operational context.

Discussions

The interfirm relationship literature presented above indicates that collaborating firms develop and nurture their relational capabilities through intensive interactions and that allow them to develop mutual trust, willingness to commit resources, and to share information and learn from each other. We have also discussed the need for collaborating firms to develop joint processes and coordination mechanism that facilitate the institutionalization of agreed procedures. The empirical evidence presented above provides additional support for some of the key conclusions found in previous studies on cross-border interfirm collaborations. It also extends some of them. First, the discussions have shown that compatibilities of motives of collaboration and resource capabilities as well as cultural and contextual knowledge are important ingredients for successful cross-border interfirm collaborations. Misalignment between partners on these key issues may result in disappointments and mistrust. These findings are consistent with the theoretical expectations about motivation discussed above. The Danish firms involved in these collaborations were relatively small and had limited international experience. Many of them had not considered entering into relationships with Ghanaian firms before learning about the PSDP and its support arrangements. The results would appear to indicate that altruistic motives do not provide a strong foundation for interfirm collaborations (even in relatively poor and underdeveloped countries). Commercial and strategic motives compel companies to carefully evaluate their capabilities before engaging in such relationships.

It is not clear from the evidence whether some of the partners and managers involved in the collaborative process had narcissistic inclinations. We have noted earlier that managers with negative narcissistic tendencies have a strong need for recognition. They are usually charming and engaging but tend not to exhibit empathy and vacillate between championing idealistic values and ruthless exploitation (Rosenthal and Pittinsky, 2006). It is possible that the Danish managers have superior feelings towards their Ghanaian partners. The reverse may also be true—i.e., the Ghanaian partners felt inferior to their Danish counterparts. It is not clear whether such inclinations contributed to the failure of the fishing net project.

Second, it is also evident that some degree of global orientation can help collaborating partners to be relatively more prepared for the challenges that they would face in collaborating with each other, especially when the partners operate in unfamiliar business environments. Previous discussions have suggested that cultural intelligence and relationship management capabilities are mutually reinforcing. Thus, following Clapp-Smith (2009: 4), we see global orientation here as including elements of "cultural self-awareness, cognitive complexity, positivity, cognitive cultural intelligence, and the ability to suspend judgment that enables individuals to integrate multiple cultural paradigms in order to understand and influence culturally diverse social events and interactions." Global orientation is also reflected in an individual's ability to intuitively adapt his/her perception and behavior to the demands of a given situation. The evidence reported above suggests that some of the Ghanaian and Danish managers appear not to demonstrate such abilities.

Third, the empirical evidence also draws attention to the importance of knowledge transfer capabilities for successful interfirm collaboration.

When communication channels are clear the partners interact frequently, it becomes a lot easier for them to learn the peculiar patterns of learning of individuals and adjust their knowledge transfer processes accordingly (Gupta and Govindarajan, 2002). The learning literature suggests two pre-conditions for successful knowledge transfer: (1) the *learning capability* of the knowledge receivers, and (2) the *transfer capability* of the knowledge providers (Kuada, 2008). Learning capability refers to the ability to absorb knowledge and integrate it into the mindset of firms. Transfer capability is determined by a combination of the teaching capability of the knowl-edge providers (i.e., the ability to appropriately communicate the required knowledge) combined with the motivation and commitment to the transfer process (i.e., the ability to commit resources and time to the transfer). Both conditions appeared not to be present in the Dixcove case.

Finally, the importance of effective communication, trust, and commit-ment has been re-emphasized in the discussions The key elements of com-munication are whether beneficial information is freely, frequently, and informally provided, and whether each party keeps the other informed on expectations, anxieties, and changes (Anderson and Narus, 1990). The fail-ure of the fishing net project can be attributed basically to problems of communication and mistrust. Commitment also helps maintain and enhance the relationship and may be built on the basis of shared interests and the adoption of mutually agreed-upon rules of conduct. There have been several situations in the Danish-Ghanaian relationships where the partners were in doubt of the commitment of their co-partners. Where commitment is felt to be absent, partners will be unwilling to cycle through the sequences of learning, re-evaluation, and re-adjustment that are considered necessary for enduring relationships (see Doz, 1996).

Conclusions

It is generally acknowledged that culture provides individuals in every society with common perspectives on making sense of the world around them. This helps shape their individual mindsets as well as sensitivity to the needs and expectations of other people. Cross-border interfirm collaborations depend on these culturally induced mental models insofar as they inform individu-als' expectations, commitment, and trust in the relationships in which they are involved. The empirical evidence discussed above shows that these fac-tors are even more important in relationships between partners from very dissimilar cultures and where there is an imbalance in the resources of the collaborating partners, making one partner more dependent on the other. Imbalances in resources make the dependent partner a lot more suspicious and sensitive to the cultural errors that the stronger partner may inadver-tently commit. Where a partner is perceived to show lower degrees of com-mitment, the spirit of reciprocity that is expected to help build trust between

partners tends to be undermined. In situations where the relationships are
facilitated by a third party (as was the case of the Danida-sponsored PSDP
presented above), the facilitative institution, through providing resources,
can serve as a balancing force that can reinforce trust between the collaborating partners.

References

Anderson, J. C. and Narus, J. A. (1990) "A model of distributor firm and manufac-
turer firm working partnerships", *Journal of Marketing* 54(1):42–58.
Andreason, A. W. (2003) "Expatriate adjustment to foreign assignments", *International Journal of Commerce & Management* 13(1):42–60.
Argyris, C. (1993) *Knowledge for Action* (San Francisco, CA: Jossey-Bass).
Asiedu, E. (2002) "On the determinants of foreign direct investment to developing
countries: Is Africa different?", *World Development* 30(1):107–119.
Aulakh, P. S., Kotabe, M. and Sahay, A. (1996) "Trust and performance in cross-border
marketing partnerships: 'Behavioural Approach' ", *Journal of International Busi-
ness Studies* 27(5):1005–1032.
Barney, J. B. (1991) "Firm resources and sustained competitive advantage", *Journal
of Management* 17(1): 99–120.
Barney, J. B. (2001) "Resource-based theories of competitive advantage: A ten-year
retrospective on resource-based view", *Journal of Management* 27(6):643–650.
Beamish, P. W. (1987) "Joint ventures in LDCs: Partner selection and performance",
Management International Review 27(1):23–37.
Beck, T., Demirguc-Kunt, A., Laeven, L. and Levine, R. (2005) *Finance, firm size and
growth* (World Bank Policy Research Working Paper No. 3485).
Beechler, S. and Javidan, M. (2007) "Leading with a global mindset", in M. Javidan,
R. M. Steers & M. A. Hitt (Eds.), *Advances in international management: The
global mindset* (pp. 131–169). (Oxford, UK: Elsevier).
Campbell, W. K., Rudich, E. and Sedikides, C. (2002) "Narcissism, self-esteem, and
the positivity of self-views: Two portraits of self-love", *Personality and Social
Psychology Bulletin* 28(3):358–368.
Capaldo, A. (2007) "Network structure and innovation: The leveraging of a dual
network as a distinctive relational capability", *Strategic Management Journal*
(Chichester) 28(6):585–608.
Clapp-Smith, R. (2009) Global Mindset Development during Cultural Transitions
(Unpublished PhD dissertation, University of Nebraska at Lincoln).
Das, T. K. and Teng, B.-S. (2000) "A resource-based theory of strategic alliances",
Journal of Management 26(1):31–61.
Datta, D. K. (1988) "International joint ventures: A framework for analysis", *Journal
of General Management* 14(2):78–91.
Doz, Y. L. (1996) "The evolution of cooperation in strategic alliances: Initial condi-
tions or learning processes?", *Strategic Management Journal* 17(7):55–83.
Driffield, N. and Love, J. (2003) "Foreign direct investment, technology sourcing
and reverse spillovers", *Manchester School Journal* (University of Manchester)
71(6):659–672.
Dwyer, R. F., Schurr, P. H. and Sejo, O. (1987) "Developing buyer–seller relationships", *Journal of Marketing* 51(2):11–27.
Earley, P. C. (2002) "Redefining interactions across cultures and organizations: Moving forward with cultural intelligence", in B. M. Staw & R. M. Kramer (Eds.),
Research in Organizational Behavior Vol. 24 (pp. 271–299). (New York: JAI).

Earley, P. C. and Ang, S. (2003) *Cultural Intelligence: Individual Interactions Across Cultures* (Palo Alto: Stanford University Press).

Eisenhardt, K. M. (1989) "Agency theory: An assessment and review", *Academy of Management Review* 14(1):57–74.

Fukuyama, F. (1995) *Trust: The Societal Virtues and the Creation of Prosperity* (New York: Free Press).

Gander, J. and Rieple, A. (2004) "How relevant is transaction cost economics to inter-firm relationships in the music industry?", *Journal of Cultural Economics* 28(1):57–79.

Geertz, C. (1973) *The Interpretation of Cultures* (New York: Basic Books).

Gulati, R. (1998) "Alliances and Networks", *Strategic Management Journal,* 19(4): 293–317.

Gullestrup, H. (2006) *Cultural Analysis—Towards Cross-Cultural Understanding* (Denmark: Aalborg University Press and Copenhagen Business School Press).

Gupta, A. K. and Govindarajan, V. (2002) "Cultivating a global mindset", *Academy of Management Executive* 16(1):116–126.

Hansen, M. and Schaumburg-Müller, H. (Eds.) (2006) *Transnational Corporations and Local Organizations in Developing Countries—Linkages and Upgrading* (Copenhagen: Copenhagen Business School Press).

Harris, M. (1997) *Culture, People, Nature: An Introduction to General Anthropology* 7th Edition (Boston: Allyn & Bacon).

Hausman, A. (2001) "Variations in relationship strength and its impact on performance and satisfaction in business relationships", *The Journal of Business & Industrial Marketing* 16 (6/7):600–616.

Hofstede, G. (1980) *Culture's Consequences: International Differences in Work-Related Values* (Beverly Hills, CA: Sage Publications).

Inkpen, A. C. (1998) "Learning, knowledge acquisition, and strategic alliances", *European Management Journal* 16(2):223–229.

Inkpen, A. C. and Crossan, M. M. (1995) "Believing is seeing: Joint ventures and organization learning", *Journal of Management Studies* 32(5):595–618.

Iyer, K. (2002) "Learning in strategic alliances: An evolutionary perspective", *Academy of Marketing Science Review* 10, available at www.vancouver.wsu.edu/amsrev/theory/iyer10–2002.html (retrieved 27 July 2004).

Kets de Vries, M. and Miller, D. (1985) "Narcissism and leadership: An object relations perspective", *Human Relations* 38(6):583–601.

Kluckhohn, F. R. and Strodtbeck, F. L. (1961) *Variations in Value Orientations* (Evanston, IL: Row, Peterson).

Kotabe, M., Martin, X. and Domoto, H. (2003) "Gaining from vertical partnerships: Knowledge transfer, relationship duration, and supplier performance improvement in the U.S. and Japanese automotive industries", *Strategic Management Journal* 24(4):293–316.

Kragelund, P. (2005) "Building technological capabilities in Ghanaian SMEs through private sector development programmes", in J. Kuada (Ed.), *Internationalisation and Enterprise Development in Ghana* (London: Adonis & Abbey Publishers) pp:217–270.

Kuada, J. (2002) "Collaboration between developed and developing country-based firms: Danish–Ghanaian experience", *Journal of Business & Industrial Marketing* 17(6):538–557.

Kuada, J. (2008) *Cultural Foundations of Management Practices in Denmark* (Aalborg: International Business Centre Working Paper Series No. 45 pp. 1–18).

Kuada, J. (2015) "Entrepreneurship in Africa—A classificatory framework and a research agenda", *African Journal of Economic and Management Studies* 6(2):148–163.

Kuada, J. and Sørensen, O. J. (2000) *Internationalization of Companies from Developing Countries* (New York, NY: Haworth Press).

Kuada, J. and Sørensen, O. J. (2005) "Facilitated inter-firm collaboration in Ghana: The case of Danida's private-sector development projects", *Development in Practice* 15(3/4):475–489.

Kumar, R. and Nti, K. O. (1998) "Differential learning and interaction in alliance dynamics: A process and outcome discrepancy model", *Organization Science* 9(3):356–367.

Lorenzoni, G. and Lipparini, A. (1999) "The leveraging of interfirm relationships as a distinctive organizational capability: A longitudinal study", *Strategic Management Journal* (Chichester) 20(4):317–338.

Mathews, J. (2006) "Dragon multinationals: New players in 21st century globalization", *AsiaPacific Journal of Management* 23(1):5–27.

Morgan, R. M. and Hunt, S. D. (1994) "The commitment-trust theory of relationship marketing", *Journal of Marketing* 58(3):20–38.

Mowery, D., Oxley, J. E. and Silverman, B. (1996) "Strategic alliance and inter-firm knowledge transfer", *Strategic Management Journal* 17(4):77–91.

Nelson, R. R. and Winter, S. G. (1982) *An Evolutionary Theory of Economic Change* (Cambridge, MA: Belknap Press of Harvard University Press).

Neshamba, F. (2006) "Why do some small businesses grow faster and become successful while others do not get beyond the 'foothills'?—Some evidence from Kenya", *Journal of African Business* 7(1/2):9–30.

Okpara, J. O. (2007) "Cultural influences on the work attitudes: A theoretical perspective", in J. Okpara (Ed.), *Management and Economic Development in Sub-Saharan Africa—Theoretical and Applied Perspectives* (pp. 209–223). (London: Adonis and Abbey Publishers).

Pfeffer, J. and Salancik, G. R. (1978) *The External Control of Organization* (New York: Harper & Row).

Pietrobelli, C. and Rabellotti, R. (2011) "Global value chains meet innovation systems: Are there learning opportunities for developing countries?", *World Development* 39(7):1261–1269.

Prahalad, C. K. and Hamel, G. (1990) "The core competence of the corporation", *Harvard Business Review* 68(3):79–91.

Reuer, J. J. and Arino, A. (2007) "Strategic alliance contracts: Dimensions and determinants of contractual complexity", *Strategic Management Journal* 28(3):313–330.

Rodrigues, C. A. (1997) "Developing expatriates' cross-cultural sensitivity: Cultures where 'your culture's OK' is really not OK", *Journal of Management Development* 16(9):690–702.

Rosenthal, S. and Pittinsky, T. (2006) "Narcissistic leadership", *The Leadership Quarterly* 17(6): 617–633.

Sabel, C. F. (1993) "Studied trust: Building new forms of co-operation in a volatile economy", *Human Relations* 46(9):1133–1170.

Schein, E. H. (1985) *Organizational Culture and Leadership* (San Francisco: Jossey-Bass Publishers).

Shapiro, J. M., Ozanne, J. L. and Saatcioglu, B. (2008) "An interpretive examination of the development of cultural sensitivity in international business", *Journal of International Business Studies* 39(1):71–87.

Stopford, J. M. and Wells, L. T. Jr. (1972) *Managing the Multinational Enterprise* (New York, NY: Basic Books).

Triandis, H. C. (1994) *Culture and Social Behavior* (New York: McGraw-Hill, Inc.).

Trompenaars, F. and Hampden-Turner, C. (1997) *Riding the Waves of Culture* (London: Nicholas Brealey Publishing).

Weitz, B. A. and Jap, S. D. (1995) "Relationship marketing and distribution channels", *Journal of the Academy of Marketing Science* 23(4):305–320.

Wilson, D. T. (1995) "An integrated model of buyer–seller relationships", *Journal of the Academy of Marketing Science* 23(4):335–345.

Wu, F., Rudolf, R., Sinkovics, C. T. and Roath, A. (2007) "Overcoming export manufacturers' dilemma in international expansion", *Journal of International Business Studies* 37(2):283–302.

Zaheer, A. and Venkatraman, N. (1995) "Relational governance as an interorganizational strategy: An empirical test of the role of trust in economic exchange", *Strategic Management Journal* 16(5):373–392.

Zinn, W. and Parasuraman, A. (1997) "Scope and intensity of logistics-based strategic alliances", *Industrial Marketing Management* 26 No.2:137–147.

10 Creating a Global Mindset in a Danish Multinational Corporation

John Kuada, Olav Jull Sørensen, Nigel Holden, Nancy K. Napier and George Tesar

Introduction

It is generally acknowledged in both academic and practitioner literature that the manner in which an international company deals with the multiple cultural and strategic realities within the global business environment depends, to a considerable extent, on its corporate mindset and the mindsets of its senior executives (Arora, Jaju, Kefalas, and Perenich, 2004; Levy, Taylor, and Boyacigiller, 2007; Miocevic and Crnjak-Karanovic, 2012). These mindsets are shaped by such factors as the company's strategic orientation, its dominant organizational values, and rules of behavior, as well as country and industry-specific characteristics (Ananthram and Nankervis, 2014). Previous studies have shown that companies and individuals that demonstrate awareness of cultural diversity, exhibit a high level of integrative capacity, and are engaged in active dialogue within and outside their organizational boundaries are able to sustain their global operational performance (Nummela, Saarenketo and Puumalainen, 2004; Miocevic and Crnjak-Karanovic, 2012). They do so partly by capitalizing on the diverse strengths of employees around the globe while providing these employees with a cohesive strategic framework around which they can focus their energies.

The concept of a global mindset has been defined and described in a variety of ways. Maznevski and Lane (2004: 172) define it as "the ability to develop and interpret criteria for personal and business performance that are independent from the assumptions of a single country, culture, or context; and to implement those criteria appropriately in different countries, cultures, and contexts." Cohen (2010: 5) sees it as the "ability to influence individuals, groups, organizations, and systems that have different intellectual, social, and psychological knowledge or intelligence from your own." To Levy et al. (2007: 27), it is "a highly complex cognitive structure characterized by an openness to and articulation of multiple cultural and strategic realities on both global and local levels, and the cognitive ability to mediate and integrate across this multiplicity." Clapp-Smith, Luthans, and Avolio (2007: 110) also see it as "the cognitive ability that helps individuals figure out how to best understand and influence individuals, groups, and organizations from diverse socio/cultural systems." Common to all these definitions is the emphasis on executives' personality traits that enable them to register signals in unfamiliar situations combined with their cognitive capacities to interpret and understand these signals and respond effectively to them.

Although the global mindset construct has received increasing research attention during the past two decades, the empirical support for the arguments presented in the literature is still relatively weak (Levy, et al., 2007; Story and Barbuto, 2011; Ananthram and Nankervis, 2014). The few empirical investigations that have been published have mainly examined the consequences of managers' global mindset without specific focus on the processes that guide the development of these mindsets. Furthermore, very few scholars have attempted to understand the diversities of mindsets that may evolve in single organizations at different levels and locations and how these differences impact behavior and performance (Murtha, Lenway and Bagozzi, 1998; Kedia and Mukherji, 1999; Nummela et al., 2004; Bowen and Inkpen, 2009; Javidan and Teagarden, 2011).

The study reported in this chapter has been inspired by the above considerations. It seeks to explore the manner in which global orientations and mindsets are developed in a Danish multinational corporation (MNC), identified in this chapter as "company A" for the purposes of confidentiality. Our main aim is to improve insights into the evolution of mindsets in international organizations in general and to understand how such mindsets guide employees in their endeavor to comprehend peoples, cultures, and local business situations.

The rest of the chapter is structured as follows. The second section provides an overview of the theoretical considerations that have informed our investigation. This is followed by sections discussing the data collection process, the empirical results, and implications for strategy and future research.

Some Contemporary Perspectives on Global Mindset

Previous reviews of the global mindset literature suggest that there is a set of organizational characteristics and personal attributes that shape corporate mindsets. The organizational characteristics include administrative heritage, internal structures (Kefalas, 1998), as well as relationships between headquarters and international subsidiaries (Levy et al., 2007). The administrative heritage is embedded in the company's operational routines, history, and the rules of accepted behavior. With respect to structures and relationships within and between organizations, some scholars argue that companies that encourage the presence of foreigners on the board of directors or in top management positions tend to promote an integrative relationship between headquarters and international subsidiaries (Nummela et al., 2004). They are also able to effectively manage potential discrepancies in the mindsets of employees at different organizational levels and in different geographical and cultural contexts (Kefalas, 1998), and to guide the socialization process of new organizational members (Sørensen, 2002). The personal attributes noted in the literature include individual cognitive and behavioral characteristics such as openness (Ananthram and Nankervis, 2014), awareness of cultural diversity (Nummela et al., 2004), learning and knowledge sharing capabilities, and the ability to balance tensions (Levy et al., 2007). Thus, Bowen and Inkpen (2009) see global mindset in terms of three important individual characteristics: intellectual, social, and psychological capital. For them, intellectual capital represents such attributes as global business savvy, cosmopolitan outlook, and cognitive complexity; social capital covers attributes such as intercultural empathy, interpersonal impact, and diplomacy; and psychological capital embraces attributes such as passion for diversity, quest for adventure, and self-assurance.

The art of balancing intraorganizational tensions has been described in terms of such dichotomies as global formalization versus local flexibility, global standardization versus local customization, global dictate versus local delegation, and differentiation versus integration (Murtha et al., 1998; Begley and Boyd, 2003; Story and Barbuto, 2011; Javidan and Walker, 2012; Cseh, Davis and Khilji, 2013). It has been argued that the performance of MNCs depends on management's ability to design strategies that ensure a workable synthesis between these dichotomies. For example, differentiation is seen as necessary because of the diverse functional requirements for successful goal attainment in global enterprises, while integration is necessary to be able to remain focused on strategic business objectives and to bring disparate elements from around the globe into a cohesive whole (Gupta and Govindarajan, 2002).

Individual employees must also balance self-confidence with humility just as they need skills such as flexibility and the ability to listen empathetically to others to be able to operate effectively in international situations (Werhane, Posig, Gundry, Powell, Carlson, and Ofstein, 2006). These attributes help configure the cognitive filters and reflective capabilities that individuals demonstrate in their relationships with others—an indication of their levels of psychological capital. Some previous studies have suggested that certain individuals, depending on their position in their organizational hierarchy, will have a stronger impact on the company's mindset than others. In fact, in some extreme cases, the personal mindset of the CEO becomes the single most important factor in shaping the organization's mindset (Cseh et al., 2013).

Some scholars draw a distinction between simple and complex mindsets. The understanding is that when firms use simple mindsets, they oversimplify their environment and make cognitive mistakes, e.g., they overlook important information (Fiol and O'Connor, 2003). Complex mindsets, on the other hand, allow firms to notice and understand varieties of stimuli (Eisenhardt and Martin, 2000).

We have been guided by these perspectives in the investigations that we have conducted in "company A." We reasoned that there may be varieties of mindsets in the company because its employees come from different cultural backgrounds, work in different parts of the world, and grapple with different challenges in their daily work processes. But the history of the company and top management's strategic direction may provide a guiding framework for organizing and coordinating these work processes.

Profile of the Case Company and Research Method

"Company A" was established within the sanitation and water management sector in a small Danish town in the mid-1950s. It quickly emerged as a key local player within the sector and gradually built up an international presence in the 1960s and 1970s. In 2015, it had more than 100 sales subsidiaries in over 70 countries, production subsidiaries in 20 countries, R&D units in 10 countries, and a total of 20,000 employees, of which approximately 5,000 were Danes. Its board and top management team has remained 100% Danish since its establishment. It has an ambition of employing over 100,000 people operating in more than 120 countries by 2030. Management is aware that such a rapid pace of growth will present serious challenges with respect to coordination and integration and has therefore initiated a deliberate process of global mindset development.

Leaning on methodology scholars such as Eisenhardt (1989), Siggelkow (2007), and Yin (2009), we reasoned that engaging in conversation-type interviews with top executives in addition to a sample of managers drawn from different departments and subsidiaries of the company would provide us with rich descriptions of the evolutionary process of the corporate global mindset. We therefore conducted semi-structured face-to-face interviews with 15 senior and mid-level executives who were involved in global management responsibilities, including the son and immediate successor of the founder. All interviews were conducted on the company's premises, their durations ranging from 60 to 90 minutes.

Results

We started the analysis by examining the conceptualization of the global mindset construct within the company and the manner in which the process of mindset formation has been initiated. We then examined the various formal and informal initiatives taken to manage the mindset evolution process and address the tensions of integration and differentiation that typically confront most MNCs. This was followed by an enquiry into the diversity and coherence of the understandings of global mindset that exist in the company and how possible varieties influence task performance within and between various units of the company.

We have been guided in our analysis by the view that a reflexive and iterative process that involves moving back and forth between the data and the extant literature will produce a deepening understanding of our data (see Bruce, 2007).

Conceptualization and Initiation of a Global Mindset in "Company A"

The general consensus among all the participants is that there is no agreed-upon understanding of the global mindset within the company, within corporate headquarters, or in the company's wider outposts. The term was perceived differently by different people and was associated with many different phenomena and activities. Some associated it with culture and cultural diversity; others associated it with knowledge and knowledge transfer. The following quotes from the interview transcripts reflect the differences in the perspectives. One of the participants describes global mindset as involving *"corporate knowledge as well as, respect, curiosity, listening, and learning from other cultures . . . many of these factors entail feelings and philosophy."* Another participant observed that a global mindset *"involves doing the same thing across countries, and doing good things for the world."* He then added, *"Our company is very good at it . . . caring for the world . . . employees need to reach a point where they think 'world' and not just Denmark, and understand they need to benefit 'the world,' not just the company; that they are 'doing good for the world,' taking care of the world."* A third participant describes global mindset as *"more of a 'soft value,' which can't be easily trained or quantified, so it is hard to show its value. Soft knowledge takes time to learn, understand, and appreciate."*

Participants also differed in their perception of the degree of pervasiveness of what they see as the company's global mindset. One participant remarked that *"global mindset is everywhere,"* but later said that there were only *"traces of it."* The first statement suggests that the global mindset is a pervasive feeling that is (1) shared by all employees and (2) influences the working climate of the company; the second hints that there is something (frustratingly) elusive about the global mindset.

There was a general consensus among the participants that the notion of the global mindset in the company stemmed from top executives. Some participants felt it was a headquarters (i.e., Danish) idea that was being presented as desirable for all parts of the company. As they explained it, the process started with informal discussions among some top executives about the need for a global mindset in the company. This was followed by a formalized process of building consensus within the company about the core values that should guide the mindset formation. This process resulted in the identification of a list of values that was endorsed primarily by senior managers within the company.

Not all managers applauded the process. Some participants expressed misgivings as to whether a corporate global mindset was necessary at all, while others expressed the view that the notion had been elevated to policy with undue haste. Thus, at the time of the interviews, the general impression conveyed by the participants was that the notion was still at a stage of being debated and it did not offer a uniform platform for practice. In the views of one of the participants, *"global mindset is in a 'state of becoming' in the company."* Several participants noted that the challenge the company faced was to translate company policies and values into behaviors that fit in with the local context. The following quotes illustrate this:

> *"The proof of the global mindset lies in how well you work with people from other cultures and your ability to draw positive synergy from those relationships."*
> *"People must think 'world,' not just Denmark."*
> *"A global mindset will be attained in this company when people find it of no interest to discuss where an employee comes from."*

Furthermore, the notion that top executives perceive global mindset to be "a good thing" and therefore the firm should "have/develop" it has been perceived particularly by those at the lower echelons of the organization as being problematic. They hold the view that the process should have been need-driven. That is, there must be a need for a company to switch from one mindset to another. One participant informed us that the general attitude among some segments of managers and employees could be summed up as follows:

> *"If we have a need we will get a global mindset . . . or even if we could formulate a need, we could have one."*

Managing the Mindset Development Process

Earlier studies have argued that the composition of the top management team and the board of directors must reflect the diversity of the markets in which a company wants to compete (Maier, 2005; Mor Barak, 2005). In terms of mindset, a multicultural board could help top executives reflect and learn by providing them with a broader perspective and context-specific knowledge about new trends and changes in different business environments. As noted earlier, although 75% of the company's employees are not Danish, all the top executives are Danes. Although there is a general acknowledgement of the need to invite non-Danes to serve on the board of directors and in top executive positions, no serious efforts have hitherto been made in that sphere. All participants agree that this remains a serious challenge in the global mindset formation of the company because only

Danish voices and mindsets are represented at the top executive level. As one participant puts it, *"our company will be deemed to have global mindset only when geography does not matter anymore or when you do not talk about where you come from."*

Building on Cseh et al's (2013) argument that the evolution of a global mindset is best seen as a learning process, we have endeavored in our interviews to examine how managers in the company learn about dynamic changes in their environment and what instruments the company adopts to ensure the transfer of its values and norms and thereby ensure a high degree of integration within its corporate entity. Furthermore, we reasoned that expatriates constitute a massive intangible resource and that harnessing their knowledge will be an important competitive factor.

Transmission of Values

We noted earlier that MNCs consist of coordinated structures distributed over wide geographical areas. They may be composed of functional departments such as marketing, production, human resource, finance, and/or a set of globally distributed units such as sales subsidiaries, production units, and R&D units. They may also consist of globally cross-cutting teams, networks, projects, and events. It is conceivable that a variety of values and mindsets will exist in these multiple sets of coordinated units. The management challenge lies in reproducing these values through behaviors without sacrificing local outlooks and attitudes. This is not an easy task, as value transmissions can only succeed when those involved have learned through experiences, and through them, find common intellectual and emotional grounds that help them coordinate their efforts to achieve common goals.

One of the mechanisms adopted by the company as a means of creating a common frame of reference for its employees is to provide them with training in the company's own "academy." The main objective of the training programs is to develop talented individuals, i.e., persons identified as having talents of the kind valued by the company. The company is also on the lookout for "global talent," and it appears to be a function of the HR department to identify these people. The company has therefore been cautious in its interference with the prevailing internal structures and modes of operation in subsidiaries in order to allow local knowledge to grow. As the HR employees explain it, HR's role is to *"unfold other people's potential . . . and see the bigger picture (through being 'a global person')—*[i.e.] *apply a holistic approach 'by building on diversity'."* That is, the desired outcome of the company's talent management policy is to facilitate global mindset development among the participants through cross-cultural knowledge sharing.

The evidence from our interviews suggests that the policy of nurturing local talents seems incompatible with the need to create interactive mechanisms that will facilitate non-Danish employees' gradual understanding and appreciation of the core values on which the company's operations are based. It was noted by several participants in the study that affiliates in, say, China are very keen to do things in a Chinese way—i.e., without too much deference to the Danish/Western way of doing things. It was also noted that in Russia, a local manager might identify a junior colleague as talented and worthy of a reward for reasons that may not necessarily be compatible with company policy (i.e., rewarding an action that may not be immediately connected to corporate performance). Top management's acceptance of such local practices is seen as a key challenge in the development of talents. As one Danish participant explains it, *"The challenge lies in encouraging foreign employees to live the values and translate them into behaviors that fit within a local context without limiting their performance."* Another participant remarked that *"we think in silos today. It will take a generation before we think globally . . . a process is needed to formulate and implement the core notion of global orientation . . ."* A third participant commented that *"the proof of the global mindset lies in how well you work with people from other cultures and your ability to draw positive synergy from the relationship . . . but it is not only ourselves who should have a global mindset. Managers in our affiliates must also have it."*

There is also a general problem of "harvesting" and sharing knowledge across departmental and geographical boundaries. We were astonished to note that the term "knowledge sharing" was only mentioned in one instance during our interviews despite top management's emphasis on talent development and knowledge transfer. This might be a reflection of other employees' reaction to the feeling that global mindset and its related knowledge transfer process is a *"head-office project,"* as one participant suggested. It was also noticeable from the interviews that discussions about knowledge transfer overwhelmingly concerned technical (engineering) know-how. Sharing of cultural and context-specific knowledge has not been presented as a corporate policy. It was therefore not surprising that expatriates of the company felt isolated and considered their international knowledge ignored on their return from assignment abroad. One of the expats described his experience as follows: *"When you return, no one wants to take care of you. You are expected to know your own way. There is no interest in what you learned . . . your experiences. Life at home has 'moved on' even if you remember it as it was before you left."* Indeed, the return to an unwelcoming "home" can be so disillusioning that the returning expats leave the company in just months. It did not appear to us that the company recognizes that this indifference to expats' knowledge constitutes a knowledge loss, which will have to be regained from scratch by other people in the company.

Discussion

The varieties of interpretations of the term "global mindset" in company A reinforce what previous research has found (see Clapp-Smith et al., 2007; Levy et al., 2007; Bowen and Inkpen, 2009). We also noted that the interpretations and perspectives tend to vary among units and levels of organizational hierarchy. Building on the evidence from our interviews, we forward the view that it is analytically purposeful to discuss the concept in terms of the following four levels of aggregation:[1]

(1) Individual (global) mindsets
(2) Multiple (global) mindsets
(3) Coordinated (global) mindsets
(4) Corporate (global) mindset

Individual (Global) Mindsets

We have argued above that global mindset has been mostly studied in the previous literature at the individual level (e.g., Kedia and Mukherji, 1999; Story and Barbuto, 2011). The underlying argument is that every individual employee develops ways of perceiving and understanding business realities, based partly on his/her upbringing, professional training, and socialization processes within the workplace. This constitutes his/her mindset. But what does it mean when we say that the individual has a global mindset? Does it mean that the individual has a lot of *knowledge* about the world, or much *experience* from working in various cultures, or specific *orientations* (e.g. multicentric or global orientation), or a specific *ability* to act and interact with people across borders? The management literature sees all these dimensions to be important in shaping the global mindset of an individual. Thus, we may postulate that the more international experience, knowledge, and international orientation an individual has, the more global mindset he/she is likely to have.

With regard to the evolutionary process of mindsets, it is important to note that the mindset at the individual level is not stable. It is in a continuously evolving state as individuals act and interact with each other within and across nations. That is, individuals create "their own" global mindset by acting locally or within their specific operational domain, by interacting with people from various cultures, and by reflecting over the local experiences. Through their actions, individuals acquire experiences that may, in turn, influence the way they perceive reality. Through the interaction, they also learn from others.

We therefore see a company as a set of units within which individuals act. Each unit is centered on a set of tasks that the employees have to perform, and it is around the tasks that they act and interact. In one way or another, these tasks are "assigned" to the unit by management or through their own initiative. This means that a mindset is formed based on "task performance." It is not based on coincidental actions and philosophical discussions. This is an important point especially when considering a global context, where cultural values may differ significantly. For example, if an R&D project or task is carried out by a team composed of members from different countries, the task is still the focal point of their interaction—not their different cultural values. Obviously, their values may come into play if certain values dictate certain behaviors and thus certain ways of handling a task. This may result in friction that could endanger the performance of the task unless the employees can creatively find solutions that can accommodate the different sets of values.

Multiple (Global) Mindsets

It is normal for organizational members to repeat actions that have proved successful, and this repetition gives rise to the emergence of routines and "best practices." At the cognitive level, the practices emerge as common or collective ways of thinking about the practice. In other words, "best practices" may be more aptly considered as both "practice" and "mindset"—i.e., ways of thinking about practices. Collective mindsets may therefore become unit-specific—i.e., formed only in and around the employees in a particular unit where particular tasks are performed. In other units, other mindsets will emerge based on the actions and interaction in that unit. This explains the emergence of *multiple mindsets* in a company. At a general level, we can argue that the more isolated and fragmented organizational units are (and the higher the task diversity in a company), the more multiple mindsets one will expect to emerge within the company.

The multiple levels of mindset that we find in Company A are consistent with results from some previous studies. For example, Javidan and Teagarden (2011) suggest in their study that a synthesis of individual- and organizational-level perspectives provides a more comprehensive framework for understanding global mindset.

Coordinated (Global) Mindsets

The function- and/or task-derived mindsets must, however, be coordinated or anchored within a common vision or set of values and guiding principles. The coordination may be formally engineered by designing structures, rules, and guidelines, and demanding adherence to them.

The evidence from this study informs that the forms of coordination considered appropriate will also depend on the characteristics of the knowledge required for the performance of the tasks. Managers involved in designing these structures see the units of the company as operating like silos. They define their tasks as developing standards that ensure alignment between the operating units, i.e., that enable them to fulfill local needs and requirements and at the same time live up to the global standards. This explains why some managers in "company A" see the global mindset in terms of a set of global standards introduced through various systems that are expected to function globally within the company.

Obviously, in a global company, the units are at a physical and cultural distance from each other, and thus they more easily develop their own mindsets. Also, when the tasks are very different (e.g., sales or production tasks), we would also expect multiple mindsets to emerge. This may be necessary to allow the units to perform their tasks efficiently and effectively. For example, salespeople will have a more local mindset, as they have to respond to local demands, while employees within production units may have a more global mindset, as they have their mind on economies of scale across units that are globally distributed.

Corporate (Global) Mindsets

We have also noted from the study that the emergence of global mindsets in MNCs may entail tensions and paradoxes. We have argued above that for a company to be locally responsive both in a cultural sense (locally responsive in a given market) and in a functional sense (sales, production, etc.), its employees will require culture- or task-specific mindsets—not a common mindset. On the other hand, such multiple mindsets may not be in harmony and thus may jeopardize the overall goals of the company. This explains why a core group within top management in "company A" decided to initiate the development of global mindset in the MNC and design processes that encourage its adoption by other management cadres and operational employees over time (see also Murtha et al., 1998). But as Begley and Boyd (2003) argue, such a mindset will not become embedded in an organization until executives pull the structure, process, and power levers to activate it.

The evidence from the study further suggests that the nature of the relationship between the global mindset and the local mindset (or mindsets) is highly complex. Understanding this relationship is perhaps the core intellectual and subsequently management challenge for "company A." The challenge has its basis in the frictions between exploring and exploiting global advantages while also being locally responsive—responsive both in the sense of adapting to local needs, but also in the sense of being able to take advantage of the diversity represented by the many localities.

Learning and Global Mindsets

The role of knowledge sharing as a mechanism for supporting the global mindset formation process has been noted in our investigation. By its very nature, knowledge, in principle, can be shared and transferred from head to head. We have noted that "company A" is, to some extent, a knowledge-resisting company—although it places emphasis on knowledge transfer. The most important knowledge flows in the company are, in the eyes of top management, those that emanate from headquarters to the affiliates. This type of knowledge is hard, proprietary, and is (unconsciously) designed for transfer. But in the subsidiary, it is received as knowledge to be shared with the local employees. This means that the quality—as opposed to the content—of the knowledge changes as it passes through the local organizational filters. For example, local staff may assign different priorities to the knowledge or may feel that the knowledge (and the way in which it has been transferred) does not suit the context of the receiving end. Thus, local employees may feel discouraged from sharing their knowledge with the headquarters.

Previous studies have shown that capturing expatriate knowledge and assigning them boundary-spanning roles appears to be a useful approach to leveraging tacit knowledge and other intangible resources within such organizations (Fiol and O'Connor, 2003; Osland, Bird, Mendenhall, & Osland, (2006). But we have noted in this study that Company A has been noticeably weak in harvesting the rich pool of knowledge that its expatriates bring home. We have noted that by allowing expatriates to leave, the company loses valuable (soft) knowledge, but it may also incur costs related to replacing some of them and/or reorganizing the staff to take over responsibilities of those who leave. Moreover, those who fill in the positions cannot draw on the experience and knowledge of those who have left the company. In other words, this kind of knowledge mismanagement process causes "reinvention of the wheel." The weakness is regrettably not peculiar to the company under investigation. Other studies report similar disregard for knowledge that expatriates bring home (see Downes & Thomas, 1999; Harzing, 2001). The available evidence suggests that headquarters staff of MNCs finds it immensely difficult to determine which types of knowledge make additional contributions to the value creation processes in MNCs. The difficulty arises partly from the nature of the knowledge acquired abroad, which is often described in the literature in such terms as thick and highly contextual (Doz, Santos and Williamson, 2001).

Implications

The discussions above carry several implications for future research into the global mindset. First, the task-centered perspective on the evolution of global mindset that we have outlined in this study challenges the dominant perspective in the existing literature and therefore suggests a shift in focus in future empirical investigations. In our view, it is more appropriate to study global mindset in terms of sets of practices. These practices may vary within functional areas of the MNCs and/or within different local contexts. But they must be guided by a common set of values. Future research must examine strategies that MNCs adopt to standardize their values while localizing their function-specific practices.

Second, previous studies have informed that the formal process of global mindset development in MNCs starts at the helm of the corporation. The present study lends support to this view. But participants in this study deem it counterproductive for top executives to "impose" a global mindset on other company employees as an ideology. The consequences of a top management-initiated global mindset development process therefore require further investigation.

We wonder if the resistance to "imposing" a global mindset in "company A" can be attributed to Danish management culture in general (see Kuada, 2008 for a discussion). If this is the case, future research must examine the possibilities and processes of building corporate mindsets through collaboration and consensus in countries where employees are generally apprehensive about top management-directed value transformation processes.

Third, although it has been suggested that the composition of the top management team and the board of directors must reflect the diversity of markets in which a company wants to compete, the present study reveals that MNCs may not take deliberate initiatives to follow this guideline unless they are pressured to do so. The implications of such reluctance for the global mindset development process require further research attention.

Conclusions

We have noted that there has hitherto been a dearth of empirical research into the manner in which global mindsets unfold within MNCs. This chapter therefore contributes to the debate by highlighting the processes of mindset formation in a specific MNC. More specifically, we have argued that global mindset in MNCs is driven less by structure and more by interactive process of managers and employees engaged in a wide variety of activities and at multiple levels of the company. Thus corporate global mindset can be said to be in a continuous "state of becoming." This perspective is in line with the suggestion forwarded in previous studies that a synthesis of individual- and organizational-level mindsets provides a more comprehensive framework for understanding global mindset.

The present study has also reinforced previous studies that have called for more research into the conditions under which repatriated knowledge might be captured in a meaningful way by MNCs, particularly at the work-unit level. We argue that unless firms understand and manage the variables that aid or hinder the transfer of knowledge acquired in international assignments, they will miss opportunities for greater competitive advantages and risk losing their investment if repatriates leave the firm.

Note

1. These levels of mindset have also been discussed elaborately in Chapter 5 of this book.

References

Ananthram, S. and Nankervis, A. R. (2014) "Outcomes and benefits of a managerial global mind-set: An exploratory study with senior executives in North America and India", *Thunderbird International Business Review*, Vol. 56, No. 2, pp. 193–209.
Arora, A., Jaju, A., Kefalas, A. G. and Perenich, T. (2004) "An exploratory analysis of global managerial mindsets: A case of US textile and apparel industry", *Journal of International Management*, Vol. 10, No. 3, pp. 393–411.

Begley, T. M. and Boyd, D. P. (2003) "The need for a corporate global mind-set", *MIT Sloan Management Review*, Vol. 44, No. 2, pp. 25–32.

Bowen, D. and Inkpen, A. (2009) "Exploring the role of 'global mindset' in leading change in international contexts", *The Journal of Applied Behavioral Science*, Vol. 45, No. 2, pp. 239–260.

Bruce, C. D. (2007) "Questions arising about emergence, data collection, and its interaction with analysis in a grounded theory study", *International Journal of Qualitative Methods*, Vol. 6, No. 1, Article 4. Retrieved March 13, 2015, from https://ejournals.library.ualberta.ca/index.php/IJQM/article/view/467/453.

Clapp-Smith, R., Luthans, F. and Avolio, B. (2007) "The role of psychological capital in global mindset development", in M. Hitt, R. Steers & M. Javidan (Eds.), *Global Mindset: Advances in International Management* (Oxford, UK: Elsevier) pp. 105–130.

Cohen, S. L. (2010) "Effective global leadership requires a global mindset", *Industrial and Commercial Training*, Vol. 42, No. 1, pp. 3–10.

Cseh, M., Davis, E. B. and Khilji, S. E. (2013) "Developing a global mindset: Learning of global leaders", *European Journal of Training and Development*, Vol. 37, No. 5, pp. 489–499.

Downes, M. and Thomas, A.S. (1999). Managing overseas assignments to build organizational knowledge. *Human Resource Planning Journal*, 22(4), pp. 33–48.

Doz, Y., Santos, J. and Williamson, P. (2001) *From Global to Metanational: How Companies Win in the Global Economy* (Boston, MA: Harvard Business School Press).

Eisenhardt, K. M. (1989) "Building theories from case study research", *Academy of Management Review*, Vol. 14, No. 4, pp. 532–550.

Eisenhardt, K. M. and Martin, J. A. (2000) "Dynamic capabilities: What are they", *Strategic Management Journal*, Vol. 21, No. 10/11, pp. 1105–1121.

Fiol, C. M. and O'Connor, E. J. (2003) "Waking up! Mindfulness in the face of bandwagons", *Academy of Management Review*, Vol. 28, No. 1, pp. 54–70.

Gupta, A. K. and Govindarajan, V. (2002) "Cultivating a global mindset", *Academy of Management Executive*, Vol. 16, No. 1, pp. 116–126.

Harzing, A.-W. (2001) "Of bears, bumble-bees, and spiders: The role of expatriates in controlling foreign subsidiaries", *Journal of World Business*, Vol. 36, pp. 366–379.

Javidan, M. and Teagarden, M. B. (2011) "Conceptualizing and measuring global mindset", in W. H. Mobley, M. Li, Y. Wang (Eds.), *Advances in Global Leadership*, Bingley, U.K. (Volume 6, pp. 13–39). (Emerald Group Publishing Limited).

Javidan, M. and Walker, J. L. (2012) "A whole new global mindset for leadership", *People and Strategy*, Vol. 35, No. 2, pp. 36–41.

Kedia, B. L. and Mukherji, A. (1999) "Global managers: Developing a mindset for global competitiveness", *Journal of World Business*, Vol. 34, No. 3, pp. 230–251.

Kefalas, A. G. (1998) "Think globally, act locally", *Thunderbird International Business Review*, Vol. 40, No. 6, pp. 547–562.

Kuada, J. (2008) *Cultural Foundations of Management Practices in Denmark* (Aalborg: International Business Centre Working Paper Series No. 45 pp. 1–18).

Levy, O., Beechler, S., Taylor, S. and Boyacigiller, N. A. (2007) "What we talk about when we talk about 'global mindset': Managerial cognition in multinational corporations", *Journal of International Business Studies*, Vol. 38, No. 2, pp. 231–258.

Maier, C. (2005) "A conceptual framework for leading diversity", *International Journal of Human Resources Development and Management*, Vol. 5, pp. 412–424.

Maznevski, M. and Lane, H. (2004) "Shaping the global mindset: Designing educational experiences for effective global thinking and action", in N. Boyacigiller, R. M. Goodman, & M. Phillips (Eds.), *Teaching and Experiencing Cross-Cultural Management: Lessons from Master Teachers* (pp. 171–184). (New York: Routledge).

Miocevic, D. and Crnjak-Karanovic, B. (2012) "The export market orientation-export performance relationship in emerging markets: The case of Croatian SME exporters", *International Journal of Business and Emerging Markets*, Vol. 4, No. 2, pp. 107–122.

Mor Barak, M. (2005) *Managing diversity: Toward a globally inclusive workplace* (Thousand Oaks, CA: Sage Publications).

Murtha, T. P., Lenway, S. A. and Bagozzi, R. P. (1998) "Global mindsets and cognitive shift in a complex multinational corporation", *Strategic Management Journal*, Vol. 19, pp. 97–114.

Nummela, N., Saarenketo, S. and Puumalainen, K. (2004) "A global mindset- A prerequisite for successful internationalization?", *Canadian Journal of Administrative Sciences*, Vol. 21, No. 1, p. 51.

Osland, J. S., Bird, A., Mendenhall, M. E., & Osland, A. (2006). "Developing global leadership capabilities and global mindset: A review". In G. K. Stahl & I. Bjorkman (Eds.), *Handbook of Research in International Human Resource Management* (pp. 197–222). Cheltenham, UK: Edward Elgar.Siggelkow, N. (2007) "Persuasion with case studies", *Academy of Management Journal*, Vol. 50, No. 1, pp. 20–24.

Sørensen, J. B. (2002) "The strength of corporate culture and the reliability of firm performance", *Administrative Science Quarterly* Vol. 47, No. 1, pp. 70–91.

Story, J. S. P. and Barbuto, J. E. Jr. (2011) "Global mindset: A construct clarification and framework", *Journal of Leadership & Organizational Studies*, Vol. 18, No. 3, pp. 377–384.

Werhane, P. H., Posig, M., Gundry, L. Powell, E., Carlson, J. and Ofstein, L. (2006) "Women leaders in corporate America: A study of leadership values and methods", in M. F. Karsten (Ed.), *Gender, Race, and Ethnicity in the Workplace: Issues and Challenges for Today's Organizations* (pp. 1–29). (Westport, CT: Praeger).

Yin, R. K. (2009) *Doing case study research* 4th Ed. (Thousand Oaks, CA: Sage).

11 Culture's Consequences for Danish Expatriates' Global Mindsets

John Kuada

Introduction

Expatriate assignments are considered by many multinational companies (MNCs) as an appropriate method of achieving a cross-border transfer of skills, attitudes, and managerial practices, and ensuring the effective management of affiliates in foreign countries (Downes and Thomas, 2000; Caligiuri and Colakoglu, 2007; Brock, Shenkar, Shoham, and Siscovick, 2008; Osland and Osland, 2006). The reasoning is that expatriates may be able to play a boundary-spanning role between host subsidiaries and headquarters, serving as the eyes and ears of the latter and exercising direct control over the operations of the subsidiaries (Harzing, 1995). In other words, people "on the spot" are able to register errors of interpretation of ideas and thoughts conveyed by their hosts and rectify them quickly enough to avoid misunderstandings that may sow seeds of mistrust. They are also likely to acquire knowledge of the host culture (national and organizational) as well as a capacity to adjust to relevant aspects of the host culture in order to fulfill their organizational objectives (Harzing, 2001). This knowledge helps transform their cognitive orientation from a home country focus to a global focus (Lovvorn and Chen, 2011). Following Kefalas (1998), globally minded individuals are more able to adapt to the needs of their host organizations and environments. They do so by balancing competing country, business, and functional concerns (Murtha, Lenway, and Bagozzi, 1998). It has, however, been argued that the ability to balance these competing concerns depends very much on individuals' personality dispositions and cross-cultural sensitivity (Collings, Scullion, and Morley, 2007).

Some previous studies have suggested that the dominant cultural characteristics of a society may influence the overall predispositions of MNCs and expatriates from that society (Gupta and Govindarajan, 2002). In other words, culture may contribute significantly to the capabilities of firms and individuals to operate successfully (or otherwise) in international settings. It has also been suggested that multinational companies tend to rely a lot more on expatriates in countries and cultures that are known to be very different from their home countries (Kedia and Mukherji, 1999). However, adjusting to a foreign work and living environment is especially difficult for expatriates assigned to cultures that are very dissimilar to their countries of enculturation (Selmer, 1999).

Although the extant expatriation literature acknowledges the roles of culture (in general) and personality in the development of expatriates' mindsets, there have been limited theoretical and empirical discussions on how the home and host country cultures may play different roles in the mindset formation process. Limited attention has also been accorded to the role of firm characteristics in individual expatriates' competence development process. There is, however, some awareness in the literature that expatriate roles might be quite different for different types of subsidiaries (Harzing, 2001), and there are also some discussions on the impact of subsidiary size, strategic importance, and autonomy needs on expatriation strategies of MNCs in general (Johnston and Menguc, 2007). But the manner in which these subsidiary characteristics (e.g., size, age, and history) impact expatriate behavior and mindset formation has received limited attention in the literature.

This chapter builds on the above observations and seeks to fill the existing knowledge gap by examining how national cultural characteristics influence Danish expatriates' global orientation, enhance their adaptation capacity, and prepare them for their assignments abroad. Its contribution to the expatriation and global mindset literature is two-fold. First, I discuss and extend the theoretical arguments underlying the impact of the home country culture on expatriates' mindset formation and their choice of management styles in foreign affiliates. I will argue that managers from low- assertiveness cultures such as Denmark are likely to be less suspicious and more caring for their host country employees and would consider it an obligation to instill these (low assertiveness) cultural values into their subsidiary organization. Second, I will extend the discussions on the impact of subsidiary characteristics on the expatriation strategies of firms by introducing the age and strategic importance of subsidiaries as factors that are likely to contribute to expatriates' choice of management style in the subsidiaries.

The remainder of the chapter is organized as follows. The next section discusses the concepts of culture and intercultural competence. This is followed by discussions of personality and corporate culture and linking both concepts to expatriate behavior. These theoretical discussions are then examined from the perspective of Danish business culture—using evidence from two cases to illustrate how Danish culture influence the behavior of expatriates posted in Lithuania and Malaysia. The last section summarizes the discussions and examines their implications for future research.

Culture and Intercultural Competence

A review of the extant literature suggests that an individual expatriate's ability to enhance his/her intercultural competencies depends on following interrelated factors: (1) home country culture, (2) personality of the expatriate and his/her degree of global orientation, and (3) the characteristics of the focal organization (Black, Mendenhall, and Oddou, 1991).

Culture is frequently described in the social anthropological literature in terms of dichotomies such as *individualism-collectivism* (Hofstede, 1980; Triandis, 1994), *vertical-horizontal* (Triandis, 1994); *masculine-feminine* (Hofstede, 1980), *active-passive,* (Triandis, 1994), and *universalism-particularism* (Trompenaars and Hampden-Turner, 1997). Other contrasting typologies used in the literature include *emotional expression* or *suppression* (Triandis, 1994; Trompenaars and Hampden-Turner, 1997), *instrumental-expressive* (Triandis, 1994), *ascription-achievement* (Triandis, 1994; Trompenaars and Hampden-Turner, 1997), and *sequential-synchronic* with respect to time (Trompenaars and Hampden-Turner, 1997). There have been suggestions in the literature that the dichotomies presented above are better seen as continua—meaning that shades of the different dimensions may be found in every culture in different areas and/or at different points in time. Previous studies have also suggested that the degree of similarities between the home country culture of a multinational company and the culture of its subsidiary will influence its choice of expatriation as an international management strategy. The more dissimilar the cultures, the more likely it is to assign an expatriate to control operations in the subsidiary (Harzing, 2001).

Although the concept of culture provides a useful cue in the analysis of human behavior in groups, it is important to bear in mind that human beings are not blank sheets of paper on which culture writes its scripts. Due to their cognitive endowments, individuals process their life experiences in their own unique manner and establish their own value sets and interior rules of behavior in addition to the cultural rules (Kuada, 1994). Different individuals will therefore perceive and react to a given situation in different ways as a result of differences in their cognitive styles and emotional flexibility. As Silverman (1970) explains it, managers are not captives of the roles, official purposes, and formalized procedures of their organizations. They have the chance to (and very often try to) reach beyond the limits imposed by existing frameworks and explore new possibilities and approaches to attaining organizational objectives. Depending on their positions within the organizational structure and decision systems, they can bring their personal convictions to bear on decisions in which they are involved and are actively engaged in implementing. It is this individual free will that shapes an expatriate's choices of management styles in unfamiliar settings.

Turning to the concept of intercultural competence, it is worth noting that it is used in the expatriation literature to describes the skills, knowledge, and attitude that allow individuals to be open and flexible to other cultures and deal effectively with people from different cultural backgrounds and understandings (Brislin, 1981; Mendenhall and Oddou, 1986; Earley and Ang, 2003; Brislin, Worthley, and MacNab, 2006). To Pusch (2009: 67), intercultural competence entails an individual's ability to cultivate the appropriate "mind-set, hear-set and skills-set that can carry across cultural boundaries." Related concepts that describe similar set of competencies are cultural intelligence (Earley, 2002; Earley and Ang, 2003; Hammer, Bennet, and Wiseman, 2003), cultural literacy (Wang, 2002), and global mindset (Levy, Beechler, Taylor, and Boyacigiller, 2007; Fee, Gray, and Lu, 2013). For example, Levy et al. (2007) identified "cultural perspective" as one of the two main perspectives on global mindset found in the literature they reviewed (the other being the "strategic perspective"; the two are combined into a "multidimensional perspective"). They described global mindset as "a highly complex cognitive structure characterized by an openness to and articulation of multiple cultural and strategic realities on both the global and local levels, and the cognitive ability to mediate and integrate across this multiplicity" (page 244).

It is important to note, however, that intercultural competence does not necessarily result in blind acceptance and adoption of ways of behavior in other cultures. It rather entails the development of critical reflective thinking that allows individuals to respectfully question the goal-fulfilling implications of existing modes of behavior in a host organization, and doing so with a view of initiating a constructive change where considered appropriate in order to fulfill organizational objectives (Kuada, 2008a).

The literature also emphasizes the learning aspects of intercultural competence development, arguing that the competence emerges out of a continuous learning process that requires deliberate and dedicated efforts from individual managers (Adler and Bartholomew, 1992). The willingness to learn enables managers to cultivate a stronger awareness of cultural differences and encourages them to strive to achieve cultural synergies in interactive processes. Properly nurtured, this awareness leads to deeper cognition, skills, and attitudes that, in turn, enhance awareness just as it is also enhanced by their development. Furthermore, as Fee et al. (2013: 302) argue, the cognitive structures allow expatriates to "engage in incremental processes of assimilating new information consistent with their current mindset or through reinforcing and strengthening existing schemas." In other words, individuals with highly developed global orientations are likely to draw varied meanings from their experiences in new environments.

Leaning on Kolb's (1984) learning theory, Fee et al. (2013: 302) draws a useful distinction between the "assimilative learning processes" and "accommodative learning processes" in which expatriates engage. Their argument is that because an incremental process of knowledge development is adequate for meaningful interactions in familiar cultures, learning becomes assimilative. But once people are placed in less familiar social environments, they experience some degree of "misfit" between their cognitive makeup and their new experiences. The unfamiliar environments may generate strange, ambiguous, and meaningless situations. They will therefore need to correct or modify their schemas to improve their "accommodation" or "fit" with the new reality. In other words, successful expatriates must be self-reflective in their learning process. Expatriates without self-reflective dispositions tend not to listen to themselves, let alone listen to people with different viewpoints. As such, they persistently fail to challenge the fundamental assumptions on which they base their actions and are unable to introduce changes that align their behavior to the new situations in which they find themselves.

Personality, Corporate Culture, and Expatriate Behavior

Personality trait theorists argue that individuals' cultural adaptation potentials are best assessed in terms of their personality dispositions. Following Miller and Toulouse (1986: 1390), managers who have high levels of flexibility as their personality trait are usually "informal, adventurous, confident, humorous, idealistic, and assertive." This compares with less flexible managers, who are described as "deliberate, cautious, worrying, industrious, guarded, mannerly, methodical and rigid . . . [They are also] pedantic in thought, overly deferential to authority, customs and traditions." Expatriates with the latter type of personality traits are most likely to be inflexible and unadaptable to the local circumstances in other organizations. Other personality traits that have featured in the literature include individuals' stress tolerance capacity (Janssens, 1995), relational skills, eloquence, and self-control (Brislin, 1981).

The personality trait literature has inspired the development of a variety of typologies that describe the adaptation potentials of individual managers abroad. Some expatriates are described as being predominantly conservative, while others are seen as flexible and therefore more capable of intercultural adaptation. Again, leaning on Miller and Toulouse (1986), it can be argued that a person with a flexible personality has a wide variety of coping repertoires and exhibits emotional shifts that make him/her comfortable in bridging cultures. He/she also displays an element of tact in minimizing conflict in social relations and therefore is relatively free of conflict-induced anxiety. Based on this reasoning, Mendenhall and Oddou (1986) have classified expatriates in terms of the following three personality orientations:

(1) *Self-Orientation*, referring to the degree to which an individual expresses an adaptive concern for self-preservation, self-enjoyment, and mental hygiene
(2) *Others-Orientation*, referring to the degree to which an individual is concerned about other peoples' well-being and desires to affiliate with them
(3) *Perceptual-Orientation*, reflecting an individual's ability to gain rich understanding of other cultures, or to show empathy in general.

They argue further that the well-adjusted expatriate managers will be those who score high on all the three dimensions—Self-Orientation,

Others-Orientation, and Perceptual-Orientation. Mendenhall and Oddou's perspective is similar to the distinction drawn in the literature between psychological, social, and intellectual capital. Self-orientation produces psychological capital, others-orientation produces social capital, while perceptual orientation produces intellectual capital. As Javidan and Walker (2012) argue, intellectual capital is usually the easiest to develop because it is cognitively based and consists of knowledge and information. Social capital is somewhat harder to develop because it is mostly relationship based and requires experiential opportunities for learning. Psychological capital is typically the hardest to develop because, as adults, our psychological makeup is already firmly set when we move to other countries.

Another important consideration in the expatriate assignment process is the culture of the MNC. Organizational cultures are reflected in the non-articulated goals of organizational members, the myths, legends, and traditions, as well as formal structures and functions—all of which combine to define what organizations consider to be "the correct approach to doing things" in any given situation (Hatch, 1993; Schein, 2004). Thus, Allaire and Firsirotu (1984) describe organizations as miniature societies, equipped with socialization processes, social norms, and structures. In Smirich's (1983) view, corporate culture conveys a sense of identity to the employees of a company and facilitates the generation of a commitment to something larger than the self.

Some MNCs strive to transfer their cultural values to their subsidiaries in other countries.

The ethnocentric-polycentric continuum of organizational dispositions presented by Heenan and Perlmutter (1979) is one of the seminal discussions of how MNCs attempt to transfer their values to their subsidiaries or allow some subsidiaries to retain aspects of their local values and rules of behavior. They argue that ethnocentrism reflects managements' belief in the superiority of the corporate culture found in the headquarters and therefore a strong inclination to transfer it to (or even impose it on) the subsidiaries. Polycentrism is the opposite. That is, MNCs with polycentric orientations allow their expatriates and subsidiaries a wider degree of latitude to draw on their host country cultural values to respond to changes in their environments. I will argue subsequently that MNCs with ethnocentric orientations tend to constrain their expatriates' learning opportunities in host countries and cut down on the variety of perspectives they bring to bear on management issues in their subsidiaries (see Chapter 12).

While home country national and corporate culture combine with expatriates' personalities to shape their intercultural competence profile and possible behaviors in their host organizations, it is important to note that the host country culture also impacts subsidiary employees' preparedness to accept and adopt the cultural values transferred to them. For example, local managers in subsidiaries whose national cultures are characterized by a high power distance (Hofstede, 1980) are likely to socialize their subordinates to be dependent on them (as centers of excellence) and hold their own capacity to take initiatives in check. Most of them would define their role as simply following, responding, and carrying out instructions from their superiors. Turning such cultures around can be extremely difficult.

Overview of Danish Cultural Traits and Management Practices

It is generally believed that most small countries tend to have relatively homogeneous national cultures. This means their cultural characteristics are uniform, internally coherent, and relatively stable. The shared meanings and values in these countries are normally institutionalized and are reflected in their legal, political, and economic systems. Their managers also tend to have relatively uniform mindsets with regard to their definition of appropriate and acceptable rules of behavior in organizations. Furthermore, they tend to be relatively ethnocentric (Punnett, 2015). The homogeneity experienced in these countries can produce positive dynamics in work situations because it facilitates the convergence of meanings and agreement on relevant courses of action, thereby encouraging quicker actions than in less homogeneous societies.

Denmark is described as a homogenous society with feminine characteristics and low uncertainty avoidance (Hofstede, 1980). Like other Western European societies, the Danish people exhibit individualistic behavioral traits and are generally short-term oriented. But the negative social consequences of individualism are cushioned by what some scholars describe as institutional collectivism—i.e., state-coordinated, collectivistic social arrangements that fit neatly with the feminine (soft value) dimensions of the society (Hofstede, 2001). Thus, the Danish society can be justifiably described as both individualistic and collectivistic. Danes interact with strangers in an informal and friendly style garnished with a generous amount of humor and self-irony. Most foreigners see Danes as modest, punctual, honest, simple, and straightforward. But others warn that although Danes may appear easy going at first glance, they can also be very reserved and rather aloof. This attitude is a reflection of the general skepticism with which Danes approach strangers, cautiously sizing them up before opening up to them.

Danish workers and managers exhibit a high preference for flat organizational structures with as few layers of hierarchy as possible, and show low preference for formalization and deference to authority (Fivelsdal and Schramm-Nielsen, 1993). Decision-making is usually delegated, and employers at all levels have significant decision-making authority in their job functions. This results in a democratic and open working environment with short channels of command from the management to the common employee. Managers usually play down their authority, talk on equal footing with every employee, and rarely give direct orders (Schramm-Nielsen, Lawrence, and Sivesind, 2004). They appear more comfortable with the terms "responsibility" and "competence" when describing their decision-making authority. Although subordinates enjoy a free hand to make decisions, they are also expected to accept the risk and consequences of making the wrong decisions.

In operational terms, Danish managers are more comfortable with elaborate consultation and consensus in decision-making situations—bringing all voices to bear on important decisions so that responsibilities for tasks can be collectively shared. Danish workers and their representatives are also expected to do the same—i.e., they devote substantial time to holding meetings during which worker-related issues are discussed and debated. The act of debating itself has a significant value; it reflects the act of listening to others and being listened to in a process of consensus seeking. Key decisions may not be immediately made at these meetings, and this may not be the main objective of the meeting: It is the process of discussing that matters most. The consultative approach to management also compensates for the Danish dislike of formalization and bureaucratic rules. If there are no specific rules to follow, people are compelled to talk with each other until they reach an agreement on important issues, no matter how long it may take. Thus, pragmatism and professionalism are also presented as dominant characteristics of Danish management style (Kuada, 2008b).

The available empirical evidence shows that there is a belief within the Danish business community that the principles undergirding Danish management practices can be successfully applied in Danish subsidiaries in other countries (Colclough, 2012; Andersen, Lauring, and Kragh, 2014). Danish managers abroad have been found to exhibit traits of openness and inquisitiveness and are generally perceived as polite and respectful in their interactions with local employees in their host environments, asking questions to seek clarifications of issues that they are uncertain about (Lauring and Selmer, 2009; Lauring, 2013). These traits tend to provide them with both social and intellectual capital in new situations. But when Danish leaders find themselves under pressure, they can appear rigid and dictatorial, particularly when their conventional leadership styles fail to encourage collaboration with host country employees and produce the desired results. They are unable to understand why some host country employees tend to reject their democratic forms of leadership. The cultural shock frequently produces perceptual bias and discriminatory behavior towards local employees. Thus, despite their good intentions, Danish expatriates may have difficulties in creating a knowledge-sharing environment for their culturally diverse employees. Under such conditions, relationship building could be fragmented and interaction patterns would not sufficiently support knowledge exchange (Andersen et al., 2014). Lauring (2009) explains the abrupt changes in Danish expatriates' leadership styles in terms of the goals of their assignment. In his view, the expatriates are usually driven by short-term financial performance objectives specified by their headquarters when deciding on which leadership styles and management practices will be appropriately adopted in a subsidiary. Thus, when the short-term goals appear unattainable due to the apparent reluctance of local employees to behave as expected by the Danish managers, they give up their democratic leadership style and resort to autocratic management—giving instructions to their local employees and supervising them closely (see Naur, 1989).

There have been studies that have questioned the preparedness of top executives in Danish headquarters to appreciate significant cultural differences that may exist in other countries and can render the transfer of Danish approaches to management rather troublesome (see Gertsen, Søderberg, and Zølner, 2012). For example, Bjørn (1995) interviewed 23 top executives of 14 Danish subsidiaries in Japan about the cross-cultural challenges that they experienced in connection with the management of these subsidiaries. The conclusion is that it took the Danish executives quite a long time and many costly wrong decisions to realize that operating successfully in Japan required a long-term strategic orientation. But this awareness was difficult to communicate to the top executives in their respective headquarters. The executives at the headquarters tended to assume that the company's accepted rules of behavior that had been successfully transferred to subsidiaries in other European countries could also be transferred to Japan (i.e., an ethnocentric orientation). This assumption rendered it difficult for them to appreciate the particularities of operating in Japan. Danish expatriates were therefore frequently caught in a dilemma in dealing with both the headquarters staff and their Japanese stakeholders.

Based on a series of studies about Danish managers' relationships with their suppliers, Andersen et al. (2014: 1) concluded as follows:

> Certain Danish management ideals, such as an open and inclusive management style, can create more problems than solutions in an international context. Employees with a different cultural background than Danish do not always understand our version of openness and inclusion. The delegation of responsibilities may be interpreted as an attempt on the part of the management to escape responsibility, and requests for employee initiatives may be seen as though the management do not have a clear idea of the direction the company is going. A derived consequence is that the manager's authority is questioned, and the Danish management principles grounded in a Danish mindset become a source of frustration, which, in turn, causes the collaboration, communication and knowledge dissemination to deteriorate.

In sum, the cumulative Danish evidence suggests that companies and expatriates from culturally homogenous and economically successful countries will tend to believe in the superiority of the values that guide their managerial behavior and seek to transfer these values to their subsidiaries. But the impact of the national cultures on expatriate behavior may be moderated by an expatriate's interpretation of top management expectations and his/

her personality (including temperament to accept a slower pace of cultural transformation in the host organization). This means that, for pragmatic reasons, expatriates who hail from homogenous and democratically oriented societies may find it difficult to adapt their management practices to fit the norms of foreign locations that are considered less democratic. Although the principle of inclusiveness enshrined in democratic management styles may be found appealing by most employees, those unaccustomed to such styles may find them initially confusing, leaving them with no clear-cut direction in their work processes. For this reason, changing organizations from authoritarian to democratic cultures requires an adoption of a gradual process. This tentative conclusion is explored further with the analysis of two Danish cases presented below.

Two Danish Cases

Case 1: Baltic Plastics (A Subsidiary of Danish Plastic Pipes A/S)

Danish Plastic Pipes (DPP) A/S is one of Europe's leading suppliers of plastic pipe systems and recycler of plastic products, with revenues totaling EUR 2.5 billion in 2014 and employing 6,700 people. It operates in 27 European countries and owns 16 manufacturing plants and has over 120 agents and licensed partners operating in Asia, Australia, Africa, Latin America, the Middle East, and North America. In 1996, it bought a Lithuanian state enterprise and established Baltic Plastics (BP), initially as a joint venture. DPP later bought the joint venture partner out and turned the company into a wholly owned subsidiary. The decision to assume full ownership of the company was made by top management due to the important role that it expected Baltic Plastics to play in Danish Plastic Pipe's operations in the Baltic countries as well as in Central and Eastern Europe.

BP was established at a time when management practices in Lithuania were still influenced by the planned economic model of the Soviet era, with deference to and respect for authority as some of the dominant characteristics. This meant that, in the main, Lithuanian employees expected their managers to give them direction and to discipline them, if necessary. Employees had to seek approval from their managers even for simple and obvious changes in their work processes. This naturally reduced employee motivation to take initiative to solve the problems that they faced in their specific work situations and reduced work efficiency.

Initially, DPP decided to take full control over the core processes and operations in Baltic Plastics. To do so effectively and quickly, a number of Danish managers were sent to Lithuania to facilitate the organizational and management development process. Mr. Kenneth Ravn, who had worked in DPP's Polish and Czech joint ventures, was appointed the deputy managing director of Baltic Plastics (a Lithuanian was appointed the managing director). He was to be assisted by two other Danish expatriates—one as marketing manager and the other as a production manager. Immediately after their arrival, the Danish management team took actions that should have improved the general work environment, raised workers' morale, and stimulated engagement within the new company. The factory was completely renovated and fitted with modern toilets and washrooms. Employees' salaries were increased to about 20% above the average salary in Lithuania. Recreational facilities (e.g., gymnastics equipment and swimming pools, etc.) were also rented for the workers.

Mr. Kenneth Ravn encouraged his fellow Danish expatriates not to be in a hurry to transfer Danish approaches to management to the Lithuanians. He advised them to give them an opportunity to learn through their own experiences, but without sacrificing the overall goals of the company. His views on the knowledge transfer process were summed up in 1998 as follows:

> They [the Lithuanian managers] say yes to everything. I would like to have more resistance. I hope I'll get it eventually. But it will take some time . . . I think it is also a question of having a good definition of their responsibilities. They don't know yet, what their responsibilities are exactly . . . Right now, as I see it, there still may be some confusion, where I feel that people do not really understand the new form of organization. They also have problems making decisions themselves . . . I am involved in very small details . . . I should not at all be involved. But with time they will learn . . . from their mistakes.

This knowledge transfer strategy proved subsequently to be easier said than done. The Danish managers believed that they had to be firm and fair if they were be able to make the required change in the organizational culture. The first Lithuanian managing director spoke limited English when appointed and this made communication between the Danish expatriates and the managing director difficult. Because the managing director was the most effective link between the Danes and the local employees, they were not sure about the extent to which their ideas were understood and communicated to the employees. The managing director was therefore given an opportunity to attend evening language classes in order to improve his English skills. But his determination faltered. Consequently, he was fired as a test case.

There were frequent conflicts between the Danish team and their Lithuanian counterparts during the first three years. Lithuanian managers did not dispute the professional abilities of the Danish managers, but they did not feel that the Danes possessed sufficient interpersonal skills to work with them. They felt that most of their initial decisions were faulty; the training programs they initiated for the local employees were poorly planned and the contents of the training were assessed to be inadequate. They were also dissatisfied with the type of technology that the headquarters transferred to BP and complained that work procedures were hastily changed without adequate preparing the local employees for the change. This is how the sales manager described the supervision and knowledge transfer process in 2006:

> Initially the Danish expatriates were visible. They virtually controlled every aspect of the management. They were unwilling to listen. So we allowed them to do things in their own way. But later on, they became less visible. They allowed us to make proposals—i.e. we would send our suggestions to them and they would assess them and make their decision. In this way we would come to the solution we both deemed correct and agreed upon. They no longer blindly ordered us to work only their way, because they noted there were differences. They have learnt from their mistakes . . . You can't compare Danish and Eastern European markets. Customers' mentality, traditions and characters are different. Now, year by year, we grow in resemblance; however, we did not have such a situation before.

It is true that the Danish expatriates did not have any specific training in intercultural management before they went to Lithuania. They felt their international experiences adequately prepared them for the assignment. For example, Mr. Ravn believed that to succeed as a manager in a foreign country, an expatriate must be flexible and learn through interactions with the local people. "You cannot learn flexibility from training courses," he observed, and continued, "I know exactly how to behave when I am in Moscow, and I know exactly how to behave when I am in Bombay . . . Knowledge is transferred in a social interaction; it is a part of the daily life and a part of the daily management."

When we interviewed him in 2006, Mr. Kenneth Ravn admitted that it had been a lot easier to transfer technical skills to the Lithuanian employees than to develop their management capabilities. In his view, the Lithuanian managers had difficulties "unlearning" the management systems they used during the Soviet era. He, however, disagreed with the Lithuanian managers' assessment that the Danish expatriates controlled all administrative activities during the early years of Baltic Plastic's existence. He thought they did the opposite, giving the Lithuanians an opportunity to learn gradually.

Case 2: ScanFirbers

ScanFirbers was established in 1974 in Denmark with the objective of producing and marketing nonwoven textile products for a variety of applications in different industries. Since its beginning, its production has been based on the latest Reicofil 4 technology, which enhanced product uniformity. Precision production requires that work standards and procedures must be strictly adhered to.

ScanFirbers started its internationalization with exports to close-by markets—e.g., the Nordic countries, as well as Germany, the UK, and

Benelux. Initially, exports were typically through direct sales or agents, distributors, and/or traders. As its internationalization process intensified, it established production subsidiaries in France, Portugal, Spain, Germany, the Czech Republic, and Malaysia. The present case covers the management of the Malaysian factory that was established as a Greenfield investment in 2010—a strategic move aimed at strengthening ScanFirbers' presence in the growing Asian market.

Malaysia was chosen as a location for the factory partly because of its good infrastructure (ports, airports, roads, etc.), relatively stable electricity supply (which is extremely critical to production), and highly skilled labor force. These locational advantages combined with the country's colonial heritage, which meant that its legal systems are based on British tradition and its business language is English. Management felt that these conditions would make its operations in Malaysia a lot easier than in other Asian countries.

Headquarters' overall strategy was to replicate the Danish system, practices, and management philosophy in the Malaysian subsidiary. Thus, when the construction of the factory was completed in January 2010, headquarters decided to send a team of 20 employees to Malaysia (six managers and 14 technical staff) in order to ensure a speedy transfer of technical and managerial knowledge to the new subsidiary and to develop a corporate culture that could ensure the attainment of the investment objectives.

The expatriates were selected on the basis of the relevance of their knowledge, experience, and work function to the needs of the Malaysian company. All of them went through personality tests that served to assess their psychological preparedness to work abroad. Each prospective expatriate was also required to make a visit to Malaysia (with their families) before making the final decision regarding the assignment.

The twenty expatriates were initially required to work as a group—i.e., without any specific leader. In this way, decisions could be made through dialogue and consensus on the actions that were assessed by the group to be necessary in the changing situations that they would experience. Contrary to top management's expectations, the group management approach quickly ran into difficulties. The team was unable to instill a strong sense of responsibility among the local employees and interdepartmental coordination was poor, creating bottlenecks and inefficiencies. There was a glaring absence of managerial direction in the company. Headquarters therefore decided to send Frank Madsen to head the Malaysian subsidiary. He had worked with ScanFirbers in Denmark for six years as an assistant to the managing director.

Although Mr. Madsen was mentally prepared for the assignment, he initially found the gravity and variety of the responsibilities to be overwhelming. There were issues of the recruitment of skilled people, problems with canteen operations, raw material supply, power outages causing lines to break down, soaring repair and maintenance costs, quality problems, cash flow challenges, and a wide range of other organizational issues to attend to.

For example, there are three major ethnic groups in Malaysia—i.e., the Indians, the Chinese, and the Malays (the latter accounting for approximately 55% of the population). The Danes admired the work attitude of the Chinese, while the Malays and Indians appeared to adopt a relatively laid-back attitude to work. But the laws of the country required that employees in each company must reflect the ethnic composition of the society.

Mr. Madsen's first task was to provide the new organization with visible leadership and strategic direction in day-to-day operations. At a meeting with the management team of the company, it was agreed that efforts must be made to optimize meeting and reporting structures as well as coordinating communications with headquarters in Denmark. The management team also found several of the local employees to be passive—waiting for instructions from their managers and supervisors before taking job-related actions. They ascribed this to Asian people's deference to authority—a disposition that also created difficulties with a free exchange of views between employees and their seniors. There were other minor challenges. For example, the religious differences between the ethnic groups produced planning challenges with respect to work schedules and even food preparation in the canteen. Even these minor issues required Mr. Madsen's attention and actions because they disturbed the overall workflow in the factory.

Frank Madsen headed the subsidiary for four years, during which the expatriate staff was gradually scaled down until there were only three expatriates in the company in 2014 when he left for Denmark—all other management positions were filled by local staff. His preferred management style during the period was to demonstrate visibility, show good examples, and maintain dialogue with the local employees as well as the Danish management group. He also insisted that the expatriate team as a whole adopted a leadership style that encouraged the local employees to adopt more proactive attitude towards their work—i.e., taking personal responsibility for their jobs. These efforts started to show positive results after his four years of tenure. The process was not entirely smooth sailing right from the onset. Due to the high power distance in Malaysia, the local employees expected the Danish expatriate managers to be unapproachable and were therefore reluctant to interact with them. But the persistence of the Danes to talk to the local employees and to relate to them socially helped them feel relaxed in their company. This enabled them to challenge the prevailing codes against hierarchical crosscutting. This paid off, as it stimulated their willingness to share context-specific knowledge with the Danes.

Discussions

The two illustrative cases describe the transfer of management practices from Danish headquarters to newly established but strategically important subsidiaries. They provide some indication of how expatriates from a culturally homogenous country like Denmark are likely to introduce changes into such subsidiaries. As noted earlier, the Danish approach to management is characterized by dialogue, implicit processes, and consensus seeking among employees combined with high expectations of employee autonomy. Danish companies assume that because this approach has been successful at home, it can work equally well in their subsidiaries abroad. They therefore seek to introduce the same processes in their subsidiaries and expect them to quickly adopt the management practices that exist at the headquarters. As the evidence from the two cases shows, Danish Plastic Pipes and ScanFirbers had clear goals of making their subsidiaries in Lithuania and Malaysia, respectively, fully integrated entities of their Danish companies. They adopted what may be called a "cultural missionary" approach to the management of the subsidiaries—a version of ethnocentrism. The Danish deputy managing director of Baltic Plastics appeared a bit impatient at the beginning to achieve his goals. For this reason, he started his relationship with a relatively authoritarian disposition, but changed a few years down the line, becoming more accommodating to local opinions and allowing the local employees to learn from their own mistakes. Frank Madsen of ScanFirbers did the opposite, using dialogue and a management-by-example approach from the onset. Judging from the reflections of the expatriates, both companies were successful in adopting the Danish management practices and could therefore transfer management to the local staff within four years (ScanFirbers) and ten years (Baltic Plastics). This means the consultative and consensus-seeking approach in decision-making situations seems to go down well with employees in both subsidiaries (after some initial hitches).

This evidence is consistent with Nonaka and Peltokorpi's (2006) argument that firms located in societies with strict status hierarchies are likely to experience a low frequency of vertical interaction, because interactions between superiors and subordinates would tend to disturb the prevailing social equilibrium within the organizations. Under such conditions, expatriates must consider it part of their obligation to encourage local employees to reflect on their own work process, learn more about themselves and their roles in the organization, and to take the necessary corrective actions on the basis of their reflections and realization. This is an approach adopted by Danish expatriates in the two companies.

It is also important to note that the Danish headquarters of the two case companies sent expatriates to affiliates that had been newly established with a view to transferring what they consider to be "best practices" in the company. This is also consistent with Reiche and Harzing's (2011) suggestion that when a subsidiary has just been established, headquarters will feel a higher need to ensure that its operations are in accordance with the headquarters' policies. But if this ethnocentric approach is adopted in companies located in high power distance societies, there is the temptation that local employees will interpret it as management's desire to control rather than allow them free hand to manage—even if the opposite is what has been intended.

Implications

Put together, the discussions in this chapter also draw attention to areas of expatriation research that deserve further attention. The first one to note is the daunting challenge that expatriates face in maintaining a working balance between consistencies in corporate policy implementation and local adaptation. The question that many expatriates ask themselves is this: "To what extent should management policies be universally standardized or locally customized?" The literature has not provided any satisfactory guideline on this issue. The challenge appears in the above discussions as well and therefore requires additional research attention. Second, the role of gender in expatriation decisions has hitherto received limited research attention, presumably because of the male dominance of management teams and the pool of those willing to do assignments abroad (Taylor and Napier, 1996). The two cases discussed above also involve male expatriates. However, Westwood and Leung (1994) suggest that, in terms of disposition, women may often be better suited for expatriate assignments than men. Future research needs to pay some attention to this issue.

Third, some scholars are now questioning the one-sided focus on foreign nationals in expatriate research. The argument is that the degree of cultural sensitivity and personality traits of host country nationals employed in the subsidiaries that expatriates manage may either facilitate or complicate the adjustment process of expatriates (Gamze and Zeynep, 2013). For example, it has been suggested that host country nationals who are high in openness to experience are expected to be more comfortable with working with expatriates, more likely to enjoy working with people from different cultures and, therefore, to have more positive attitudes toward them (Wang, 2008). Furthermore, ethnocentric dispositions of host country nationals will negatively impact their attitude to expatriates as well as their willingness to collaborate with them. This also deserves further empirical investigation.

Conclusions

Expatriate assignments remains one of the essential tools for cross-border transfer of skills, attitudes, and managerial practices by MNCs. The successful performances of expatriates have been found to depend partly on the national and organizational cultural values that have shaped their management experiences, their personalities, as well as their degrees of global orientation. The discussions above have suggested that expatriates from homogenous cultures that have been economically successful tend to adopt ethnocentric approaches to their knowledge transfer. Furthermore, cultures that are associated with less respect for authority and less regard for organizational status tend to encourage participatory management style globally—i.e., expatriates from those cultures tend to encourage local employees to make their voices heard on important decisions so that responsibilities for tasks can be collectively shared. This approach to management resonates well in all organizations. But it must not be imposed on employees in highly power-distant cultures because they are usually unaccustomed to democratic process of management.

References

Adler, N. J. and Bartholomew, S. (1992) "Managing globally competent people" *Academy of Management Executive*, Vol. 6 No. 3, pp. 52–65.

Allaire, Y. and Firsirotu, M. E. (1984) "Theories of organizational culture" *Organization Studies*, Vol. 5 No. 3, pp. 183–226.

Andersen, P. H., Lauring, J. and Kragh, H. (2014) "The manager as the company's global competitive parameter" Available at http://bss.au.dk/currently/news/newsitem/artikel/the-manager-as-the-companys-global-competitive-parameter-1/ Accessed on September 18, 2015

Bjørn, L. (1995) *Danske datterselskaber i Japan: Ledelse og Organization* (Copenhagen: Handelshøjskolens forlag).

Black, J.S., Mendenhall, M. and Oddou, G. (1991) "Towards a comprehensive model of international adjustment: An integration of multiple theoretical perspective" *Academy of Management Review*, Vol. 16, pp. 291–317.

Brislin, R.W. (1981) *Cross-cultural Encounters: Face-to-Face Interaction* (New York: Pergamon Press).

Brislin, R., Worthley, R. and MacNab, B. (2006) "Cultural intelligence: Understanding behaviors that serve people's goals" *Group and Organization Management*, Vol. 31, pp. 40–55.

Brock, D. M., Shenkar, O., Shoham, A. and Siscovick, I. C. (2008) "National culture and expatriate deployment" *Journal of International Business Studies*, Vol. 39 No. 8, pp. 1293–1309.

Caligiuri, P. M. and Colakoglu, S. (2007) "A strategic contingency approach to expatriate assignment management" *Human Resource Management Journal*, Vol. 17 No. 4, pp. 393–410.

Colclough, C. J. (2012) *Building Social Capital—A Joint Venture between Management and Employees in a Danish MNC* (Copenhagen: Unpublished PhD thesis, University of Copenhagen).

Collings, D. G., Scullion, H. and Morley, M. J. (2007) "Changing patterns of global staffing in the multinational enterprise: Challenges to the conventional expatriate assignment and emerging alternatives" *Journal of World Business*, Vol. 42 No. 2, pp. 198–213.

Downes, M. and Thomas, A. S. (2000) "Knowledge transfer through expatriation: The U-curve approach to overseas staffing" *Journal of Managerial Issues*, Vol. 12 No. 2, pp. 131–149.

Earley, P. C. (2002) "Redefining interactions across cultures and organizations: Moving forward with cultural intelligence" In B. M. Staw & R. M. Kramer (Eds.), *Research in Organizational Behavior Vol. 24* (pp. 271–299). (New York: JAI).

Earley, P. C. and Ang, S. (2003) *Cultural Intelligence: Individual Interactions Across Cultures* (Palo Alto: Stanford University Press).

Fee, A., Gray, Sidney J. and Lu, S. (2013) "Developing cognitive complexity from the expatriate experience: Evidence from a longitudinal field study" *International Journal of Cross Cultural Management*, Vol. 13 No. 3, pp. 299–318.

Fivelsdal, E. and Schramm-Nielsen, J. (1993) "Egalitarianism at work: Management in Denmark" In David J. Hickson (Ed.), *Management in Western Europe* (pp. 27–45). (Berlin: Walter de Gruyter).

Gamze, A. and Zeynep, A. (2013) "Host country nationals' attitudes toward expatriates: Development of a measure" *The International Journal of Human Resource Management*, pp. 1–21.

Gertsen, M. C., Søderberg, A-M. and Zølner, M. (2012) *Global Collaboration: Intercultural Experiences and Learning* (Basingstoke: Palgrave Macmillan).

Gupta, A. K. and Govindarajan, V. (2002) "Cultivating a global mindset" *Academy of Management Executive*, Vol. 16 No. 1, pp. 116–126.

Hammer, M. R., Bennet, M. J. and Wiseman, R. (2003) "Measuring intercultural sensitivity: The intercultural development inventory" *International Journal of Intercultural Relations*, Vol. 27, pp. 421–443.

Harzing, A-W. (1995) "The persistent myth of high expatriate failure rates" *Human Resource Management Journal*, Vol. 6 No. 4, pp. 457–475.

Harzing, A-W. (2001). "Of bears, bumble-bees, and spiders: The role of expatriates in controlling foreign subsidiaries" *Journal of World Business*, Vol. 36, pp. 366–379.

Hatch, M. J. (1993) "The dynamics of organizational culture" *The Academy of Management Review*, Vol. 18 No. 4, pp. 657–693.

Heenan, D. A. and Perlmutter, H. V. (1979) *Multinational Organization Development: A Social Architectural Perspective* (Reading, MA: Addison-Wesley).

Hofstede, G. (1980) *Culture's Consequences: International Differences in Work-Related Values* (Beverly Hills, CA: Sage Publications).

Hofstede, G. (2001) *Culture's Consequences: International Differences in Work-Related Values* (Second edition, Thousand Oaks, London, New Delhi: Sage Publication).

Janssens, M. (1995) "Intercultural interaction: A burden on international managers?" *Journal of Organizational Behavior*, Vol. 16 No. 2, pp. 155–167.

Javidan, M. and Walker, J. (2012) "A whole new global mindset" *People & Strategy*, Vol. 35 No. 2, pp. 36–41.

Johnston, S. and Menguc, B. (2007) "Subsidiary size and the level of subsidiary autonomy in the multinational corporation: A quadratic model investigation of Australian subsidiaries" *Journal of International Business Studies*, Vol. 28 No. 5, pp. 787–801.

Kedia, B. L. and Mukherji, A. (1999) "Global managers: Developing a mindset for global competitiveness" *Journal of World Business*, Vol. 34 No. 3, pp. 230–251.

Kefalas, A. G. (1998) "Think globally, act locally" *Thunderbird International Business Review*, Vol. 40 No. 6, pp. 547–562.

Kolb, D. A. (1984) *Experiential Learning: Experience as the Source of Learning and Development* (Upper Saddle River, NJ: Prentice Hall).

Kuada, J. (1994) *Managerial Behaviour in Ghana and Kenya: A Cultural Perspective* (Aalborg, Denmark: Aalborg University Press).

Kuada, J. (2008a) *Cultural Foundations of Management Practices in Denmark* (Aalborg: International Business Centre Working Paper Series No. 45 pp. 1–18).

Kuada, J. (2008b) *Leadership, Culture and Management in an International Context* (Aalborg: International Business Centre Working Paper Series No. 46 pp. 1–38).

Lauring, J. (2009). "Managing cultural diversity and the process of knowledge sharing: A case from Denmark" *Scandinavian Journal of Management*, Vol. 25 No. 4, pp. 385–394.

Lauring, J. (2013) "International diversity management: Global ideals and local responses" Under review with *British Journal of Management*, Vol. 24 No. 2, pp. 211–224.

Lauring, J. and Selmer, J. (2009) "Expatriate compound living: An ethnographic field study" *International Journal of Human Resource Management*, Vol. 20 No. 7, pp. 1447–1463.

Levy, O., Beechler, S., Taylor, S. and Boyacigiller, N. A. (2007) "What we talk about when we talk about 'global mindset': Managerial cognition in multinational corporations" *Journal of International Business Studies*, Vol. 38 No. 2, pp. 231–258.

Lovvorn, A. S. and Chen, J-S. (2011) "Developing a global mindset: The relationship between an international assignment and cultural intelligence" *International Journal of Business and Social Science*, Vol. 2 No. 9, pp. 275–283.

Mendenhall, M. and Oddou, G. (1986) "Acculturation profiles of expatriate managers: Implications for cross-cultural training programs" *Columbia Journal of World Business*, Vol. 21 No. 4, pp. 73–79.

Miller, D. and Toulouse, J-M. (1986) "Strategy, structure and EEO personality and performance in small firms" *American Journal of Small Business*, Vol. 10 No. 3, pp. 47–62.

Murtha, T. P., Lenway, S. A. and Bagozzi, R. P. (1998) "Global mind-sets and cognitive shift in a complex multinational corporation" *Strategic Management Journal*, Vol. 19, pp. 97–114.

Naur, M. (1989) *Eksport og Kultur—Danske Projekter i Udviklingslande* (Frederiksberg: Samfundslitteratur).

Nonaka, I. and Peltokorpi, V. (2006) "Objectivity and subjectivity in knowledge management: A review of 20 top articles" *Knowledge and Process Management*, Vol. 13 No. 2, pp. 73–82.

Osland, J. and Osland, A. (2006) "Expatriate paradoxes and cultural involvement" *International Studies of Management & Organization*, Vol. 35 No. 4, pp. 91–114.

Punnett, B. J. (2015) *International Perspectives on Organizational Behavior and Human Resource Management* (New York: Routledge).

Pusch, M. D. (2009) "The interculturally competent global leader" In D. K. Deardorff (Ed.), *The sage handbook of intercultural competence* (pp. 66–84). (Thousand Oaks, CA: Sage).

Reiche, S. and Harzing, A-W. (2011) "International assignments" In A. W. K. Harzing, A. Pinnington, (Eds.), *International Human Resource Management* (pp. 185–226). (London: Sage Publications).

Schein, E. H. (2004). *Organizational Culture and Leadership* (3rd ed.) (San Francisco, CA: Jossey-Bass).

Schramm-Nielsen, J., Lawrence, P. and Sivesind, K. H. (2004) *Management in Scandinavia: Culture, Context and Change* (London: Edward Elgar).

Selmer, J. (1999) "Western business expatriates: Coping strategies in Hong Kong vs. the Chinese mainland" *Asia Pacific Journal of Human Resources*, Vol. 37 No. 2, pp. 92–107.

Silverman, D. (1970) *The Theory of Organisation* (London: Heinemann).

Smircich, L. (1983) "Concepts of culture and organizational analysis" *Administrative Science Quarterly*, Vol. 28 No. 3, pp. 339–358.

Taylor, S. and Napier, N. (1996) "Working in Japan: Lessons from women expatriates" *Sloan Management Review*, Vol. 37 No. 3, pp. 76–84.

Triandis, H. C. (1994) *Culture and Social Behavior* (New York: McGraw-Hill, Inc.).

Trompenaars, F. and Hampden-Turner, C. (1997) *Riding the Waves of Culture* (London: Nicholas Brealey Publishing).

Wang, I. (2008) "The relations between expatriate management and the mentality and adjustment of expatriates" *Social Behavior and Personality*, Vol. 36 No. 7, pp. 865–882.

Westwood, R. I. and Leung, S. M. (1994) "The female expatriate manager experience: Coping with gender and culture" *International Studies of Management & Organization*, Vol. 24 No. 3, pp. 64–85.

12 Advancing Global Mindset Research
Opportunities and Challenges

John Kuada

Introduction

The concept of global mindset has been described by the contributors to this volume as important but ambiguous/ephemeral (Napier and Crow, Chapter 3), slippery (Holden, Chapter 4), or illusive (Sørensen, Chapter 5). It also conveys different connotations within the extant literature and does not represent a permanent set of competences. Holden (Chapter 4) sees it as a set of individual attributes that help global leaders better influence those who are different from them. Sørensen (Chapter 5) describes it as a state of mind, capability, and process—attributes that, in combination, reflect an individual's preparedness to learn and adapt to changing contexts and situations. In the same vein, Vuong (Chapter 8) argues that those with a global mindset must constantly update their knowledge in the light of changes that they experience within their operational environments. He uses "mindsponge" as a metaphor to describe the learning process. The preparedness to learn strengthens individuals' awareness of diversities and contradictions within the operational environments of global organizations as well as their abilities to adopt strategies that respond effectively to the complexities. Tesar and Moini argue that the formulation of global strategies is not the preserve of only large firms with a global presence. In other words, small and medium-size international firms (SMEs) can also develop global mindsets and global strategies. But what makes global mindset creation a particularly trying task for SMEs is that they are forced to develop such a mindset in a shorter period of time, if they want to keep abreast of the ever-increasing pace of change in their varied operational environments. The challenges that firms face in creating and applying their global mindsets in various management contexts have been illustrated in the empirical investigations reported in Chapters 8, 9, 10, and 11.

In addition to the practical importance of global mindset to the operations of small and large international companies, we have also noted that the concept has become very useful for researchers who endeavor to understand the managerial decision-making processes of these companies (see the discussions by Tesar and Moini in Chapters 6 and 7). Thus, an overriding objective of the discussions above has been to provide insight into the current level of knowledge on the subject with the hope to stimulate further research into how managers can improve the processes by which they develop global mindset in their organizations both as individuals and in groups. To achieve this goal, we have explored following issues in the various chapters presented:

(1) Why the notion of "mindset" is situational and dynamic, especially in a global setting
(2) How global mindset could be conceptualized
(3) Why scholars and managers should continue to engage themselves in debate on the topic
(4) What directions might be possible for future research.

The purpose of this last chapter is to provide summaries and highlights of the ideas presented and delineate the key issues that have received attention in current research in the field and some of the knowledge gaps that remain to be filled. The chapter also seeks to discuss how the existing knowledge may profitably be harnessed (and combined, where necessary) to push the field forward. I forward the view that because contemporary organizational science literature reflects multiple ways of engaging in organizational research (Deetz, 1996), insight into contemporary research practices and debates on global mindset also requires an understanding of the meta-theoretical perspectives that have informed past investigations. Building on this thinking, I revisit the notion of the global orientation of multinational corporations, discussing the challenges of universalization and particularization of values and practices and the conditions that augur well for one or the other. I have also argued that metaphysical constituents of life lie at the core of human attitudes and priorities. The same holds true for employee behavior in all parts of the world. Thus, a reflexive awareness of this core is necessary for a deeper and meaningful understanding of mindsets in general and global mindset in particular. This means that issues of human energy, spirit, and emotion are as essential considerations in global mindset discussions as values, rules, structures, and processes. I present this perspective as marking a new frontier of research in the field.

Views of Organization and Their Implications for Global Mindset Research

The literature review presented in Chapter two suggests that the global mindset research agenda can be framed in many different ways, depending on the fundamental presumptions that researchers hold about organizations. These fundamental presumptions are succinctly described in the philosophy of science literature with the concept of paradigm (Kuhn, 1970). Kuhn argues that every field of research is characterized by a set of root assumptions that are usually taken for granted by those who endorse them. They influence the kinds of questions that researchers consider useful to ask about the phenomenon under investigation, how to design the research to answer the research questions, and how the results should be interpreted. Every paradigm is, however partial, evolving, and in competition with others in time and space, because researchers may subscribe to divergent perspectives on a given issue that represents an aspect of a complex and dynamic world (Deetz, 1996).

The Burrell and Morgan Paradigmatic Classification

One of the influential classifications of paradigms in organizational studies is that presented by Gibson Burrell and Gareth Morgan (1979) in their book *Sociological paradigms and organizational analysis—elements of the sociology of corporate life*. They drew a distinction between what they called the "sociology of regulation" and the "sociology of radical change." They used the term *sociology of regulation* to describe those approaches to sociology that concentrate on explaining the nature of social order and equilibrium. *Sociology of radical change* describes those studies in sociology that are concerned with the problems of change, conflict, and coercion within human social units. The radical change paradigm borrows from thoughts found in critical social research inspired by the writings of Marxist scholars. Critical theories draw attention to inequalities, malpractices, injustices, and exploitations in social worlds, and seek to give voice to marginalized groups. Burrell and Morgan leaned on these perspectives to produce four paradigms for organizational analysis, labeled (1) functionalist, (2) interpretive, (3) radical structuralist, and (4) radical humanist.

A functionalist holds the view that an organization (as social systems) is made up of interconnected parts that work together in harmony to maintain a state of equilibrium. This means an organization cannot function effectively without some degree of agreement on the norms and principles that regulate relationships among individuals. Scholars subscribing to the functionalist paradigm therefore endorse the need for individuals within a group, organization, or society to agree on value systems that will guide their behavior. This usually takes place through the socialization processes that employees in a given organization undergo. Thus, functionalists will analyze employees' actions in terms of their functions and contributions to the attainment of overall organizational objectives. Seen from this perspective, mindset must be collective and goal-oriented—i.e., it must be seen from an overall organizational perspective, with limited emphasis on the individual. It also means that researchers subscribing to this perspective will seek to explore issues of harmony, stability, and uniformity that collective mindsets produce.

An interpretive paradigm is based on the view that people socially and symbolically construct their own organizational realities (Berger and Luckman, 1967). Thus, scholars subscribing to interpretive paradigm will tend to emphasize the need to understand peoples' definition of situations in which they are involved and the meanings they derive from their experiences. That is, while functionalists are preoccupied with explaining events or experiences as objective evidence separate from those experiencing them and often without direct reference to the contextual setting, an interpretive paradigm requires investigators to perceive their actors as engaged in continuous interpretation, meaning creation and sense-making of events and their contexts. Investigators therefore focus their work on understanding rather than explaining.

Thus, from an interpretive perspective, executives and employees construct their mindsets through reflections and interpretations of events within their organizations and operational environments. This means that individuals may hold multiple and changing mindsets in response to the perceived variability within their environments. Scholars subscribing to this perspective will therefore investigate personality traits that shape managers' sense-making processes. For example, it has been argued that openness enjoins managers to be willing to accept local meanings grounded in context-specific social and organizational practices. The concept of "native views" (Gregory, 1983) aptly captures what drives this evolutionary process.

The radical structuralist paradigm assumes that structures, or social formations, contain contradictory and antagonistic relationships within them. This generates crises and acts as seeds of instability in organizations and societies. Thus, scholars subscribing to this perspective will focus on conflicts, inconsistencies, and deprivation in organizations. They will be less interested in individuals than the collectives—i.e., groups, departments, and organizations. Their research objective will not be to identify shared values, but rather reveal modes of domination and the social practices and institutional structures that create and sustain power differences within and across organizations and business contexts.

Radical humanists argue that the consciousness of individuals is usually dominated by the structures in which these individuals are embedded. These structures tend to nurture "false consciousness" and prevent individuals from reaching their highest possible potential within their organizations. In other words, this perspective sees individuals in organizations as victims of domination. Researchers adopting this perspective will focus on developing understandings of these structural and mental dominations and seek to develop mechanisms by which individuals could be freed. They do so by gaining insight into the experiences of these individuals. A global mindset research that adopts this perspective will focus attention on the imposition of a specific mode of thinking by executives on individual employees and the alienation of the individual within the organizational structures. They will also emphasize the manner in which these "imposed sense-making structures" constrain individual creativity and accomplishment.

The literature review presented in Chapter 2 shows that most previous researchers have not explicitly articulated the root assumptions underlying their discussions of global mindset. But the functionalist perspective appears to dominate the existing literature. For example, Levy, Beechler, Taylor, and Boyacigiller (2007: 237) see global mindset creation as an executive action space and define it as "the extent to which management encourages and values cultural diversity, while simultaneously maintaining a certain degree of strategic cohesion." At the same time, they also see it from an individual perspective, describing it as reflecting "openness, an ability to recognize complex interconnections, a unique time and space perspective, emotional connection, capacity for managing uncertainty, ability to balance tensions, and savvy." But these individual attributes are seen from an organizational goal-attainment perspective rather than as a sense-making process.

Our own discussions of the global mindset construct in this book have been guided largely by a functionalist perspective. This is consistent with the dominant perspective in business economics (see Rask, Strandskov, and Håkonsson, 2008; Kuada, 2009). None of the chapters has adopted the radical structuralist and radical humanist perspective. This indicates an ontological gap that future researchers may consider to explore.

Viewing the multiple factors and processes that shape global mindset creation, it is perhaps appropriate not to endorse any one of Burrell and Morgan's four paradigms in its purest form, but rather engage in some kind of paradigmatic combinations in specific research projects. For example, global mindset may be seen as emerging out of the interpretations that individuals accord events and experiences within their organizational structures and environments (i.e., with less emphasis on the structures themselves). This may represent an adoption of a structural interpretive perspective. Others may subscribe to the view that mindset is normatively regulated modes of behavior that emerge through social interactions—i.e., with an emphasis on interactions. Sørensen's contribution in this volume (Chapter 5) leans partly on this perspective. He argues that mindsets emerge out of interactions of employees in their normal course of work. Interactions create history and norms that influence current and future behaviors. This perspective will combine functionalist paradigm with interactionism. The value of paradigmatic combinations in global mindset research appears to have motivated some scholars to advocate for a synthesis of different frameworks in order to produce "a more comprehensive framework" (see Javidan and Teagarden, 2011). This thinking also underlies the suggestion that ambidexterity can be a useful construct in explaining global mindset because it illustrates the multidimensionality of the concept (Tushman and O'Reilly, 1996).

Revisiting the Notion of Global Orientation of Multinational Firms

From an operational perspective, the extant literature is replete with the observations that global organizations strive to achieve behavioral consistency across their affiliates. This explains why many scholars perceive organizations with a global mindset as those in which the underlying vision, values, and management approaches found in a firm are widely shared and intensely held and orchestrated throughout the organization (Rhinesmith, 1996). Consistency in management practices in all affiliates is believed to speed up group action and create transnational cohesion based on an accepted corporate logic. However, it also means that the assumptions that govern the behavior of employees are very rarely questioned. This, inevitably, blocks new learning and cuts down on the variety of perspectives brought to bear on management issues. It has, therefore, been suggested that global organizations must scout for novel ideas from near and wide and satisfy local needs in locally appropriate ways in order to sustain their competitive advantages. Furthermore, empirical evidence suggests that management practices embedded in the home country administrative heritage of MNCs are frequently rejected in host country subsidiaries when transferred there (Brock, Shenkar, Shoham, and Siscovick, 2008). Thus, successful global organizations must learn to balance "global consistency with local responsiveness" (Begley and Boyd, 2003).

Perlmutter's (1969) ethnocentric, polycentric, regiocentric, and geocentric management model has been frequently presented as an illustration of the challenges that companies face in deciding on the appropriate management practices to adopt globally. MNCs with an ethnocentric orientation would want to transfer the rules of behavior that are accepted and applied in the headquarters to employees irrespective of location. A polycentric company gives its subsidiaries a wider degree of latitude to respond to changes in their environments. Its managers tend to think that host-country cultures and organizations have mindsets that are very different from theirs but equally valid in their unique contexts.

Neither ethnocentric nor polycentric orientations (in their pure forms) have proved to be successful management models in practice. Thus, the dominant view (echoed in several of the contributions above) is that mangers of multinational companies must combine high global integration with high local responsiveness in order to compete effectively in host country environments. This perspective is usually captured in the phrase "think global and act local," the starting point being a global strategy focusing on the standardization of rules of behavior but allowing local adaptation, where appropriate.

The discussions in the previous chapters have inspired me to suggest an extension of the "think global and act local" guide in this chapter. I forward the view that organizations can address their integration-responsiveness challenges in four concurrent ways:

(1) Think global and act global
(2) Think global and act local
(3) Think local and act global
(4) Think local and act local

These four possibilities are illustrated in Figure 12.1.

Figure 12.1 Thinking and Acting in Global and Local Contexts

		THINK	
		Global	Local
ACT	Global	**Supra-National Issues** E.g., Environmental sustainability	**Innovation and Creativity** E.g., co-creation and sharing of knowledge
	Local	**Leadership and Human Resource Management Issues** E.g., expatriation	**Marketing Issues** E.g., communication with customers & product adaptation

Think Global, Act Global

The first strategic option is to think and act global. MNCs may choose to think and act globally in relation to issues that are of global concern and require global strategies to address. A familiar example is global environmental protection issues that enjoin companies to formulate corporate social responsibility (CSR) strategies. The adoption of a CSR strategy that is applied in all affiliates of an organization serves to demonstrate corporate citizenship, with corporate image, goodwill, and branding as outcomes (Irwin, 2003; Kuada and Hinson, 2012). The concept of shared value creation suggested by Elkington's (1994) and Porter and Kramer's (2006) sustainable development perspectives represent additional examples of the manner in which companies can both think and act global. Elkington argues that companies must assess their performance in terms of "the triple bottom line" (TBL)—i.e., profit, people, and planet. In his view, only a company that produces a TBL is taking account of the full cost involved in doing business. Thinking and acting in response to the challenges of the planet and people must be universal and consistency in doing so will improve an international company's overall profitability.

Think Global, Act Local

The second strategic option is to think global but act local. This is usually captured in the phrase "unity without uniformity." Some organizations seek to address the integration-responsiveness challenge by formulating superordinate vision or standardizing overall organizational values while allowing individual organizations to fit their strategies to specific local conditions (Adler, 2002). It requires the MNC to decide on which aspects of its values and practices it may universalize and which to particularize.

An example of a Danish company that has done this quite successfully may illustrate this option in practice. Since its establishment, the Danish toy company LEGO has pursued a consistent strategy in communicating its foundational principles and corporate identity to its affiliates and has therefore been successful in binding the company's business units into an integrated whole. Top management would want the LEGO name to be a universal concept associated with three notions: *ideas, exuberance,* and *values.* LEGO ideas are to be captured in concepts such as creativity, imagination, un-limitedness, and discovery. The notion of exuberance is also to be captured by concepts such as enthusiasm, spontaneity, and self-expression. The values come from concepts such as quality, caring, development, innovation, and consistency. In other words, LEGO's brand identity has been based on abstract concepts although its original product—the brick toys—is tangible. The consistency between the brand image, the abstract concepts, and the tangible product is seen in the design of the products—the flexibility that the bricks offer in construction stimulates children's imaginations to combine the bricks in a wide variety of novel ways.

Since the early 1990s, LEGO has ventured into three new and strategically important business areas: the LEGOLAND parks, lifestyle products, and media products for children. In many cases, these developments have entailed LEGO setting up a presence in countries outside Denmark. For example, in spring 2000, LEGO acquired a high-technology toy firm, Zowie Entertainment, in Mateo—about 30 kilometers from San Francisco. The American company specialized in innovative smart toys and with this acquisition, LEGO made a big jump into the computer-driven toy sector. In order to integrate the new company into the LEGO family, the Danish headquarters encouraged Zowie Entertainment to develop and market its products in a way that is consistent with LEGO's underlying values. This was done through the formation of a number of task forces that aimed at providing employees from the headquarters and the new company with a mental space in which they could work together on joint projects. The headquarters' employees acted as carriers of the core values of the LEGO culture to the new environment. But together with the local employees, they were encouraged to engage in new interpretations of these values within the local environment in order to achieve compatibility without sacrificing the underlying core principles of top quality, good service, and creativity. Through these interactions, employees from the headquarters and the acquired company were able to gradually challenge their respective comfort zones and at the same time avoid the destructive conflicts that personality clashes could produce.

Think Local, Act Global

This strategic option enjoins the MNC to develop structures and processes that encourage reverse learning—i.e., allow the companies to feed local experiences and lessons into the pool of internationally shared sources of knowledge. Previous studies of reverse knowledge flows have been focused on the types of knowledge that host country employees can provide expatriates who have been assigned to their organizations to train them and ensure that they abide by the corporate logic received from the headquarters. The understanding is that host country workers can help an expatriate gain cultural and contextual knowledge that can facilitate their interactions with the host society and improve their performance (Vance and Ensher, 2002). Later studies have shown that host country nationals also can effectively contribute to the pool of technical knowledge that helps develop new products for markets in different parts of the world. This emerging understanding draws on creativity theory. It has been argued that although creative breakthroughs may occur by chance, bringing ideas together from a variety of sources may speed up innovation processes in work organizations (Kuada, 2010). This requires that MNCs must be willing and able to receive and process knowledge gained from employees in host country organizations (Napier, 2006).

Think Local, Act Local

The "think local, act local" strategy implies understanding local needs and expectations and satisfying them fully at profit, drawing on available resources within the MNC. Companies have realized that no matter what mix of products, service, and prices they offer in some markets, customers will have different perceptions of its value and remain not fully satisfied. This is a drawback in many local adaptations of global value propositions. In other words, there are situations in which companies still need to craft local solutions to local problems for them to effectively serve the needs of local stakeholders and occupy a market space previously unexplored even by local firms. This requires giving local people the opportunity to analyze local needs using context-specific knowledge, enabling them to bring perspectives previously not considered in the operational history of the company to bear on the situations they identify and using corporate resources in novel ways. Hitherto, MNCs have shunned away from this approach, considering local adaptation as the most cost-effective way of creating "local" value propositions. But as the pockets of middle-class consumers emerge and grow in the developing parts of the world, local-specific solutions are becoming profitable propositions that MNCs can hardly ignore. Further research is required to explore the usefulness of the "think local, act local" strategy to corporate performance.

New Research Frontiers

Another field requiring additional research is the socio-psychological influences in the global mindset formation process. Following Wheatley and Kellner-Rogers (1996), human beings are identities in motion, searching for the relationships that will evoke more from them. Through these relationships, they seek meanings, create systems, and rearrange their lives. They invariably bring these characteristics into their work organizations, seeking from their co-workers, as individuals and collectives, the opportunities to explore their potentials in life. Understanding human relationships takes us beyond the physical persons and to a higher level of human beings, the metaphysical energy that engulfs us as persons.

Aspects of the discussions in Chapters 9 and 11 of this volume are in line with this thinking. We have drawn attention to the role that personality traits can play in the mindset development process in these chapters. We have argued that personality influences peoples' openness as well as the degree to which they are seen as "agreeable" (i.e., demonstrate empathy, courtesy, cooperative capability, and conflict avoidance in their relationships with others). Previous studies have also suggested that people who are open-minded are also willing to learn from their mistakes and try new behaviors (Ket de Vries and Miller, 1985; Campbell, Rudich, and Sedikides, 2002). Furthermore, some managers may have personalities that reflect narcissist tendencies—i.e., they are driven by their own egotistical needs for control, power, and self-importance, even if they outwardly appear to champion the needs of others (Rosenthal and Pittinsky, 2006). Managers with such personality profiles tend to demonstrate a sense of superiority and vanity in their behavior and relationships with others. They also demonstrate a weak ability to maintain relationships and never learn from their mistakes. Many of them believe that they are superior in ability and competence to all others and are comfortable with building parental relationships with their followers—talking down to them as if they were children (Campbell et al., 2002). Thus, the psychological profiles of employees therefore influence their mindsets and ability to tap into the reservoir of resources embedded in the networks and relationships between people. Tapping into this reservoir can open up innovative pathways for creating and capturing new opportunities in different business situations.

Another stream of research with consideration is the impact of organizational energy on mindset creation. The metaphysical perspective on work-life has entered management literature from the beginning of the 21st century (Luthans, 2002; Dutton, 2003; Cameron, Dutton, and Quinn, 2003). It has encouraged the introduction of the concept of human *energy* as a summary construct for the inner constituents of human beings and organizations (Cleveland and Jacobs, 1999; Luthans, 2002). Others refer to it as the soft side of organizations (Kuada and Serles, 2010). The emerging understanding is that individuals are transmitters of energy within organizations. The transmission takes place during interpersonal relations and/or group interactions. Here, language and emotions combine to transmit the latent energy inherent within the individuals to one another.

A typical situation in which energy transmission occurs within organizations is during interactions between employees at different levels of an organizational hierarchy. The transmission process is often self-reinforcing. That is, positive energy manifestation sets off a spiral of positive energies, while an initial negative energy manifestation produces the reverse effect (Dutton, 2003). Negative energy manifestations are most frequently reflected in behaviors that promote greed, selfishness, manipulation, secrecy, distrust, anxiety, self-absorption, fear, burnout, and feelings of abuse that tend to derail organizational efforts. In contrast, an organization in which energy flows positively tends to be characterized by such attributes as appreciation, collaboration, virtuousness, vitality, and meaningfulness. Members of such organizations are characterized by trustworthiness, resilience, wisdom, and humility. Their social relationships and interactions are characterized by compassion, loyalty, honesty, respect, and forgiveness (Kuada and Serles, 2010). Thus, the mindset creation and manifestation process is greatly influenced by the energy flows between people in interactive situations. However, this socio-psychological perspective has not as yet received much attention in the global mindset stream of research. But to the extent that the drivers of human and organizational energy may vary across organizations, industries, and countries, it is a potential source of new insights into global mindset development.

One field of enquiry (with a solid theoretical foundation) that can serve as an initial source of inspiration for this strand of global mindset research is the emotional intelligence stream of research, which started seriously in the 1990s with the publication of Gardner's Multiple Intelligences (1993) and Goleman's Emotional Intelligence (1995). These studies opened up inquiries into the manner in which the management of emotions can contribute to individual capability enhancement and improved interpersonal relationship development.

Emotional intelligence is described in the literature as the capacity to recognize and manage emotions and to solve problems effectively in real-life situations (Zeidner, Matthews, and Roberts, 2004). It is often related to social learning processes and described in the concept of social and emotional learning (SEL). SEL is then described as the process of acquiring and effectively applying the knowledge, attitudes, and skills necessary to recognize and manage emotions; develop attributes of caring and concern for others; establish positive relationships; and make balanced decisions in handling issues that may appear challenging in specific human interactions (Mayer, Salovey, and Caruso, 2004).

Emotional competence is important in business management as well because people feel things first before assigning meaning to them (i.e., cognitively reflecting on it). Thus, without the emotional experience, the cognitive processes (if they happen at all) become divorced from real life. Thus, global mindset as a cognitive process becomes more meaningful when linked to the emotional processes that individuals engage in when dealing with specific life situations. Emotional competence has also been shown to be a prerequisite for learning a wide range of job-related skills and translating them into capabilities and behavioral attributes. Thus, an understanding of this process therefore enriches any understanding of the mindset development process.

Concluding Remarks

The discussions in this book suggest that a global mindset is both an individual and a collective feature in organizations. But its manifestation is seen mainly in individuals' behavior. The empirical evidence presented in the various chapters shows that individuals will most likely develop different mindsets as their perceptions are shaped by their personality, emotional configurations, and their own particular experiences. They will therefore react differently to the same situation irrespective of the collective mindset of their organizations. Thus, navigating the chaotic and irregular trajectories of a global business environment requires the adoption of a strategy that encourages individuals to develop the emotional and cognitive capabilities to respond to new situations and learning from the experiences. We have also argued that mindsets can change because individuals are likely to change their perspectives as they attempt to accommodate different experiences through critical reflection on these experiences. In that sense, mindsets are constantly evolving and must not be conceived as fixed frames of reference. The discussions in this chapter have also drawn attention to knowledge gaps in the existing literature and have suggested that future research must be aware of the different root assumptions underlining current conceptualizations.

References

Adler, N.J. (2002) *International Dimensions of Organizational Behavior* 4th Ed. (Canada: South-Western).

Begley, T.M. and Boyd, D.P. (2003) "The need for a corporate global mind-set" *MIT Sloan Management Review*, Vol. 44 No. 2 pp: 25–32.

Berger, P. and Luckman, T. (1967) *The Social Construction of Reality: A Treatise in Sociology of Knowledge* (Penguin: Harmondsworth).

Brock, D.M., Shenkar, O., Shoham, A., and Siscovick, I.C. (2008) "National culture and expatriate deployment" *Journal of International Business Studies*, Vol. 39 No. 8 pp: 1293–1309.

Burrell, G. and Morgan, G. (1979) *Sociological Paradigms and Organizational Analysis: Elements of the Sociology of Corporate Life* (London: Heinemann).

Cameron, K.S., Dutton, J.E., and Quinn, R.E. (2003) *Positive Organizational Scholarship* (San Francisco: Berrett-Koehler).

Campbell, W.K., Rudich, E., and Sedikides, C. (2002) "Narcissism, self-esteem, and the positivity of self-views: Two portraits of self-love" *Personality and Social Psychology Bulletin*, Vol. 28 No. 3 pp: 358–368.

Cleveland, H. and Jacobs, G. (1999) "Human choice: The genetic code for social development" *Futures*, Vol. 31 Nos. 9–10 pp: 959–970.

Deetz, S. (1996) "Describing differences in approaches to organization science: Rethinking Burrell and Morgan and their legacy" *Organization Science*, Vol. 7 No. 2 pp: 191–207.

Dutton, J.E. (2003) *Energize Your Workplace: How to Create and Sustain High-Quality Connections at Work* (San Francisco: Jossey-Bass).

Elkington, J. (1994) "Towards the sustainable corporation: Win-win-win business strategies for sustainable development" *California Management Review*, Vol. 36 No. 2 pp: 90–100.

192   John Kuada

Gardner, H. (1993) *Multiple Intelligences: The Theory in Practice* (New York: Basic Books).

Goleman, D. (1995) *Emotional intelligence* (New York: Bantam Books).

Gregory, K. L. (1983) "Native-view paradigms: Multiple cultures and culture conflicts in organizations" *Administrative Science Quarterly*, Vol. 28 No. 3 pp: 359–376.

Irwin, R. (2003) "Corporate social investment and branding in the new South Africa" *The Journal of Brand Management*, Vol. 10 No. 41 pp: 303–311.

Javidan, M. and Teagarden, M. B. (2011) "Conceptualizing and measuring global mindset" In William H. Mobley, Ming Li, & Ying Wang (Eds.), *Advances in Global Leadership Bingley, U.K.* (Volume 6, pp: 13–39). (Emerald Group Publishing Limited).

Kets de Vries, M. and Miller, D. (1985) "Narcissism and leadership: An object relations perspective" *Human Relations*, Vol. 38 No. 6 pp: 583–601.

Kuada, J. (2009) *Paradigms in International Business Research: Classifications and Applications* (Aalborg: Centre for International Business, Department of Business Studies, Aalborg University).

Kuada, J. (2010) "Creativity and leadership in a cross-cultural context: The role of expatriates" In J. Kuada & O. J. Sørensen (Eds.), *Culture and Creativity in Organizations and Societies* (pp: 9–23). (London: Adonis & Abbey Publishers Ltd.).

Kuada, J. and Hinson, R. E. (2012) "Corporate social responsibility (CSR) practices of foreign and local companies in Ghana" *Thunderbird International Business Review*, Vol. 54 No. 4 pp: 521–536.

Kuada, J. and Serles, D. (2010) "Creative human and organizational energy" In J. Kuada & O. J. Sørensen (Eds.), *Culture and Creativity in Organizations and Societies* (pp: 51–63). (London: Adonis & Abbey Publishers Ltd.).

Kuhn, T. S. (1970) *The Structure of Scientific Revolutions* (Chicago: University of Chicago Press).

Levy, O., Beechler, S., Taylor, S., and Boyacigiller, N. A. (2007) "What we talk about when we talk about 'global mindset': Managerial cognition in multinational corporations" *Journal of International Business Studies*, Vol. 38 No. 2 pp: 231–258.

Luthans, F. (2002) "Positive organizational behavior: Developing and managing psychological strengths" *Academy of Management Executive*, Vol. 16 No. 1 pp: 57–72.

Mayer, J. D., Salovey, P., and Caruso, D. R. (2004) "Emotional intelligence: Theory, findings and implications" *Psychological Inquiry*, Vol. 15 No. 3 pp: 197–215.

Napier, N. K. (2006) "Cross cultural learning and the role of reverse knowledge flows in Vietnam" *International Journal of Cross Cultural Management*, Vol. 6 No. 1 pp: 57–74.

Perlmutter, H. V. (1969) "The tortuous evolution of the multinational corporation" *Columbia Journal of World Business*, Vol. 4 No. 1 pp: 9–18.

Porter, M. E. and Kramer, M. R. (2006) "Strategy and society: The link between competitive advantage and corporate social responsibility" *Harvard Business Review*, Vol. 84 No. 12 pp: 78–92.

Rask, M., Strandskov, J., and Håkonsson, D. D. (2008) "Theoretical perspectives on the internationalization of firms" *Journal of Teaching in International Business*, Vol. 19 No. 4 pp: 320–345 Available online at http://www.haworthpress.com Downloaded on 15 August 2015.

Rhinesmith, S. H. (1996) *A Manager's Guide to Globalization: Six Skills for Success in a Changing World* (2nd ed.). (New York: McGraw-Hill).

Rosenthal, S. and Pittinsky, T. (2006) "Narcissistic leadership" *The Leadership Quarterly*, Vol. 17 No. 6 pp: 617–633.

Tushman, M. and O'Reilly III, C. A. (1996) "Ambidextrous organizations" *California Management Review*, Vol. 38 No. 4 pp: 8–30.

Vance, C. M. and Ensher, E. A. (2002) "The voice of the host country workforce: A key source for improving the effectiveness of expatriate training and performance" *International Journal of Intercultural Relations*, Vol. 26 No. 4 pp: 447–461.

Wheatley, M. J. and Kellner-Rogers, M. (1996) *A Simpler Way* (San Francisco: Berrett-Koehler Publishers).

Zeidner, M., Matthews, G., and Roberts, R. D. (2004) "Emotional intelligence in the workplace: A critical review" *Applied Psychology: An International Review*, Vol. 53 No. 3 pp: 371–399.

Index

absorptive capacity 66, 71
acknowledged values 116; *see also* values
adaptation 38, 62, 66, 67, 78, 162;
  cultural 133, 165; local 176, 185, 188
adventure, quest for 19, 52, 68, 148
adverse selection 129
alien values 116; *see also* values
Americanization 51
appropriate values 115, 122
assertiveness 162
autonomy, intellectual and affective 42,
  113, 162, 175

Baltic Plastics (BP) 170–2
Barnevik, Percy 43–4
boundary-spanning 19, 157, 161
bounded rationality 63, 65, 66
bourgeoisie 50
business culture 112; *see also* corporate
  culture
businesses *see* emerging market
  multinational enterprises (EMNEs);
  multinational corporations (MNCs);
  multinational enterprises (MNEs);
  small and medium-sized enterprises
  (SMEs)
business orientation, global 15
business savvy, global 19, 52, 68, 148

capabilities: cognitive 17, 18, 64, 75,
  191; relational 129, 130–1, 139;
  situational 4, 73–5
capital: intellectual 19, 52, 68, 148,
  166; psychological 15, 19, 21, 52, 68,
  148, 166; social 19, 52, 68, 148, 166
CCS (cross-cultural sensitivity) 18, 21,
  133
Cemex 58–9
cities 54

cognitive capabilities 17, 18, 64, 75, 191
cognitive complexity 3, 8, 19, 52, 68,
  111, 140, 148
cognitive feedback 132
cognitive mistakes 19, 148
collaboration: challenges of 135–6;
  interfirm 5; *see also* cross-border
  interfirm collaboration
collectivism vs. individualism 112, 163
comfortable values 116; *see also* values
communication: in cross-border
  interfirm collaboration 141; IT
  systems 49; and knowledge transfer
  141; methods of 42–4
The Communist Manifesto (Marx and
  Engels) 50
competence/competencies 74, 121,
  127, 129, 138; emotional 190; of
  entrepreneurs 111; of expatriates
  162; intercultural 129, 162–5
competence-based perspectives 128
complexity: cognitive 3, 8, 19, 52, 68,
  111, 140, 148; environmental 111; of
  globalization 53, 64, 111; of global
  business 8, 18, 51, 72; organizational
  111, 135; role 37; task 135
confidence building 110, 116, 117
Confucianism 117, 121
context: business 183; changing 52,
  63–4, 146, 180; cultural 18; domestic
  62; dynamic 4; emerging economy
  5; global 21, 51, 65, 106; in the GM
  conceptual framework 63, 65, 76–8;
  international 169; local 6, 67, 151,
  153, 157; situation/situational 71, 74,
  76–9, 86
convergence 66, 67, 167
core values 109, 114–17, 119, 122, 150,
  152, 187; *see also* values

For Product Safety Concerns and Information please contact our EU
representative GPSR@taylorandfrancis.com
Taylor & Francis Verlag GmbH, Kaufingerstraße 24, 80331 München, Germany

www.ingramcontent.com/pod-product-compliance
Ingram Content Group UK Ltd.
Pitfield, Milton Keynes, MK11 3LW, UK
UKHW021608240425
457818UK00018B/444